PALM BEACH

Hawkesbury River

Cowan Creek

Berowra Creek

Ku-ring-gai Chase
National Park

HORNSBY

T A S M A N

CHATSWOOD

CASTLECRAG

BALMORAL

*Sydney
Harbour*

HUNTERS
HILL

MOSMAN

Watsons Bay

NORTH
SYDNEY

NEUTRAL
BAY

Parramatta

River

VAUCLUSE

Harbour Bridge

SYDNEY

S E A

PADDINGTON

HABERFIELD

BURWOOD

NEWTOWN

*Sydney
Airport*

Ⓐ

ANKSTOWN

HURSTVILLE

LA
PEROUSE

*Botany
Bay*

rges River

SYDNEY

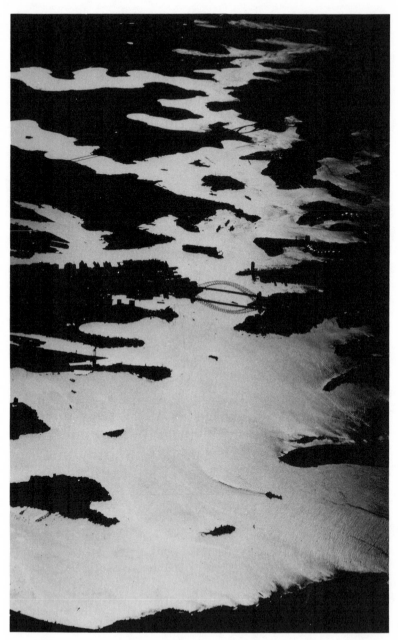

Sydney Harbour from 16,000 feet, 1966. Photograph by David Moore.

SYDNEY

JAN MORRIS

RANDOM HOUSE

NEW YORK

Copyright © 1992 by Jan Morris

All rights reserved under International and Pan-American Copyright Convention.
Published in the United States by Random House, Inc., New York.
This book was originally published in Great Britain by Viking, a division of
Penguin Books Ltd., London.

Grateful acknowledgment is made to the following for permission to reprint
previously published material:
Hamish Hamilton Ltd.: Two lines from "Australia" from *Collected Poems 1930-1965*
by A. D. Hope (Hamish Hamilton, 1966). Copyright © 1966 by A. D. Hope.
Reprinted by permission.
David Higham Associates: Excerpts from *HMS* Glory *at Sydney* from *Collected Poems*
by Charles Causley, published by Macmillan. Reprinted by permission.
The Society of Authors and Mrs. Nicolete Gray on behalf of the Laurence Binyon Estate:
Excerpt from "For the Fallen" (September 1914) by Laurence Binyon from *Collected
Poems of Laurence Binyon: Lyrical Poems*. Reprinted by permission of Mrs. Nicolete
Gray and The Society of Authors on behalf of the Laurence Binyon Estate.

Library of Congress Cataloging-in-Publication Data

Morris, Jan.
Sydney/Jan Morris.—1st ed.
p.   cm.
ISBN 0-394-55098-6
1. Sydney (N.S.W.)—Description.   I. Title.
DU178.M64   1992
994.4'1—dc20   91-41141

Manufactured in the United States of America

9 8 7 6 5 4 3 2

First U.S. Edition

The text of this book is set in 11/15 Palatino.
Book design by Jo Anne Metsch

For
SAM PROVSTGÅRD MORYS
born 1988

CONTENTS

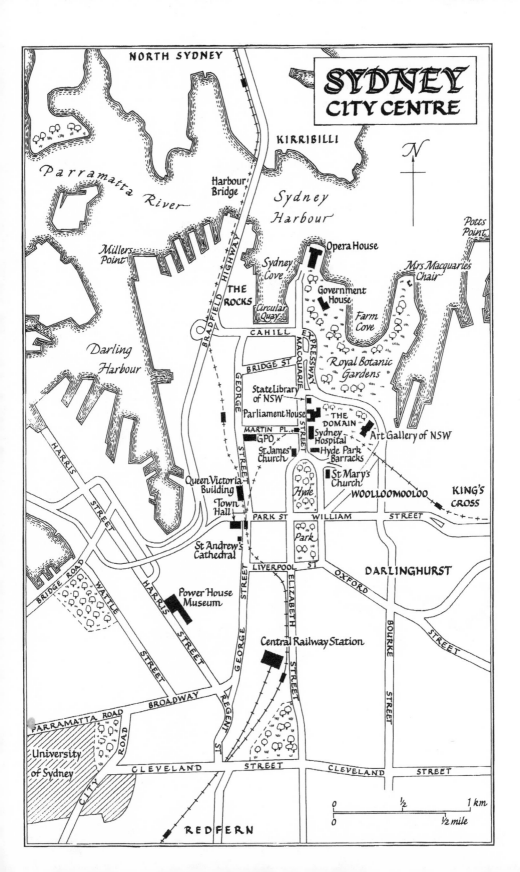

SYDNEY CITY CENTRE

NORTH SYDNEY

KIRRIBILLI

Parramatta River

Harbour Bridge

Sydney Harbour

N

Potts Point

Millers Point

Sydney Cove

Opera House

Mrs Macquaries' Chair

THE ROCKS

Circular Quay

Government House

Farm Cove

Darling Harbour

CAHILL

BRIDGE ST

Royal Botanic Gardens

BRADFIELD HIGHWAY

GEORGE STREET

MACQUARIE

EXPRESSWAY

State Library of NSW

Parliament House

THE DOMAIN

MARTIN PL.

GPO

Sydney Hospital

Art Gallery of NSW

St James' Church

Hyde Park Barracks

Queen Victoria Building

Hyde

St Mary's Church

WOOLLOOMOOLOO

KING'S CROSS

Town Hall

St Andrew's Cathedral

PARK ST

WILLIAM

STREET

HARRIS STREET

Park

ST

DARLINGHURST

BRIDGE ROAD

WATTLE STREET

LIVERPOOL

ELIZABETH

OXFORD

BOURKE STREET

STREET

Power House Museum

GEORGE STREET

Central Railway Station

PARRAMATTA ROAD

CITY ROAD

BROADWAY

REGENT ST

University of Sydney

CLEVELAND STREET

CLEVELAND STREET

0   ½   1 km
0   ½ mile

REDFERN

SYDNEY

VIEWPOINT

On a Sunday afternoon in late summer two elderly people in white linen hats, husband and wife without a doubt, and amiably married for thirty or forty years, stand at the parkland tip of Bradley's Head on the northern shore of Sydney Harbour in Australia—a promontory whose eponym, Rear-Admiral William Bradley, R.N., was sentenced to death in 1814 for defrauding the Royal mails. She wears a flowery cotton dress, he is in white shorts, though not of the very abbreviated kind known to Australians as stubbies. They are leaning on a rail below a white steel mast, the preserved fighting-top of His Majesty's Australian Ship *Sydney*, which sank the German sea raider *Emden* in 1914. In front of them a Doric column, protruding from the water, marks the beginning of a measured nautical mile; it used to form part of the portico of the Sydney General Post Office. Across the water the buildings of the south shore glitter from Woolloomooloo to Watson's Bay. Both husband and wife have binoculars slung around their necks, both have sheets of paper in their hands—lists of bird species, perhaps?—and even as we watch them, with a sudden excitement they raise their binoculars as one and look eagerly out across the water.

At such a time—Sunday arvo in the Australian vernacular —Sydney Harbour is prodigiously crowded. It is a kind of boat-jam out there. Hundreds upon hundreds of yachts skim, loiter, tack and race one another in the sunshine, yachts slithery and majestic, yachts traditional and experimental, solitary or in bright flotillas. Stolid ferryboats plod their way through the confusion. The Manly hydrofoil sweeps by. An occasional freighter passes on its way to the Pyrmont piers. A warship makes for the ocean. Distantly amplified guidebook voices sound from excursion cruisers, or there may be a boom of heavy rock from a party boat somewhere. And presently into our line of sight there burst the eighteen-footers of the Sydney Flying Squadron, which is what our dedicated pensioners have really been waiting for—not bowerbirds or whistle ducks, but furiously fast racing yachts.

They are hardly yachts in any ordinary sense. Their hulls are light rafts of high technology, with immensely long bowsprits, and they carry overwhelming, almost impossible masses of sail. Their crews, laced into bright-colored wet suits, faces smeared with white and yellow zinc, lean dizzily backward from trapezes. Their sails are emblazoned with the names of sponsors, the Bank of New Zealand, Xerox, Prudential, and they come into our vision like thunderbolts. Dear God, how those boats move! It makes the heart leap to see them. Foaming at the prow, spinnakers bulging, purposefully, apparently inexorably they beat a way through the meandering traffic, sending more dilettante pleasure craft hastily scattering and even obliging the big ferryboats to alter course. They look perfectly prepared to sink anything that gets in their way, and so like predators from some other ocean they scud past the *Sydney*'s mast and the pillar from the G.P.O., sweep beyond Bradley's Head, and disappear from view.

Romantics like to think that the eighteen-footers have developed from the hell-for-leather cutters of rum smugglers, and in evolving forms they have certainly been a beloved and familiar facet of this city's life for more than a century. Behind them, in the harbor mélange, we may be able to identify a smallish ferryboat pursuing them up the harbor: this is a beloved and familiar facet too, for unless it has lately been raided by plainclothes policemen, its passengers include a complement of punters, elderly people many of them, who go out each Sunday to place their illegal bets on the flying yachts before them—and some of whom, we need not doubt, were once themselves those sweating young toughs, brown as nuts, agile as cats, driving so tremendously before the harbor wind.

I choose to start a book about Sydney with this scene because I think it includes many of the elements which have created this city, and which sustain its character still. The glory of the harbor, the showy hedonism of its Sunday afternoons, the brutal force of the eighteen-footers, the mayhem aboard the gamblers' ferryboat, the white-hatted old lovers— the mixture of the familiar, the illicit, the beautiful, the nostalgic, the ostentatious, the formidable and the quaint, all bathed in sunshine and somehow impregnated with a fragile sense of passing generations, passing time, presents to my mind a proper introduction to the feel of the place.

Books about Sydney are innumerable, but they are mostly guidebooks, works of civic history or social analyses, and they have nearly all been written by Australians. No foreigner has tried to write a full-scale study or evocation, and this is not surprising; it is only in the last years of the twentieth century that Sydney has joined the company of the great metropoles. To inhabit a "world-class" city was always an aspiration of Sydney people, but it took them two centuries to achieve it.

Of course everyone had long had an idea of the city—if the world thought of Australia at all it generally thought of Sydney. Its harbor was popularly ranked for beauty with those of San Francisco, Rio de Janeiro, Hong Kong, Naples, Vancouver and Istanbul. Its sad origins as an eighteenth-century penal colony exerted an unhealthy fascination, and fostered many a gibe about criminal tendencies. Its accent was a gift to humorists. Its harbor bridge had been one of the world's best-known structures since 1932, and since 1966 its Opera House had provided one of the most familiar of all architectural shapes. Bondi beach was an archetypal pleasure beach, the quarter called Kings Cross was an international synonym for Rest and Recreation of the racier kind, and the interminable suburbs of Sydney, so vast that in built-up area this city is twice as large as Beijing and six times as large as Rome, had long figured in travelers' tales as an epitome of urban error. As for the people of Sydney, they had impressed themselves upon the universal fancy as an esoteric subspecies of Briton—sunburned, healthy, loud, generous, misogynist, beery, lazy, capable, racist and entertaining, strutting along beaches wearing bathing caps and carrying banners, exchanging badinage or war memoirs in raw colonial slang, jeering at unfortunate Englishmen at cricket matches they nearly always won.

It was a vivid image, but it was essentially provincial. Sydney was thought of, by and large, as second-rate—far from the centers of power, art or civil manners, a place of uncouth beginnings and ungentlemanly presence. Throughout the twentieth century visiting writers, mostly British, had been variously condescending and abusive about the city. At the turn of the century the radical Beatrice Webb thought it chiefly notable for its bad taste: its people were aggressive in manner and blatant in dress, while its mayor and aldermen were one and all "heavy common persons." In 1923 D. H. Lawrence, who spent two days in the city, declared it no more than a substitute London, made in five minutes—"as margarine is a substitute for butter." Robert Morley the actor, in

1949, thought the city misnamed—"Why didn't they call it Bert?" Neville Cardus the music critic, in 1952, said it was just like Manchester, except that the harbor was at the bottom of Market Street instead of the River Irwell. Denis Brogan the political philosopher, in 1958, thought the old-fashioned ladies' underwear on display in the big stores revealed "all too plainly the acceptance of a non-competitive mediocrity." "By God, what a site!" cried Clough Williams-Ellis the architect in the 1950s, "by man, what a mess!" And nobody was ruder than I was, when I first went to Sydney in the early 1960s. It was, I wrote then, no more than a harbor surrounded by suburbs—its origins unsavory, its temper coarse, its organization slipshod, the expressions of its society ladies "steely, scornful, accusatory and plebeian, as though they are expecting you (which Heaven forbid) to pinch their tight-corsetted behinds." It was five full years before the last letter of complaint reached me from down under.

The world turns; societies, like authors, age and mature; today Sydney really is, by general consent, one of the great cities of the world. Its population, though still predominantly British and Irish in stock, has been alleviated by vast influxes of immigrants from the rest of Europe and from Asia. Modern communications and the shifts of historical consequence mean that it is no longer on the distant perimeter of affairs, but strategically placed upon that frontier of twentieth-century change, the Pacific Rim. Its prickly old parochialism has been softened by a perceptible ability to laugh at itself, and a flood of Sydney talent has been unleashed upon us all, greatly changing perceptions of the city. When in 1988 the bicentennial of European settlement in Australia was spectacularly celebrated around the harbor, with fireworks and operas and tall ships, a new vision of Sydney, resplendent, festive and powerful, was once and for all stamped upon the general imagination.

I have often visited and written about the city since that reckless foray of 1962, and I return now primarily as an aficionado of British imperial history. Having commemorated in a series of books the rise and decline of the Victorian Empire, having written its elegy in a study of the last great colony, Hong Kong, I wanted to conclude my imperial commitment with a book about something grand, famous and preferably glittering left on the shores of history by Empire's receding tide. Preeminent among such flotsam, it seems to me, is the city of Sydney—not I think the best of the cities the British Empire created, not the most beautiful either, but the most hyperbolic, the youngest in heart, the *shiniest*. I do not entirely retract my judgments of thirty years ago, but like the rest of us I have come to view Sydney in a different light, and I think now that of all the strangers who have written about the city, since it first emerged from those origins I was fool enough to emphasize then, perhaps the poet Charles Causley got the municipal flavor most nearly right in his *H.M.S.* Glory *at Sydney*, (1951), which celebrates all the mixed offerings of a shore leave in this city, barmaids and tram rides, theaters and hangovers, besides the beauty of a sea entrance:

> *O! I shall never forget you on that crystal morning!*
> *Your immense harbour, your smother of deep green trees,*
> *The skyscrapers, waterfront shacks, parks and radio towers,*
> *And the tiny pilot-boat, the* Captain Cook,
> *Steaming to meet us . . .*

Back to Bradley's Head; and as we watch the eighteen-footers storm out of view, that crystal light and smother of trees is all around us, and the skyscrapers look back at us from over the water (though alas the elegant *Captain Cook* long ago sailed its last). And to add to the authenticity of the scene, now it turns out that our friends in the white hats have a little money on the boats too. *"Betting?"* they say with poker faces, "We don't know the meaning of the word." But those papers in their hands are race cards, not bird-spotting charts, and when Xerox and Prudential disappear behind the trees cheerfully they hasten down the woodland track around the point the better to follow their fancies. The contest lasts for another couple of hours, and sends the boats twice scudding up and down the harbor along courses dictated by the weather; thus making sure that whether it is the dry west wind that is blowing that day, or the maverick they call a Southerly Buster, or a humid nor'-easter out of the Tasman Sea, in one direction or another the Flying Squadron is sure to go pounding through, as our old enthusiasts might say, like a Bondi tram.

GENESIS

A gap between rocky scrub-covered headlands, about a mile wide, is the entrance to Sydney's harbor and thus the sea gate to the city itself and all its history. It stands at 151°10′ east longitude, 33°55′ south latitude, and the welcome it offers voyagers is allegorically benevolent. Outside, the Tasman Sea stretches away toward South America, New Zealand, South Africa and the Antarctic; inside, the landlocked haven promises every kind of comfort—navigational, climatic, sensual and domestic. Sydney Harbour is really a twisted valley, flooded by the sea a few millennia ago. It has two principal arms and a myriad smaller bays, and it disperses in the west into two channels which, though they are really more sea inlets than freshwater streams, are called the Parramatta and the Lane Cove rivers. The harbor is 16 miles long, covers an area of 21 square miles, reaches a depth of 160 feet, and despite the presence of the great city that lies around its shores, remains organically antipodean. Inland the low line of the Blue Mountains, for years the frontier of white settlement, still seems to speak of a wilderness beyond, especially when a golden-gray haze, like the suggestion of a desert, masks the suburbs at its feet, or when a bushfire smokes and flickers on the horizon;

and even within the easy limits of the harbor itself, to a stranger from the north matters can feel sufficiently esoteric.

Over Sydney Harbour the moon wanes and waxes topsy-turvy, and on its shores, as everyone knows, water goes the wrong way down the drain. The climate is benign in reputation and enviable in statistic (mean averages range from 22.3° in February to 12.3° in July), but in practice rather queer. It is said most closely to approximate that of Montevideo, in Uruguay, and can be disconcertingly capricious—hot one moment, cold the next, wet in one part when it is dry in another, with abrupt rainstorms and terrific winds which suddenly blow everything banging and askew, or instantly make the temperature plummet. It never snows in Sydney, but on an average it rains 140 days each year; while the winter can be superbly bracing, the summer often drags on week after week in muggy debilitation. Allergies and asthmas are common; in earlier times, before the European metabolism was acclimatized perhaps, Sydney people often complained of chronic sleepiness—"born tired," they used to say.

Then the green which is still the predominant color of the harbor shores is a peculiarly Australian olive-green, overlaid sometimes with a pinkish veil which is said to come from the vaporous essence of gum trees, and interspersed with a drab primordial gray of rocks. Many of the trees look to a foreign eye somehow inside out, with a ghostly glint of silver to them, and an indolent drooping of leaves: eucalyptus trees of many kinds, cabbage palms, blackboys, ironbarks, turpentines, mangroves, trees whose barks look as though they have been scribbled all over, trees bearing huge squashy figs, mighty pines of the South Pacific, strangely mixed with old familiars like limes and chestnuts and often encouched in ferns, orchids and casuarinas, or attended by plants with strange and lovely names—milkmaids, parrot-peas, lillypillies. Botanists still find surprises here: the scraggy pseudo-oak *Allacasuarina Portuen-*

sis was first identified in 1989, and only ten specimens have yet been discovered.

Swaths and patches of this evergreen foliage are every-where around the harbor. Wild ravines survive below busy streets, tangles of scrub lap commuters' houses. There are fine windy headlands above the ocean cliffs, and the Great North Walk, a 160-mile bush track, starts in the heart of the suburbs. Heaven knows what fauna you will encounter if you explore these glades, gullies and inlets. Possums will certainly be about, and wallabies perhaps, and multitudes of cackling, shouting, and coughing birds—mynahs, cockatoos, kookaburras, lyrebirds, egrets, languorous pelicans, sea eagles, the red-whiskered bulbul, the black-faced cuckoo shrike, or most maddeningly a kind of cuckoo called the koel, which emits for hours on end a tuneless cry like a small boy's early attempts at whistling. There may be koalas, or bandicoots, or possibly even duck bill platypuses. The cicadas will be shrilling in the various timbres attributed to their kinds—the black princes in one key, the yellow mondays allegedly in another. Crayfish skulk on the beds of streams. At night little aerial marsupials called sugar-gliders saunter from tree to tree. Even the Sydney gulls seem to me particular to the place: in grassy spots I have sometimes seen them staring fixedly between their legs for minutes at a time, yawning a great deal and settling them-selves amply in the green like hens.

Some of these creatures sound alarming. Watch out for the tiger snake, which has enough toxin in it to kill 6,000 mice.[1] Beware the nephila spider, whose web can be strong enough to snare a small bird, or worse still the Sydney funnel-web spider, which lives only in these parts, and is one of the most venomous arachnids on earth. An awful fish, the goblin fish,

---

[1] Or in the case of the most prolific recorded specimen, milked of its venom in 1934, enough to kill 40,000.

swims the Sydney waters, carrying poison in its spines. And the terrible star of all Sydney creatures is undoubtedly the shark, which is surrounded by legend, fear and wry humor. Pieces of human limbs have frequently been discovered in the bellies of sharks, or regurgitated from them, and more than one murder case has been linked to a shark's digestion. A Maginot Line of permanent nets, stretched across twenty-three beaches, protects Sydney from this monster, but still the most persuasive of Sydney injunctions is the one in many languages, accompanied by a grisly picture, warning people that there may be sharks about.

For the most part, though, it is a kindly enough strangeness that informs the Sydney setting. Very few people are really vomited by sharks. You are extremely unlikely to be stung by the goblin fish, or to feel in yourself the twitching of muscles, the profuse flow of sweat, tears and saliva that shows the funnel-web has got you. Sydney Harbour's allegory is just: it really is a haven, for people as for ships.

W e are told that natives of Australia have been living in the region of the harbor for 20,000 years, but no literate person is known to have set eyes on the Sydney Heads, the sea entrance, until 1770. In that year Lieutenant James Cook, Royal Navy, accompanied by the scientist Joseph Banks and the Swedish botanist Daniel Solander, brought H.M.S. *Endeavour* to this coast, made the acquaintance of its native tribespeople, and called it New South Wales.[1] He spent a week ashore at a large inlet some ten miles south of Sydney Harbour, and that

[1] Mysteriously, it may be thought—there is no record of his having seen South Wales, the coast is very different, and there was a New South Wales already, on Hudson Bay in Canada; but the name was apparently chosen as a favor for the Welsh patriot and botanist Thomas Pennant, who was a great friend of Banks's, and perhaps really means the New Wales of the South.

he called Botany Bay.[1] When he sailed on to the north, he passed the Heads, and noting that there appeared to be a safe anchorage within, named it Port Jackson.[2] However, after many months at sea he was doubtless in a hurry to get home, and he did not enter the haven.

It was accordingly Botany Bay, rather than Sydney Harbour, that the British government had in mind when, seventeen years later, it dispatched a fleet to colonize New South Wales in the name of the Crown. No European had been there in the meantime, and Cook was dead by then; but it had been decided that this arcane far corner of the world would be a suitable site for a penal settlement. The American colonies having lately been lost, the West African colonies being generally more lethal than even villains deserved, a new dumping-ground was needed for Britain's felons. The prison hulks of the Thames and Medway were hideously overcrowded, and there were thousands of miscellaneously convicted criminals, rebels, layabouts and ne'er-do-wells that the British Establishment wished to be rid of. Botany Bay was far away, relatively temperate, and might one day prove strategically or commercially useful; that it was already occupied by its native people was no handicap, in the political morality of the time; for a start 775 luckless misfits, 582 males, 193 females, average age twenty-seven, were packed into six chartered transports and sent to the Antipodes.[3]

Many of them were habitual offenders, though their crimes were mostly trivial. Their sentences were for seven years, fourteen years, or life, but good behavior might earn them tickets-of-leave before the expiration of their sentences, giving

---

[1] More obviously, since on its shores Banks and Solander collected scores of plants hitherto unknown to science.
[2] After George Jackson, a Secretary of the Admiralty, who presently spurned this gift of immortality by changing his name to Duckett.
[3] I take these figures, which are uncertain, from Mollie Gillen's *The Founders of Australia*, Sydney, 1989.

them limited freedom within the settlement, and the right to a grant of land. They might indeed be pardoned altogether at the government's discretion, but for the vast majority transportation to Botany Bay meant perpetual exile—very few would ever accumulate enough cash to buy a passage home. The convicts were accompanied by a couple of hundred marines, with 27 wives and 25 children, and by miscellaneous livestock.[1] With the transports sailed two small warships and three ships carrying supplies.[2] The route took the First Fleet of Australian history via Rio de Janeiro and the Cape of Good Hope—13,950 miles in all—and never before had so many people traveled so far together.

For most of the convicts, never having heard of Captain Cook, let alone read his reports (for they were almost all illiterate), it must have been like sailing to the moon. It is hard to imagine a more violent contrast between departure point and destination. In England Jane Austen was at work, the Marylebone Cricket Club had lately codified the rules of cricket and the House of Commons was considering a motion for the abolition of slavery. In New South Wales the cicadas chafed, the parrots squawked, and aboriginals speaking unknown tongues hunted inconceivable marsupials. Cowering in their creaking ships, often in chains, the prisoners of the First Fleet went all unknowing from one to the other.

Thus it was that on January 21, 1788, the first Europeans passed through the Sydney Heads. The First Fleet's commander, Captain Arthur Phillip, R.N., was also to be governor of the colony, and he very soon decided that Botany Bay was not after all the right place for a settlement, being wan of vegetation and short of fresh water. Instead he took a party of

---

[1] Including the chaplain's cats.
[2] Including, for instance, 40 wheelbarrows, 747,000 nails, and 250 women's handkerchiefs.

three boats northward along the coast to investigate Port Jackson, and spent two days exploring its waters.

We have a contemporary description of him in a boat—"his face shrivelled, and his aquiline nose under a large cocked hat, gathered up in a heap, his chin between his knees"—and so perhaps we may imagine him as his boat crews of sailors and marines rowed up the harbor toward a historic landfall. I suppose that after all those months at sea any coast looked pleasant, and Port Jackson was certainly more welcoming than Botany Bay. Even so, with its low and featureless shores covered with dense green, its rocks, as somebody said at the time, like bones that have had the fur rubbed off them, it must have looked desolate and monotonous enough. Here and there a parklike effect gladdened the English eye—the tribespeople regularly burnt brushwood to make hunting easier—but for the most part the bush was thick and forbidding. A few naked black people stared impassively as they passed, standing with fishing spears on rocks, or hunched over cooking fires in flimsy bark canoes. There were flashes of strange birds, no doubt, and perhaps glimpses of gray wallabies. Otherwise, only the rocks, the water and the changeless bush: to one of my own temperament Sydney Harbour in 1788 would have offered a discouraging spectacle.[1]

Not, however, to the naval eye. As he was later to report, Phillip realized this to be "one of the finest harbours in the world, in which a thousand sail of the line might ride in perfect security." Persevering well past Bradley's Head, almost to the mouth of the Parramatta River at the western end of the harbor, presently the boat crews found a place where fresh

---

[1] As it certainly did twenty years later to the litterateur Barron Field, who came to Sydney as a Supreme Court judge, thought evergreen trees inimical to the poetic urge, and said he could "hold no fellowship with Australian foliage." When Field left Australia in 1824, the British *Dictionary of National Biography* delicately tells us, "the complimentary address of the lawyers did not represent every shade of public opinion."

water ran into an anchorage down a gentle declivity in the bush—"a small snug cove on the southern side," is how Captain Watkin Tench of the marines described it. They called this V-shaped inlet Sydney Cove, after the home secretary, Thomas Townshend, first Baron Sydney of Chislehurst[1]; and on its banks, on January 26, 1788, they ran up the Union flag and founded a city. They intended to call it Albion, but somehow or other it became known as Sydney too.

No great city, not even Rome which was founded by wolf's sucklings, has had more unlikely beginnings, and the first years of Sydney were predictably tough and lonely. The merchantmen of the fleet soon sailed away, three to China to pick up tea, five to England in ballast, leaving only one storeship and the two little naval vessels. The convicts were set to building work—houses for the officers, huts for themselves—but there were few skilled craftsmen among them, and at first mud, reeds, wattles and unseasoned wood were their only materials, together with lime made from crushed mussel shells. The soil was poor. The fauna was unnerving. The natives, belonging to a tribe called the Iora, proved largely incomprehensible. A second fleetload of convicts, arriving in 1790, discharged a horrifying complement of dead and dying, and for a time it seemed that everybody might starve—a convict was given 1,000 lashes for stealing three pounds of potatoes, and dinner guests at the governor's table had to bring their own victuals. The whole colony was in a state of dejec-

---

[1] And last, the title dying with him. Why he called himself Sydney the *Dictionary of National Biography* does not say, and it suggests that were it not for the Australian city named after him he would probably be best remembered by a line of Oliver Goldsmith's about Edmund Burke: *"Though fraught with all learning, yet straining his throat / To persuade Tommy Townshend to give him his vote."* However, citizens of Sydney, Nova Scotia, founded 1785, might disagree.

tion, and there were moments when even the most sanguine of Phillip's officers thought it might be better to give up. It was the poorest country in the world, wrote Lieutenant Ralph Clark of the marines. Nature there was nearly worn out, wrote Major Robert Ross. There was hardly anything to see but rocks, reported the Reverend Richard Johnson, chaplain to the colony, and hardly anything to eat but rats. The first suicide soon occurred: an aged perjurer named Dorothy Handland, said to be the oldest person in the colony, hanged herself from a gum tree.

Yet Phillip himself was convinced that one day this miserable settlement might outgrow its origins to become a free British nation on the other side of the earth. Bolstered by this conviction he held things together until he went home in 1792, and by the turn of the century the worst was over. The place was still generally known in England as Botany Bay, as the penal colony always would be, but in fact the city of Sydney had taken root. It was no longer the only Australian settlement—it had founded its own subsidiary penal colony at Norfolk Island, a thousand miles out in the Pacific. Nor was it now utterly isolated in the world at large, because trading ships had begun to find their way there in the wake of the transports. A third convict fleet from England had raised the population to rather more than 7,000, including some 500 free citizens, and around the cove a proper town had arisen, built by now largely of brick and the local reddish-brown sandstone. The rivulet that had first attracted Phillip to the site had been channeled into small reservoirs and named the Tank Stream, and a stone bridge had been built across it; this formed a rough boundary between more disreputable quarters on the west side of the cove, more respectable on the east —a social demarcation which was to linger for a century and more.

A bumpy sandstone outcrop formed the western arm of the

cove. Along its edge ran a track called Serjeant-Major's Row, and in lines above stood the huts the prisoners had built for themselves, single-room houses put together of mud, wood and thatch in the old English way, with small gardens and lines of washing. There were a few more sizable houses up there too, and a hospital of single-story buildings, one of them brought out in prefabricated parts from England. Not far away were the gallows, and the stocks, and the barracks of the New South Wales Corps, which had by now replaced the marines as a garrison and police force. On the promontory at the end stood a signal tower, a simple observatory and a gun embrasure. At night a beacon fire burned for the guidance of ships.

On the other side of the cove, the bourgeois side, lived the Establishment. There were no quays then, ships anchoring offshore, but to the east of the Tank Stream a jetty protruded, announcing the portals of Sydney officialdom. On the slope immediately behind it the governor occupied a two-story white house with a veranda, looking over a garden to the water and picturesquely supplied with tame wallabies, and nearby were substantial houses for his chief officials. The superintendent of convicts lived there *ex officio,* and the garrison commander, and the chaplain, and the surveyor general, and to the east, over a low ridge, gamely struggled a government farm, where the first attempts had been made to grow European vegetables in an uncongenial soil.

A guardhouse next to the bridge protected one half of the town from the other. Near it was the government lumber yard, where convicts worked at saws and forges, and beyond it the settlement straggled away to the south, meandered through by mud roads. A pair of windmills crowned the higher ground behind the waterfront, together with the tower of Sydney's only church: it was named St. Phillip's, with two *ls*, in honor of the first governor.[1] On the northern side of the harbor there were a few houses, too, and from them tracks went off to the infant farming settlements already established on the Hawkesbury River, twenty miles to the north. To the west the first proper road in Australia, shaded by thick foliage, led to the ancillary village of Parramatta, where the government had a second experimental farm, and the governor a second Government House. By now there were about a thousand head of cattle in the settlement, together with six thousand sheep and four thousand pigs, and several thousand acres had been sown with wheat, corn and barley.

Pictures of the time make Sydney look quite elegant and well ordered, with ships on the stocks at the government shipyard on the cove, neat rows of cottages, boats scurrying here and there, the hospital spanking clean and Government House gracious above its gardens. Decorous natives generally appeared in these scenes, and sometimes well-dressed stockmen drove cattle down pretty lanes. All this was largely artistic convention however, and was often heightened when, far away from the discomforts of Sydney Cove, on-the-spot sketches were turned into engravings. In reality those buildings were rickety, amateurish, riddled with white ants and spongy with wet rot. Government House was horribly damp, besides being plagued by vile and unexplained smells from its foundations, while the hospital on the ridge, which looks so commendable in the pictures, was appallingly filthy and overcrowded. Sydney was a prison, but a kind of open prison; the only jail was a primitive lockup, and the convicts were still left to house themselves as best they could. Their homemade cottages were generally no more than hovels, often simultaneously serving as *ad hoc* taverns and brothels; many of the more

[1] A common imperial practice: St. Stephen's at Ootacamund, for example, is named not for the protomartyr but for Stephen Lushington, Esquire, Indian Civil Service.

feckless transportees lived in caves among the rocks, in sea-shore crannies, or even in holes in trees. The bush around was still like a somber green cage. Convicts who ran away into it generally returned disoriented, and no European had ever crossed the Blue Mountains, only thirty miles to the west.

Besides, we must add to our mind's picture the truly extraordinary features of everyday life in Sydney circa 1800, which seldom show in the watercolors: tatterdemalion gangs of male convicts clanking about in irons, incorrigible female prisoners screeching ribaldry and obscenities, soldiers everywhere with high hats and enormous fixed bayonets, petty offenders sitting in the stocks, sex-starved sailors raunching around the grogshops and aboriginals wandering stark naked or in cast-off English finery. Wallabies and chickens strayed here and there, caged cockatoos screeched, and in the public cemetery pigs and goats scavenged among the graves, the pigs sometimes interrupting themselves to eat the goats. Hundreds of ragged homeless children mooched through the streets; on the island called Pinchgut, off the cove, swung the skeletonic remains of a hanged Irishman, as a *memento mori* for the rest.[1]

The convicts formed an extremely rough-and-ready proletariat. Many of them had no idea where they were, and some thought that China lay just beyond the Blue Mountains. Governor John Hunter, in the 1790s, said of them that "a more wicked, abandoned and irreligious set of people had never been brought together in any part of the world," and they were kept under control largely by the use of the cat-o'-nine-tails, with which a quarter of a million strokes were administered in an average year. If they remained intractable they

---

[1] Pinchgut is said to have got its original name either because of the poor convicts deposited there in punishment, and fed only bread and water, or (more probably) because the harbor narrowed around it. It is now officially called Fort Denison.

could be sent off to still worse punishment on Norfolk Island, the end of the road. The soldiery, their guards, were hardly more reassuring than the felons. The rankers were brutal riff-raff, the officers, scoured one assumes from regiments not anxious to retain their services, soon congealed into a rapacious clique of opportunists, and grabbed a near-monopoly of the colony's commerce. The local aborigines were already being debased with alcohol, mockery, abuse and condescension, besides being decimated by smallpox and other diseases. There were virtually no machines, and few draft animals; almost every labor had to be done by hand, with the help of the flogger's whip.

Probably no city has ever been so meticulously pictured from the day of its foundation, by naval and military officers professionally trained to sketch and map, and by variously gifted amateurs. The atmosphere, though, is quite another thing, and perhaps we can never quite conceive what it was like to live in such a place, where the gentry were jailers, where the people were prisoners, where the natives were like creatures out of another age, and where the terrible sound of the scourge was heard so often above the cries of the birds, the parade-ground shouts, and the wind through the gum trees all around.[1]

All changed in the Victorian century, as further British colonies were founded one by one elsewhere in Australia, and Phillip's dream was fulfilled. There was a slight coup d'état in 1808—the so-called Rum Rebellion, when Governor William Bligh of *Bounty* fame was deposed in a military putsch. Order however was soon restored, and Sydney became a thrusting

---

[1] We shall return to the penal environment; for a complete evocation of convict Sydney, Robert Hughes's *The Fatal Shore* (1986) has no rival.

enclave of capitalism in the south. A civilian establishment took over from the military. A thriving sea trade developed. The merino sheep, imported from Spain, gave the colony a profitable commodity. A governor of artistic leanings, Lachlan Macquarie, gave it some sense of style. Penal transportation to New South Wales was ended in 1840; by then about 83,000 convicts had been shipped in, but they were almost balanced by some 70,000 free Britons given government-subsidized passages in the cause of imperial development. Soon both categories would be outnumbered by native-born Europeans. The illimitable bush still hemmed in the town—when his parishioners left church after evensong, the vicar of St. Thomas, North Sydney, once remarked, their hurricane lamps disappeared into the empty valleys "like stars into infinity"—but there was a road across the Blue Mountains now, and the town had a well-populated hinterland. No longer were these alien people fumbling their way through the strangeness of climate, fauna and flora; a generation had grown up that felt at home with the land, and knew the tricks of survival.

In 1856 Sydney became the capital of the self-governing Colony of New South Wales. Its economy was distinctly of the boom-and-bust variety, and in size and wealth it was rivaled by Melbourne to the south, but still as the imperial century proceeded toward its apogee, and Victoria the Queen-Empress toward her Golden Jubilee, the former penal settlement matured into a proper imperial outpost, peer to Toronto and Singapore, Durban and Madras. The poor indigenes had all but disappeared; the British had made a city in their own image. In the second half of the century Sydney's population increased by about 100,000 in every decade. By the 1880s, the centenary decade, it was approaching 400,000, and the city government moved into a new Town Hall proper to its responsibilities, a mile or so to the south of the cove. This was almost excessively municipal, extravagantly towered and housing a terrific organ, and beside it stood a hardly less diocesan Anglican cathedral, with three towers and much stained glass. Here was the nexus, functional and symbolical, of High-Victorian Sydney.

As a very simulacrum of Britishness in the age of free trade and imperial expansion, the Sydney of the 1880s was intensely self-conscious. Among the professional people, the civil servants, the landowners who maintained their town houses in the city, life seems to have been almost suffocatingly genteel. All the paraphernalia of Victorian decorum flourished. Etiquette was severe, morality ostentatious, social behavior was derived directly from the example of what was still generally thought of as Home, or the Mother Country. Families competed in splendor of transportation and fashionableness of costume, and we read of incessant visiting among the ladies, of busy club life, political activity and sporting enthusiasm among the gentlemen, the whole revolving around the governor in his new and far grander Government House in the green Domain above the harbor. People from Melbourne thought it all absurd, and called Sydney Sleepy Hollow; visitors from England thought it rather charming.

The central city looked very British, too. "The houses," Charles Dilke had written sourly in the 1860s, "are of the commonplace English ugliness, worst of all possible forms of architectural imbecility." Sydney's chief park was called Hyde Park, its lovely botanical gardens looked consciously toward Kew, its university was a transplanted fragment of Oxbridge and its best shops were modeled on the London style—W. H. Soul the pharmacists, for instance, blue and white and heraldically crested, or David Jones the draper, which prided itself upon its silky service.[1] A mighty post of-

[1] And which was founded, like several of the great London stores, by a "Cardi"—a Welshman from Cardiganshire.

fice, with a Renaissance tower and elaborate decoration, stood in the heart of the business district. Overlooking Sydney Cove was a solid Customs House with a bust of Queen Victoria above the door, and behind it sundry great government buildings had arisen, portentous in golden sandstone and rich in symbolism. The Treasury Building had a portico with Ionic columns, just like something in Whitehall. The brand-new Lands Department Building had an onion-domed tower and was equipped with forty-eight niches for statues of famous citizens. The colonial secretary's office was guarded by images of Wisdom, Justice and Mercy. The Legislative Assembly and the Mint were housed in some of Governor Macquarie's ambitious Georgian buildings, and Macquarie Street upon which they stood was lined with handsome town houses, some of them very opulent, looking out across a green expanse of parkland in genuinely English style.

Utterly English too were the villas which now speckled the outskirts of town, and were implanted on suitable promontories throughout the harbor—gardened white mansions in classical style, with ornamental gates, leafy drives and lodges. The chief secretary lived in one such pleasant house, the bishop of New South Wales in another, and sometimes there were cottages appended for servants, for all the world like an English estate. In less advantageous parts of town the middle classes occupied pleasant terraced houses, and the better-off artisans lived in rows of cottages that were often charming, and were decorated ornately with iron filigree.

All the symptoms of British imperial system were apparent. Big warehouses dominated the harbor front, and around Sydney Cove had been built a modern landing place, the Semi-Circular Quay—later, though if anything squared up rather by then, renamed the Circular Quay. There were steam trams in the streets, and steam ferries across the harbor, and trains to Parramatta. There were up-to-date hospitals and water supplies, and the Tank Stream had been diverted into underground channels. A brand-new sewerage system discharged its effluent not into the harbor but into the open sea. There was an *Illustrated Sydney News,* and a Sydney *Punch.*

But of course, here as in Victorian Britain itself, behind these complacent scenes there teemed an underclass, some of it extremely raw. Slums festered, for all the civic propriety. Public health was terrible despite the sewerage system. Society was still full of mayhem and corruption—political shenanigans, drug abuse, prostitution—and most vices were legal. As a contemporary said even of the Imperial Temperance Hotel in King Street, "there is no knowing what you can do, if you only know how to work the ropes." And if you could sin at the Imperial Temperance in King Street, just think what you could do at the sailors' taverns at the Rocks, that sandstone outcrop above the Cove where the convicts had built their huts! Down the years the Rocks had developed into one of the Pacific's most notorious sailor towns, where some of the toughest people in the world lodged hugger-mugger among the courts and narrow alleys, drinking furiously, banding together in ferocious street gangs, living by thievery and prostitution and frequently given new blood by deserting seamen and peripatetic rascals from all the oceans.

The bishop and the chief secretary lived handsomely enough in their villas; the poor of Sydney lived miserably enough down below, despite the sunshine, the space and the freedom. *"Drifting past, drifting past, / To the beat of weary feet,"* is how Henry Lawson the poet thought of them, *"In the filthy lane and alley, / and the cruel heartless street."* Perhaps, after all, the city had not quite transcended its beginnings; sometimes, as we read about its aldermanic pride and prosperity, the grand celebrations with which it greeted its own centennial and Victoria's fifty years upon the throne, we can just see poor old Dorothy Handland still swinging from her eucalyptus.

Not for much longer. The Rocks were largely demolished when in 1900 a bubonic plague fell upon Sydney. The worst of the slums disappeared then, most of the vices were made illegal, and in a generation or two the physique of Sydney working people almost miraculously improved. In the new century, as the various Australian colonies banded themselves together into a Federal Commonwealth, Sydney became an epitome of the Workers' Paradise—as democratic a city as any on earth, with powerful trade unions to fight the poor man's cause and a burning sense of social equality. Its standards of living were said to be higher than those of any British or American city, and its people had developed, said a local writer in 1907, "a sort of clever hecticness, an almost unnatural sharpening of the wits in the furious race for wealth, and a constant and all but unappeasable itching for excitement and amusement and change for its own sake." When the city's young men went to war, in 1914, they went with terrific brio. In Victorian times they had been described as "wanting in power and weight"; now John Masefield, the English poet, could compare them to "kings in old poems."

Australia became a nation, people still like to say, upon the battlefields of Gallipoli, and the Sydney that emerged from the Great War was a different Sydney too. Conscious of itself as an Australian city, no longer just a transplanted city of the English provinces, Sydney had acquired an urban character of its own. Although its people were still 98 percent British in origin, by now they looked, sounded and dressed differently. Let us visit them finally at the start of the 1930s, when the Great Depression was falling upon Sydney as it was falling upon every city of the capitalist West. All the miseries of the slump were visible here then, the shantytowns and the soup kitchens, the unemployed thousands sleeping in parks, at railway stations, on ramshackle houseboats, the mothers with their children scavenging among the seashore flotsam. Communism was strong. Organized crime was rampant. Mutilated survivors of the Great War haunted the city streets, reproachfully begging. Amidst this unhappiness the personality of the community, now more than a million strong, had reached some kind of climax.

The economy had been more or less stagnant throughout the first quarter of the twentieth century, but the city now extended in immense swaths of suburbia far out from the Town Hall: beyond Parramatta toward the Blue Mountains in the west, down to Botany Bay in the south, joining up with the old Hawkesbury River settlements to the north. At the same time the beach culture was developing fast—the Sydney preoccupation with sun, sand and surf, exemplified in bright oceanfront suburbs and in the competitive pageantry of the lifeguards. The city felt more southern, more Pacific than it had seemed in the 1880s, as though it was consciously changing direction. Even the architecture, so slavishly British fifty years before, had acquired extra subtropical mannerisms— eaves, overhangs, arcades, verandas, and the canopies over sidewalks which had become characteristic of the Australian urban style.

After generations of sunshine and general plenty, the people themselves had been mutated, too. The women were tall and robust, the men had acquired that somewhat louche, shambling, easygoing but powerful gait that for a time was to be their hallmark. This was the real heyday of the dinkum Aussie—the Aussie of the slouch hat, the long-short trousers and the knee-length socks, with his Sheila who stuck with the rest of the girls at the far end of the room, and his well-known place at the bar. It was a macho, philistine, cocky Sydney, or as Kenneth Slessor the poet preferred, "gaslight, straw hat, bunch-of-bananas, tram-ride Sydney."[1] "In things of the mind," declared the Sydney cartoonist Will Dyson in 1929, "we show about as much spirit as a suburban old maid."

It was Sydney at its most truly provincial. Inevitably the place still half thought of itself as an imperial metropolis, and figured in works of imperial self-gratification as The Second City of the Empire. But it was really neither one thing nor another. Though it was still a state capital, it was now only one of six in a self-governing Australia whose federal capital was at Canberra, 180 miles away. Its governing classes remained, by and large, almost ridiculously royalist and conventional, but many of its working people were generally indifferent to the British link, often republican of tradition, often Communist of sympathy, militantly organized and Irishly inclined.

It was not really much of a place, by international standards. Its Victorian landmarks and Georgian relics had been swallowed up in run-of-the-mill commercial development, of no particular style. Its suburbs, often cruelly deprived of trees, were mostly unlovely. Since the Great War hardly a public building had gone up which was worth a second look, or would seem in future decades worth preserving. The cockiness was probably largely chip-on-shoulder, and I would think it fair to say that the early 1930s were Sydney's nadir. The city looked back still with bitterness to its squalid start; it was torn between a sickly imperial loyalty and a raucous independence; one would hardly guess, surveying its philistine parochialism and sense of resentment, that within another fifty years it would have burst into the buoyant postimperial prodigy that this book is going to describe.

---

[1] From his text for the picture book *Portrait of Sydney*, 1950.

Yet only two years later, in a gesture of anomalous exhilaration, at the worst time of the Depression Sydney opened its Harbour Bridge, one of the talismanic structures of the earth, and then by far the most striking thing ever built in Australia. At that moment, I think, contemporary Sydney began—perhaps definitive Sydney. Another world war, a few more booms and slumps, confirmed Sydney's economic status. The decline of the British Empire shifted its attitudes to the world. A tremendous migration of continental Europeans and Asians drastically altered its manner. We have arrived at our Sunday arvo of the 1990s, with the eighteen-footers storming past Bradley's Head, and the skyscrapers gleaming on the foreshore.

Sydney people often say their city lacks a sense of history, but I do not find it so. I find the past more easily retrievable in Sydney than in most cities, so familiar to us are the people who founded this place, whether we know them by name or simply as generic figures, and so easy is it to imagine the scenes of earlier times. Many a monument of the Victorian age stands grandly Victorian still. David Jones now claims to be "The Most Beautiful Store in the World," and W. H. Soul the Pitt Street pharmacy offers a SOULCOLOR fast film service. The Treasury's cortile now shelters the coffee shop of the Intercontinental Hotel. The Lands Department Building has vacant niches for twenty-five heroes. When George Street (né Serjeant-Major's Row) swerves near its northern end, it is avoiding the vanished boundary of the original government shipyard; when it veers to the east and back again by the Town Hall it is shying away from the ghosts of the first city graveyard, where the pigs molested the goats. The unpredictable street pattern of downtown Sydney relates still to the site of Phillip's malodorous little mansion. The Tank Stream, sometimes fierce with storm water, still empties itself into Sydney Cove beside Pier 6 at Circular Quay. Graffiti remain from the days of the First Fleet. Often in the evening, around the harbor, I see solitary meditative figures sitting on rocks just as the aboriginals sat long ago; and after dark, when the riding light of some small fishing craft swims across the water, I find it easy to expect one of those elementary canoes to come paddling out of the night, with a naked black woman in the stern and a cooking fire burning amidships.

And the bush survives. We will end this skim through the Sydney past with a glimpse of the wild present—more than mere *rus in urbe,* more nature indestructible. We stand on a road bridge in one of the northern suburbs, looking down upon one of those tangled gullies of bush far below the sidewalk. It is dusk. A full moon is rising, and little groups of people, in twos and threes, are fitfully assembling on the bridge. The traffic is light, the evening is sultry, there is not much sign of life in the houses which are scattered among the trees. Below us a stream glints through huge ferns. A youth with tattooed forearms throws a cigarette end over the bridge, and it floats into the gully in a scatter of sparks. A couple of small children race each other up and down the sidewalk. We are waiting for the Sydney fruit bats, the big flying foxes, which nest somewhere down there in their hundreds of thousands, allegedly emitting a frightful vespertilian smell.[1] Each evening they leave their perches in the wood to go foraging through the city, all over the northern suburbs and far across the harbor, where they are often to be felt, rather than exactly seen, fuzzily passing apartment windows. They are among the southernmost fruit bats, the largest community in Sydney, and they have survived everything that history has been able to do to them. Today they have many admirers, and I went once to a protection society meeting, up the road in the well-

---

[1] Transmitted, I am told unnervingly by one who has tried, into the sweat of those who eat them.

heeled suburb of Gordon, whose enthusiasm the bats themselves would have been astonished to discover—bat-friends of all ages were there, wearing bat-badges and bat-ornamented T-shirts, listening to zealous bat-lectures, examining a bat-skeleton in a glass case and distributing bat-pamphlets of missionary zeal.

Night begins to fall. The little audience crowds to the parapet. Out of the murky bush there emerges a solitary *Pteropus poliocephalus,* flapping over our heads and wheeling southward toward the harbor. After a minute or two another follows, and then a couple more. It seems a desultory progress, and the children begin to lose interest, and start racing up and down the pavement again. "Is that all?" says a girl to her young man. "Fucking hell," says the youth with the tattoos. But after a few minutes the pace theatrically quickens, the bats appear in threes and fours, and then in batches, and then in squadrons, and then in fleets, until the whole darkening sky is full of them, and they pour out of the bush in an apparently endless stream, hundred upon hundred, thousand upon thousand, like a furious reassertion of old supremacies.

After a while their interminable passage into the night becomes a bit of a bore, and long before the last bat has flown over that bridge the children have seen enough of them, and are clamoring to go home.

APPEARANCES

1 URBS

For most people in the world the look of Sydney is the grand-slam look, the whole-hog, flag-and-fireworks look. This can certainly be magnificent. Little in contemporary travel beats flying down the coast from Newcastle on a fine spring day, following the line of the northern ocean beaches and abruptly turning westward at the Sydney Heads to make the home run down the harbor. It makes you feel majestic even in an elderly shuddering seaplane. It gives you a triumphant feel, as though there ought to be incidental music in the air, preferably "Waltzing Matilda."

The Heads fall away below you, bashed by their Pacific waves, the Middle Harbour runs off to the north, and then there are wide red-roofed suburbs below, splodged with green wooded protrusions, with the gleam of innumerable swimming pools, and glorious splashes of flame trees and jacarandas. A couple of small islands slide beneath your wings. The harbor is streaked with the wakes of ships, freighters off to sea, hydrofoils rushing to and from the city, and here and there stand fine white villas on desirable sites. There goes Bradley's Head, with the *Sydney*'s fighting-top, and there is the little island citadel of Pinchgut, and then—*tara! tara!*—the heart of Sydney splendidly greets us, the great old arch of the bridge, the splayed shells of the Opera House, the skyscrapers all flash and swank. Beyond it, as in diminuendo, the suburbs fade away dingy around the maundering Parramatta River, and beyond them again is the gray-blue ridge of the mountains, that *ne plus ultra* to the early settlers. Few cities on earth can offer so operatic an approach.

Somebody once lent me five videocassettes of the bicentennial celebrations in 1988, which were the most spectacular of all the city's spectacular occasions. I played them on fast forward, and never was there such an exhilarating succession of images: yachts and symphony orchestras and flags and dancing aborigines—airships, fire-floats spouting, princes arriving, bands playing—vast cheering crowds, curtsies, soldiers saluting, gabbled speeches—now a wide shining shot of the harbor, now the Opera House from the air—gun salutes I think, helicopters certainly, flowers, children singing, and as the day rapidly changed to night before my eyes, a violent eruption of rockets into the sky, and a pyrotechnical waterfall over the lip of the bridge.

Speeding it up in this way seemed perfectly proper to me—aesthetically Sydney is made for the instant exciting impact, not five full cassettes of contemplation—but I slowed the tape down in the end when, as the city broke into a last tremendous blaze of rejoicing light, they really did play "Waltzing Matilda."

The original city, on the south shore of the harbor, was built upon shallow hills and outcrops—the gentle bumps and slopes that surrounded Phillip's Tank Stream. This gave it pictorial advantages, but it also meant a certain meanness of scale, and time and again efforts were made to endow the place with a more formal dignity. Phillip himself apparently envisaged a Sydney of inspirational quality, like Raffles's Singapore—"built in characters of light." He decreed that its principal streets should be 200 feet wide, and he imagined a waterfront square with the chief buildings of state grouped around it, and Government House above—perhaps he was thinking of Greenwich on the Thames. It never happened, anyway. When the Italian navigator Alessandro Malaspina arrived at Sydney in 1793 with two Spanish corvettes, he was assured that there *was* a city plan, but could not make out how it operated.

Governor Macquarie, who arrived in 1810, also had visionary plans for the city, in which he was abetted by a convict architect, Francis Greenway of Bristol, transported for fourteen years for forgery but pardoned after six. Like Phillip, Macquarie wanted to minimize the convict taint, visually at least, and he fancied a city centered not upon the waterfront but around a cathedral square a mile or so inland; upon this piazza all the city streets, named after members either of the British royal family or of the Macquarie clan, would ornamentally converge, affording both splendor and the easy control of riots. Macquarie's inspiration was probably Edinburgh, with a touch of British Calcutta thrown in. At the same time his protégé Greenway dreamed of building a castle on the Rocks, and a monumental colonnade around the cove to be Sydney's ceremonial gateway. Once again the greater designs came to nothing, but before accusations of extravagance stifled them Macquarie and Greenway did manage to get some agreeable building done—a church or two, civilized-looking convict barracks, a beguiling fort on the water's edge, a nice lighthouse, a turreted tollhouse like a Gothic folly, a market with a street to its own wharf and a gubernatorial stable block which, if it was not in fact the castle of Greenway's dreams, looked remarkably like one.

Ever since then there have been sporadic proposals for the monumentalization of Sydney, usually based upon some variation of Phillips and Greenway—majestic harbor-front developments, that is, together with broad boulevards into town. Sir Robert Garran, solicitor-general of the Commonwealth of Australia, mused in the 1930s that a Great Fire might be a good idea; they could give the rebuilt city "impressive exits and entrances, open up a scenic drive along the harbour foreshore, and provide a fair allowance of stately boulevards." In the 1950s a redevelopment scheme for William Street, one of the chief east-west thoroughfares, imagined it transformed into a café-lined, tree-shaded, eight-laned ceremonial highway, elegant with plazas, malls, and colonnades and with a stream running down the middle—"at least the equal," as the plan's chief progenitor foresaw, "of the Champs-Elysées of Paris."[1] More recently the Sydney Planning Committee (ever hopeful as planners must be, or they would lose heart) has envisaged a downtown divided into twelve zones each of "unique character"—a zone for cinemas, for instance, an educational zone, a "business area with heritage flavour," a Chinatown zone and a ceremonial civic zone.

There was a time when the Victorians did manage to give this city, as they gave to so many others throughout the British Empire, a discernible unity of style and purpose. The Town Hall complex had definite authority, and pictures of the Circular Quay in the late nineteenth century show it, too, handsomely balanced, the Customs House centrally presiding, sandstone offices of state on the slopes behind, Gothic Government House stately in its gardens above. The govern-

---

[1] William Street in 1992 is chiefly notable for car salesrooms in the daytime, prostitution at night, and is bounded at its eastern end by an enormous Coca-Cola sign.

ment's private Domain had become a superb park, stretching in uninterrupted green down the eastern flank of the city center, and lively sandstone devices of baroque and rococo gave the downtown streets exuberance. For a few years, too, in the early 1880s, the scene was majestically crowned by the domed Garden Palace of Sydney's first International Exhibition, looking rather like a basilica from Central Europe; but this was made only of wood, and burned down in a matter of hours in 1882.[1]

With the turn of the twentieth century the balance was lost, and by the time I first reached this city, at the start of the 1960s, its center was uncompelling indeed. Its principal streets were dowdy, its older quarters were run-down, and its skyline, limited until 1957 to a height of 150 feet, lacked either panache or romance. Sydney Cove, far from being grandly colonnaded, had been crassly masked by the Cahill Expressway, an overhead ring road which hideously blocked the city's central vista, and went on to cut the lovely Domain in two.[2] On the point where the Opera House now stands there was a tram station thinly disguised as a fort, and the tallest structure in town was a radio mast on top of an office block, forlornly pretending to be the Eiffel Tower.

Things are not half so dull today. The Victorian balance has never been restored, and architecturally Sydney is certainly not one of the most distinguished of the New World's city centers. Nevertheless the explosion of steel, glass and concrete in the past twenty years has given it a cohesive excitement, and the central clump of high rise is nothing if not energetic. It is capped by the burnished gold steeple of the Sydney

---

[1] "In a great lustrous sea," the *Sydney Morning Herald* reported with relish at the time, "of red-hot metal and burning woodwork." The palace gates are still there, on Macquarie Street.

[2] Passing, by an act of rare justice, within a few feet of the dining-room windows of the Royal Automobile Club.

Tower, the tallest structure in the Southern Hemisphere, and though the caprices of postmodernism have hardly affected it yet, it does present a lively variety of shapes, levels and angles. The radio tower has long been submerged in the mass, but many of the Victorian monuments still manage to assert themselves, if only in daintily preserved façades, and here and there graceful survivors of Macquarie's day stand assiduously preserved amidst the frenzy.

Downtown Sydney, the square mile or so south of Circular Quay, remains somewhat warrenlike. A kind of grid system has been imposed upon its streets, but only just, and visitors are surprised to discover that it is really rather picturesque—in character not unlike lower Manhattan, and far more crannied and quirky than most of the other great modern cities of the world. This is partly because of its irregular terrain, which has required steep streets, unexpected staircases, and interesting variations of level, but partly because of its improvised origins.

The early planners having failed in their designs, the city was to retain forever a touch of the ramshackle, and even now it is possible to discern in corners of inner Sydney glimpses of ancient social styles—styles Dickensian or Hogarthian, or older still, inherited from England. Deep-worn steps in waterside lanes, unexpected squares, the occasional unimproved pub, back alleys littered with leaves and blown blossoms, smells of rot and damp wood in about-to-be-gentrified cottages—all these easily evoke for me times and manners long gone. Anthony Trollope thought the same, when he came to Sydney in 1873. He was baffled by Sydney's sense of antiquity, since it was then less than a century old, but charmed by its intricacy. It was not, he remarked approvingly, parallelogrammatic. Then years later Richard Twopenny, also direct from England, thought its tangled streets "like old friends," and the artist Lloyd Rees, entering the city center for the first time in 1917, was delighted by its sense of enclosure—"one cannot see *through* Sydney."

Flower, fruit and food stalls add to this feeling of organic age, together with the crowded arcades, full of small shops like medieval markets, that burrow between the streets. The Rocks have long been prettied up for the tourists, but still cherish a few nooks of suggestive shadow, lanes where the whores once lurked, steps where you might once have had your throat cut for your cash, taverns where unscrupulous landlords might have dropped you through a trapdoor and shanghaied you off to sea. Sometimes there are glints of the harbor, between the office blocks, as one used to see snatches of the Thames down waterside staircases of Wapping or Limehouse. Sometimes the enormous girders of the Harbour Bridge loom high above a row of terrace houses, cast their shadow over a park or close the prospect of a busy street: and this always suggests to me the presence of a mighty cathedral, in whose lee for a thousand years some far more antique town has flourished and suffered.

Within the general jumble there are several enclaves or patches of distinction. There is Macquarie Street for a start, a fashionable residential street when we visited it in the 1880s, now a street of politicians, doctors, lawyers and institutions. Parliament is here, and the State Library of New South Wales, and the modern Supreme Court, and the rambling Sydney Hospital, and the whole street looks out over the Domain, part park, part the purlieus of Government House, still all a prodigy of light and color running down to the water's edge through the flowers, trees, lawns, and greenhouses of the Royal Botanic Gardens.[1]

This quarter of Sydney has the air of a true capital, and Government House within the Domain is the nearest thing Sydney has to a palace—as the home of the governor of New South Wales it is indeed the proxy palace of the British monarchy far away. People sometimes confuse it with its nearest neighbor, the battlemented pile that Greenway built as the gubernatorial stables, but which now houses the Conservatorium of Music. Government House is battlemented too, but was built a quarter of a century later by Edward Blore, designer of Sir Walter Scott's mock-feudal home at Abbotsford in Scotland, and is a jolly caprice of *Ivanhoe* Gothic, described by John Hood, when it went up in 1843, as being "somewhat in the Elizabethan style, but not exactly." The buildings of upper Macquarie Street look toward it across the green rather as the apartment blocks of Manhattan look over Central Park, and all in all there is something very invigorating about this thoroughfare, especially when you reach it up the gentle hill from the cramped financial district, to be greeted by its wide sunny space and its air of consequence, its palm trees, its flags, its flowers and its general impression of statuary.

Just up the road is Hyde Park, and this green oblong, frequented by lovers, tramps and chess players, is properly metropolitan too. The ornate Great Synagogue overlooks it from the western side, on the east is the heavily pilastered Australian Museum, and among the trees stands the Anzac 1914–18

---

[1] It was Melbourne's Botanic Gardens, not Sydney's, that the prime minister, Sir John Gorton, eulogized in a famous speech in 1970, but I cannot resist quoting his words anyway: "If this collection here in these gardens is not thoroughly matchless and I think it probably is, but if it's not, and if it's not unique of its kind, then I have no doubt that under the guidance of Mr. Shoobridge it very shortly will be, if it isn't already."

War Memorial, for my tastes one of the noblest things in the city. Hyde Park's most admired monuments, however, stand to the north, around the site Governor Macquarie envisaged as the ceremonial center of the city. They include two of Francis Greenway's best buildings—his graceful St. James's Church, which would be unremarkable perhaps in London or in Boston, but which looks exceptionally urbane here, and his Hyde Park Barracks across the way. This he designed for Macquarie in 1819 to provide, for the first time, a place of confinement for male convicts; for nearly thirty years its initials, HPB, were stamped on their clothing. As an ex-con himself Greenway was presumably reluctant to design anything too gloomy (though there was a triangle in the yard for floggings) and he created a building that has remained an ornament to the city ever since. A big rectangular block with a pitched roof, a cupola and a fine old clock, it stands in a wide courtyard behind grand gates, and always suggests to me some mellow institutional building, an examination hall or a proctor's office, within the precincts of academe.[1]

Hyde Park's other dominant building is St. Mary's Catholic Cathedral, at the northwest corner. This is huge. It is not quite as long as Lincoln Cathedral, its model, but it is probably the largest Christian church anywhere in the overseas British Empire, and I suspect that when it was completed in 1882 it may have been the largest building of any kind erected by the British in their imperial territories—astonishing to contemplate, when one remembers how small was the city it was built to serve. It is a kind of standard Gothic cathedral, such as you might order from an ecclesiastical catalog, with high

---

[1] Although wandering around it one day when it was being converted into a museum, and wondering at its gentlemanly proportions (far more civilized than many a barracks I have myself been obliged to occupy), I was chilled to see faintly legible on a wall a relic from some intermediate stage in its career, announcing the Master in Lunacy's Office, Top Floor.

pointed arches, dim transepts, a crypt and three towers;[1] two
heroic statues outside the south door are not of saints or mar-
tyrs, but of recent archbishops.

The area around the Town Hall, the pride of the 1880s, still
has some swagger. St. Andrew's Anglican Cathedral, it is
true, is infinitely less grandiose than its Roman rival, and is
indeed curiously unobtrusive nowadays; its main entrance
used to open to the west, but when in the late nineteenth
century new streets and buildings hemmed it in the arrange-
ments were turned back to front, so that the entrance is now
where the high altar ought to be, giving the structure a
slightly shamefaced air. The Town Hall itself, on the other
hand, is as cocksure as ever, and could well serve as a manual
of architectural styles. Eleven architects are said to have had a
hand in its design at one time or another, and the result is a
defiantly eclectic mix of intentions, crowned with a five-
layered, arched, columned, windowed, porticoed, archi-
traved, buttressed, domed, urned and flag-staffed clock
tower.

Even better is the adjacent Queen Victoria Building. This
was built in 1898 as a market, and after housing a library, a
wine store and various bureaucratic offices, has now been
gloriously done up by Malaysian entrepreneurs to be one
of the most sumptuous shopping centers on earth. Not only
is its exterior wonderfully entertaining, with a galaxy of
domes, domelets and roof pavilions, but its complex galleried
interior suggests to me a happier Piranesi at work; also
there is a glorious hanging clock which, every hour on the
hour, displays a series of mechanically moving tableaux of
British kings and queens, heralded by loud automaton

---

[1] All three originally intended to have been surmounted by steeples, which
are optimistically shown in all their glory in one of the best-known Victorian engravings of Sydney.

trumpeters and ending with the very slow beheading of Charles I.[1]

Not far away is the city's newest architectural set piece, Darling Harbour. Called by the early settlers Cockle Cove, this is the next harbor inlet west of Sydney Cove, and until a few years ago was one of the city's chief dock areas. Now it is a tourist and convention center of a certain slapdash splendor. It straggles around the old wharves in a sequence of white-and-glass buildings like so many winter gardens, linked over the inlet by the Pyrmont Bridge, the oldest working electrical bridge in the world, and crossed by the concrete viaduct of a motorway. There is a funfair and an aquarium, a Chinese garden, a huge convention center, multitudinous shops and two museums: strewn as it all is around the water, and backed by some fairly drab old industrial buildings, it has a frisky fancy to it, and is linked to the city center by a monorail train which sweeps over the water, circles around those spiky white buildings, like a portly red-and-cream worm. On a sunny Saturday Darling Harbour is a caldron of activity, and on one such day I came across a group of stilt dancers, painted and feathered, prancing in weird silence beneath the motorway bridge; their tall gliding motions, with the spinning of the funfair mechanisms, the comings-and-goings of the boats, the wavering of fugitive toy balloons and the crowds sauntering here and there, gave Darling Harbour that afternoon an unexpected air of power.

S ydney's substitute for a truly ceremonial center is Martin Place, three blocks back from the waterfront in the heart of the business district. This has been developed from one of the old

[1] "Well worth waiting for," as a bystander with a pronounced Irish accent once remarked to me.

crosstown streets; widened, cleared of traffic and planted with trees, it now extends from George Street, the city's original main thoroughfare, to Macquarie Street on the edge of the Domain. It is the pulse of downtown Sydney, especially at lunchtime on a working day, and an index to the city's style and sensibility. The Cenotaph is there, guarded by sculpted servicemen with bowed heads. An unfortunate essay in modern imagery, like a tower of aluminum kites, commemorates the Sydney artist William Dobell and is nicknamed the Silver Shish Kebab. There is a small sunken arena with a stage, and a big splashy fountain at the western end.

All is dominated by the General Post Office, which after nearly 120 years still has a claim to be Sydney's central and archetypal building. It holds its own bravely against the mass of the surrounding skyscrapers, and its Italianate colonnades greatly add to the dignity of the street. Its series of noble Letter Boxes (officially called Apertures and certainly worthy of capital letters) are set in magnificent brass surrounds.[1] There are brass railings inside, too, and flags, and a picture of the queen, and big ball lights, while on the Pitt Street façade there are some cheerful sculptures illustrating the ever-obliging attitudes of the postal service. These were thought to be downright indecent when they were first unveiled; the worst I can see in them, however hard I try, is a possibly slightly lascivious smirk on the face of a postman delivering the morning mail to a perhaps too-invitingly smiling housewife in the right-hand panel.

Martin Place is lined with big banks and insurance houses, and crossed by four busy streets that unfortunately reduce the plaza effect. Nevertheless at its best it can be delightful.

[1] Maintained in varying degrees of polish: when I asked one of the cleaners why OVERSEA, SPECIAL POSTINGS AND INTERSTATE was so much more shiny than SUBURBAN, COUNTRY, A.C.T. AND SYDNEY CITY, he just said, "Ah, well, SUBURBAN AND COUNTRY's the other shift."

Flower stalls and newsstands give it color. The Coolibah Hut offers satay and Asian food. There are always people doing nothing in particular on the big semicircular benches beneath the trees. Sometimes street musicians strike up, guitarists, Irish harmonica players, and when there is a concert in the arena, as there generally is at noon, hundreds of young people give the scene a cheerful animation, unwrapping their sandwiches on the rim of the fountain, doing frantic things on skateboards (penalty $A200), queuing for cut-price theater tickets at the Halftix kiosk or dancing to disco music outside the Commonwealth Trading Bank. One Friday lunchtime I saw an elderly paralyzed lady drawing a picture with a pencil attached to her head, watched by a large admiring audience.

Martin Place is Sydney's Trafalgar Square; Sydney Cove, where it all began, is its Piccadilly. There are pedestrian ways around it now, and it is dominated by the great pavilion of the Opera House, whose soaring and eccentric silhouette almost everyone knows. With its nine flying roofs of off-white tiling, its varying planes and mingled textures, Sydney Opera House is the hardest building I have ever tried to draw, and it has not been universally admired. Beverley Nichols the English journalist thought it was like something that had crawled out of the sea and was up to no good. The writer Blanche d'Alpuget likened it to "an albino tropical plant rootbound from too small a pot." I myself find it unattractive seen head-on from the harbor side, when its big teethlike windows, framed by their hoods, have a distinctly rapacious look, likened by a Brisbane wit to that of Sydney's heroine Joan Sutherland in the mad scene from *Lucia di Lammermoor*.

It is an immensely suggestive building. When I walk down its wide shallow steps, with those soaring roofs above me, I feel remarkably like one of the minute stereotypical figures to be seen in architects' drawings of visionary cities—figures almost irrelevant to the scene, and impelled only by the momentum of the future all around them. But there is also something *unguent* about the Sydney Opera House, something enveloping, so that when I have got over feeling like an extra in an architect's scenario, I feel rather like an insect in an ice cream.

Yet in many ways the building is very sensible, and is far more than an opera house in any conventional sense.[1] Sydney citizens use it almost as a club, so accessible are its halls, cafés and restaurants, and so handy its lesser buttresses for small boys to slide down. One rainy Sunday afternoon I went there to hear the Sydney Youth Orchestra playing in one of the foyers, and thought the place seemed positively cozy. The orchestra bravely played, and all around it people wandered about, leaned on rails, drank tea, pointed out their daughters among the cello players or sat on the floor reading newspapers. Through the windows I could see slanted umbrellas and hurrying laughing women, Japanese taking each other's pictures in the wet, gulls scudding around, yachts hastening home, ferries laboring through the rain; snugly indoors the orchestra played Brahms, while the teacups tinkled, the crowd amiably chatted, and a little boy left behind scuttled down the foyer stairs, two paces to a step, calling "Daddy! Daddy!" through the music.

Sydney Cove is attended by some of the ugliest buildings in Sydney, making for a meanness beneath the shine of it, but it is given character by the remains of gabled old warehouses,

---

[1] Far less, too, opera people say, since it is primarily a concert hall really, and its operatic facilities are sadly inferior to those of the visually far less exciting Melbourne Arts Centre. This has given rise to the quip that Australia has the best opera house in the world—its exterior in one city, its interior in another.

like something from Bergen, now serving as restaurants on the western side. There is a patch of green above the Rocks, where the Observatory stands, and the Ocean Terminal is properly hefty, and the skyscrapers rise behind, and to complete the ensemble the Harbour Bridge lumbers immensely away across the narrow harbor channel to the west. This is certainly not the world's loveliest bridge, but it is one of the world's old friends by now. It speaks of familiar loyalties, it does a good workaday job, and is thus in every way a proper complement to the esoteric folly of the arts below.

Nothing can quite match the particular sensations of this scene. The cove foams with the passage of the ferryboats. Cafés and bars are lively and sunshaded. Perhaps there is a cruise ship moored at the terminal, towering above us with bunting and fresh paint. Cars rumble incessantly over the bridge, and sometimes when a train crosses it the earth seems to shake. Excursion boats circle around, their loudspeakers echoing; there is often a tinkle of zither, a thin strain of violins, a beat of drums from buskers (as the Australians, like the British, call their street performers). It always seems to me Australia idealized—so young and energetic, so hopeful. The Opera House is like a very emblem of fresh starts, and the old bridge above, the jumble of the harbor front, the ceaseless turmoil of the water traffic, the sense of dazzle superimposed upon grubbiness, once more bring home to me Sydney's peculiar sensation of time truncated.

2 SUBURBS

In a satellite photograph Sydney looks less like a city than a geological feature, and among its expanses of dark gray and red, between the sea and the mountains, the downtown quarter scarcely shows. The Central Business District—C.B.D. as everyone calls it—has hardly grown in size since the last century. It is about as big as downtown Birmingham, England, or Dallas. Greater Sydney, though, that slab on the satellite picture, is as big as London. With a population of about 3.5 million it is one of the most sprawling of all the earth's cities, covering 670 square miles. It can take a couple of hours to drive out of Sydney, whichever way one goes, and there are said to be people in the remoter districts who have never set eyes on the Harbour Bridge. This is preeminently a city of suburbs—*the* city of suburbs, perhaps; a city which has whole books written about its suburbs, gazetteers and directories of its suburbs, architectural studies of its suburbs, social analyses of its suburbs, suburban governments, suburban styles, suburban loyalties and intense suburban prides.

The city's epicenter is supposed to be somewhere around Parramatta, some fifteen miles inland from the Circular Quay. This is proper, for Parramatta was the earliest of the outsettlements, and for a time at the end of the eighteenth century was bigger and busier than Sydney itself. Over the generations several such towns and villages have been absorbed into the metropolis, but the chief reason for Sydney's unnatural extent has been the inexorable outward growth of the city itself. Immigrants landing in Sydney were generally reluctant to go far into the interior, preferring to settle on the edge of town, and as long ago as 1900 the suburbs became more populous than the city proper. Since then they have expanded ever further, ever more coagulatively into the bush—it was in the 1950s that the last of Sydney's black swans, seeing the way things were going, flew away en masse from their lagoon in the suburb of Dee Why. Suburbia came naturally to Sydney. In 1836 Charles Darwin likened the entire city to a London suburb[1]; almost a century later D. H. Lawrence described it as "crumbling out into formlessness and chaos."[2]

The old inner city suburbs are mostly of terraced houses of the European kind, economical of space. They line the streets convivially with small front gardens, verandas, assorted ornamental addenda and a profusion of the fancy ironwork known as Sydney Lace—of which it is claimed that twenty different patterns can be seen in one row alone, Argyle Place above the Rocks. The outer suburbs are more absolutely Australian. They are mostly of bungalows, often built of a kind of cement known in Sydney as fibro, with red terra-cotta roofs, and their size has been dictated by one of Australia's most fervent and admirable beliefs, the conviction that a family should own its own house, with a garden all around it (in later years with a garage too, and nowadays preferably with space for a boat). Mile after mile the Sydney suburbs illustrate this creed, with varying degrees of beguilement. The main roads that connect them must be among the least attractive city roads on earth, a dismal mixture of English provincial humdrum and tacky American display. The roads themselves are often narrow and twisty, being based upon the coach roads of long ago. The buildings that line them make the heart sink—not quite hideous enough to shock, but monotonous enough to make you feel, as you lurch from traffic light to stop sign, through one unenticing shopping center after another, as though they will never end. For myself I will do almost anything to avoid these gruesome arteries: but the suburbs themselves are another matter.

---

[1] He thought it perfectly marvelous at first, but when he saw more of it "perhaps my admiration fell a little."

[2] In *Kangaroo* (1923), of which by the way an anonymous letterwriter in the Sydney *Bulletin* wrote: "God save Australia from these cheap writers from semi-literate countries. . . . There are plenty of Australian writers of rubbish, and local rubbish should have the preference."

Robin Boyd the architect launched a famous attack on the more recent suburbs in his book *The Australian Ugliness* (1960), using a fine vocabulary of invective: destructive . . . pretentious . . . stealthy crawl like dry rot . . . cold-comfort conservatism. There is no denying that many Sydney suburbs are less than lovely, their plans tedious, their streets (as Lawrence thought) like children's drawings—"little square bungalows dot-dot-dot. . . ." I can see that socially progressive architects and planners must detest them. Nevertheless they represent, for several hundred thousand people of many national origins, true human fulfillment—the very antithesis of the crowded tenements from which so many of them or their forebears came. Besides, they often turn out to be more interesting than you expect, when at last you reach them along those interminable highways.

Some are historically interesting. Parramatta in particular illustrates the development of Sydney almost as well as the city center. Its original plan was devised in 1790 by a naval officer of the First Fleet, Lieutenant William Dawes. He laid out a grid system of five wide streets, with one main highway running from Government House to the Parramatta River, and another terminating in a plaza with a Town Hall in it. Symmetrically around them were to be disposed the institutions of Church and State. Much of this plan, overlaid by urban sprawl, is apparent as in palimpsest still.

Grand as ever Government House stands in its park, with the lodge at its gates and the very tree where in 1847 Lady FitzRoy, the governor's wife, was dashed from her carriage to her death. George Street runs away to the river's bank. St. John's Cathedral with its twin towers stands in a rather Mediterranean way above its little gravel close. The cavalry barracks are elegant in their compound. The Town Hall still presides over its wide plaza, and nearby are the Centennial Clock Tower of 1888 and the Bicentennial Fountain of 1988 (which portrays three ghoulish figures apparently about to be drowned in a waterfall, and was put up during the town clerkship of Mr. R. G. Muddle). It may not be all as Dawes foresaw it, but the shape of Parramatta is recognizably his memorial.

Other interesting suburbs are simply rich. Not all rich suburbs are interesting, by any means, but Sydney's often are. All around the harbor, and intermittently along the ocean shore, houses of an infinite variety of styles are encouched in opulent green, their gardens dripping with bougainvillea or frangipani, rich old trees shading their yards. Sometimes they stand defiantly on the edges of cliffs, or deep in bushland, or are built on hillside declivities so steep that cars and boats are parked on their roofs. Sometimes they have tree houses, gazebos, or private external elevators ("inclinators" in the vernacular) connecting them with the harbor front. They have pools, they have awnings, they have sprinkled lawns, they have appropriated picturesque steps or urns from antique shops. They have two cars in the garage, and on their sidewalks, in good times at least, crates of empty champagne bottles habitually await the garbagemen.

Some of these houses do strike me as arid and artificial, in the Hollywood manner. Many others seem all too enviably organic. I know of no city with so many houses that I would be extremely happy to acquire, and it is no surprise that the plutocratic old suburbs like Vaucluse, Point Piper or Clifton Gardens, sun-splashed on their headlands, like to call themselves generically The World's Best Address. Almost since the beginning of Sydney the rich have been building themselves homes in these parts, and many an old villa or cottage *orné* still basks among its flower gardens as it has since some lucky official or wool factor commissioned it long ago; so that even in districts now glitzy with boutique and high rise, a sense of privileged continuity prevails.

Most of the suburbs have developed piecemeal, but some have been sociologically planned. The first was Woolloomooloo Hill, not far to the east of downtown and now more usually called Potts Point. In the 1820s Governor Ralph Darling earmarked this pleasant promontory as a place of residence for senior functionaries, well away from the penal quarters or the homes of vulgar emancipated convicts. Generous lots were granted to people like the high sheriff or the surveyor-general, and rigid planning restrictions were imposed—all buildings must face the town of Sydney, for instance, and no home was to be of less value than £1,000. Woolloomooloo Hill was fastidiously developed, with Gothic villas, well-wooded gardens of imported trees and shrubs, and stately nostalgic names—Craigend, Brougham Place, Telford Lodge. Few mansions remain, Woolloomooloo in general having long since been overwhelmed by urbanism, but the names of some have been inherited by the apartment blocks ("home units," they are called in Sydney) which now occupy their sites, and Potts Point remains, as Darling would have wished it, decidedly posh.

Several planned enclaves were built around the turn of the twentieth century, in the heyday of the Garden Suburb idea. The grandest was a very upmarket development called Appian Way, completed in 1911 within the otherwise undistinguished suburb of Burwood. It was, and still is, like a very small slice of Newport, Rhode Island, and is now a popular location for filmmakers. Its thirty-odd villas are set in wide gardens, surrounded by picket fences and shaded by magnificent brush boxtrees. In the middle is a small park, communally owned by the householders, in which one used to be able to play croquet, and can still play tennis, resorting for gossip and lemonade, I like to think, to a follylike pavilion beside the green. At another social extreme was Daceyville, in the south. This was the first state-planned suburb, created in 1912 as an example of how it should be done. It was an extremely ambitious project, and architects' plans show it as an immense swath of symmetry—ovals, squares, and residential oblongs interspersed with ample parks; but it rather petered out when in 1924 an inquiry convicted the State Housing Board of gross carelessness, incompetence and improper management, and all one can see of it now is a kind of fizzled ghost of its pretensions, festooned with telegraph wires, speckled lamely with ornamental palms and made all too spacious by brownish grass medians.

Then in 1924 the American architect Walter Burley Griffin, fresh from designing the new Australian capital at Canberra, arrived in Sydney with his wife, Marion, herself an architect (and supposed to be of American Indian blood). Appalled at the general standard of Sydney suburbia, he set out to build an enclave in the Frank Lloyd Wright manner, blending imperceptibly with nature and housing a community of artistic or philosophic temperament. No tree was to be unnecessarily felled, no inch of bush needlessly destroyed. There were to be no fences, no boundaries and certainly no red terra-cotta roofs. Griffin acquired 750 acres of land at Castlecrag, overlooking Middle Harbour in the north, and laid out his streets around the contours of a rock known locally as Edinburgh Castle. Half-buried in bush and boulder, all different but united in conservational spirit, the houses were built either of local sandstone or of a rough precast concrete. There were also a couple of shops, a golf club, and a small amphitheater in a gully, where the Griffins put on ecologically compatible plays. The suburb flourishes still. It may have lost its metaphysical cohesion, but many of Griffin's houses still stand, and the romantically rambling streets of Castlecrag still bear their original castellan names—The Bulwark, The Redoubt,

The Citadel, The Parapet, The Rampart, The Postern, The Bastion. "We want to keep Castlecrag for ever part of the bush," declared the Griffins, and they have succeeded, for those of their buildings that have survived are half-obliterated by the foliage.[1]

The ultimate planned suburb, though, the Sydney suburb *in excelsis,* is Haberfield, which survives only partly violated on the south side of the Parramatta River, and is one of the most truly Sydneyesque places in Sydney. Early in the present century a developer named Richard Stanton, together with his architect J. Spencer-Stanfield, set out to create the perfect urban living environment. It would be conveniently linked by rail and ferry to the city center, and was to be everything Australians wanted, everything they deserved—unashamedly Australian in every way, and unashamedly profitable too. It would be, so the publicity said, a suburb "Slum-less, Laneless and Pub-less," where every house would have a bathroom, and every householder would be able to say "this is my own home—this is mine for life." Some 1,500 houses were built, on a 200-acre site. They were all designed by Spencer-Stanfield, and most of them are still there.

The bungalow was the prime Sydney building form by then, and Haberfield is a town of them, sometimes extending into attics and even turrets, but for the most part compactly single-storied. They are built in the style called in Australia the Federation Style.[2] This is a blend of English, European

---

[1] Griffin built six houses elsewhere in Sydney, besides a number of monumentally styled and technically progressive incinerators.

[2] Because its emergence coincided with the federation, in 1901, of the six Australian colonies. It is the one truly Australian style, though the Central Sydney Heritage Inventory categorizes eighty-four, including Immigrants' Nostalgic and Postwar Stripped Medieval.

and American influences, medieval to Victorian, suffused in specifically Australian allusions. It has a touch of Prairieism from the United States, and a hefty dose of Arts and Crafts from England, and grace notes of Art Nouveau. Its characteristics are, to my mind, hard to isolate. It is a Queen Anne–ish, Tudory, semicountrified, sometimes whimsical sort of style, with eaves often, and fancy chimneys, and ornamental ridge cappings, and much woodwork. Stained-glass windows go well with the Federation Style, and tiled floors, and bargeboarding, and a veranda is almost essential. It is a style easy to mock or patronize, but on the whole it is humane, attractive, practical and fun, and it is a worthy instrument of the Australian Dream—to live in that house of one's own, with that garden all around it, in a respectable, healthy and thoroughly Australian neighborhood. Such a neighborhood was quintessentially Haberfield, and they call it still The Federation Suburb. It extends in unpretentious serenity, its streets lined with diverse trees, from the Parramatta Road to the edge of Iron Cove, an inlet of the Parramatta River, which has a tropical-looking island picturesquely wooded in the middle of it.

A good deal of shabby building has crept in since Stanton's day, much unadvised improvement has occurred, but part at least of Haberfield is protected as an urban conservation area, and it remains an endearing place. Although from its highest points you may see the skyscrapers in the distance, its streets are wonderfully quiet, its gardens are lush, people sit on porches reading newspapers, and in the air, even now, one hears the cooing of pigeons, the humming of insects and the gossiping of neighbors over fences. Every single house in Haberfield is different. If one house has a hexagonal glass conservatory, the next has a conical turret. Here is a veranda decorated in fretted woodwork, here an elaborately tiled garden path. There are fancy roof ridges. There are gables and wide eaves. There are stained-glass windows rich in kooka-burras, waratahs, wattles or sinuous Art Nouveau abstractions. Stanton kept his promises. There are no back alleys, there are no slums, and to this day there is no pub.

But it is really only an apotheosis of your average Sydney suburb. Haberfield is occupied nowadays largely by Italian immigrants, but its aspirations have not changed. Wandering around it one day I happened to notice a crude sign tacked beside a modest house gate, and thought that while its lettering and style were perhaps not up to Spencer-Stansfield's standards, its message was purest Federation:

"STRICTLY". RESIDENTS. CARS. ONLY. CAN. PASS. BEYOND. THIS POINT. THANK. YOU. ("OWNER")

There are many surprises in the suburbs—corners of survival, anomalies, sudden glimpses of eccentricity—and of all these serendipities my favorite happens at Lavender Bay, a small inlet of the northern shore just west of the Harbour Bridge. Long ago barrack ships were moored here, some to house stonecutters and limeburners, others waiting to take some of the more recalcitrant of the Sydney convicts to still worse banishment on Norfolk Island. Nowadays it could hardly be more innocuous. On its east shore stand the dilapidated buildings of the once-famous Luna Park amusement center, deprived now of the huge laughing face that constituted the entrance and was one of Sydney's trademarks, and left in a kind of stagnancy between purposes. On the west shore a suave restaurant sits at the water's edge. There are two ferry jetties and a sailing school, lots of yachts are moored offshore, and a couple of apartment blocks stand on the waterfront.

High above the bay rise the office towers of North Sydney, a formidable financial and commercial center in its own right, but below them is a settlement of a very different kind. There a handful of old houses tumbles down the hillside in the seclusion of a small and well-wooded park. This is a favorite artists' and actors' quarter, and the houses possess a strong sense of languid Bohemianism. They are built variously of sandstone and clapboard, and one has a merry little tower. At the top there is an Indian restaurant, and this is apposite, for with their gables, bleached railings and balconies these houses have an evocatively Simla look. Clustered tightly together there, thickly shaded by the trees, embedded in ferns and jacarandas, almost out of sight either from the land or from the water, they ought to have white-robed bearers preparing teas on their verandas, and memsahibs in floppy hats.

Back we come, though, inevitably to the harbor itself, toward which all these suburbs, however remote and landlocked, instinctively seem to strain: in Sydney, the playwright David Williamson once said, nobody cares about the meaning of life—it's a harbor frontage that counts. The harbor was the original raison d'être of this city, and remains its visual saving grace. Trollope said of it, in one of Sydney's favorite quotations, that he thought it might be worth a man's while moving to Sydney just so that he might look at it "as long as he could look at anything." It is the Sydney standard, by which all else is measured.[1]

The harbor is ringed with sensuous delights, pleasant little coves, waterside parks all green and welcoming, fine houses to look at. Sometimes it reminds me of the Bosphorus—notably at Kirribilli, where the apartment blocks stand side by side at the water's edge, their inhabitants to be waved at from

[1] In many ways the Australian standard too: for example I learn that Australian engineers measure reservoirs by a unit called the "Sydarb."

passing ferries. Sometimes the glitter of its waterside commerce is like Manhattan. Sidney Nolan once painted it looking like a lake in a barren desert, while the nineteenth-century
watercolorists gave it a gentle Home Counties allure, alleviated only by the odd kangaroo, or by groups of natives ornamentally disposed.

All the same, the harbor seems to me less a spectacle than
an event. It is like a perpetual pageant, punctuated by aston-
ishments. Something is always happening on it, even in the
small hours of the morning—always a ship passing, a helicopter flying by, unexplained lights wavering in the distance,
dim white sails loitering. I looked out of my balcony one
morning to see an enormous pair of inflatable sunglasses
perched high upon a wing of the Opera House as upon its
nose: they had been placed there by a group of ecological
activists, including the first three Australians to reach the
summit of Everest, in protest against the depletion of the
ozone layer, and I could see those adventurers scrambling
over the high roofs pursued by policemen. The very next day,
when I looked out again, I saw a man sitting on the gantry at
the highest point of the Harbour Bridge, threatening with angry gestures to jump off: policemen and white-coated medics
were up there trying to persuade him to come down, a police
helicopter hovered above him, a police launch cruised below,
police cars and ambulances jammed the bridge approach, and
on both sides of the harbor hundreds of people were staring
up at that high arch, half hoping despite themselves that the
man would jump.

He never did, and the police soon deflated the Opera
House sunglasses, but anyway on Sydney Harbour there is
always another day, another drama. It is by no means always
blithe and sunny there. When one of those sudden winds
blows up, and everything is flying, scudding, racing, flat-
tened, flecked with white, the whole pace of the haven seems

feverishly quickened. When one of Sydney's thunderstorms comes raging in, suddenly all turns bronze or ocher, the lowering clouds hang like doom over the skyscrapers, and the whole harbor seems to be catching its breath, waiting for the lightning and the rain.

I once crossed the harbor in a tossing small launch during one of the most ferocious of these downpours, described at the time indeed as Sydney's worst natural disaster, and seeing the city grotesquely distorted through our water-streaked windows, as in an old surrealist movie, now the bridge swooping above us, now the office towers crooked and bent, made me feel that another and altogether more sinister city had been conjured.

STYLE

Years ago, in the public ice rink near the Central Station, I came across a Sydney boy whose style I have never forgotten. He was about five years old, tough, blond and capable. He could not actually skate, but he was adept at hobbling about the rink on his blades, and his one purpose was to gather up the slush that fell off other people's boots, and throw it at more accomplished skaters. Hop, hop, he would abruptly appear upon the rink, and choosing a suitable target, staggering his way across the ice, zealously he would hunt that victim down until *splosh!* the missile was dispatched— and quick as a flash he was out of the rink again, gathering more ammunition.

I could not help admiring him. He hardly ever fell over, he seldom missed, and he did everything with dexterity. When I asked him his name he grimly spelt out GORGE with his finger on the rail of the rink; and in my mind's eye I could see him thirty years from then, exploding into a company meeting with an irresistible takeover bid, relentlessly engineering the resignation of a rival, or (it occurs to me now) bashing his way down the harbor in command of an eighteen-footer.

Of course he made me think of the convict children. It used

to be popular to see penal origins in everything about Sydney, and occasionally I fall into this romantic fallacy myself—it is all too easy to fancy the mug of an eighteenth-century London footpad in a passing loveless face, or to imagine in a well-fed child at a skating rink some apotheosis of those poor little abandoned creatures in the streets of Sydney 200 years ago. The chances are remote indeed that Gorge is connected in any way with the transportees: if his grandparents were not homely souls from Macclesfield they were probably hard-working fishing folk from the Aegean. Still, it is fair to conjecture that the existence of the original penal settlement may have permanently affected the style of the city, and thus of Gorge himself.

In many ways, indeed, Gorge's style is Sydney's style. He was a delightful boy, but not exactly tender; Sydney is a genial and generous city, but with a streak of malice to it. A well-recognized characteristic of the place is called "the tall-poppy syndrome"—the tendency to cut you down to size, if you are seen to be too successful. This is the municipal equivalent of throwing ice-slush at you.

The transportation policy was not all evil. Its methods were ghastly and its chief intention was certainly to rid Great Britain of as many unwanted persons as possible, but it was seen also as a chance for the miserable discards of British life to make a new beginning. Once their sentences were worked out they were "emancipated." They became free citizens of New South Wales, very likely with grants of land, and this gave thousands of people a better chance of success than they would ever have found at home. Many spent the second halves of their lives as respectable run-of-the-mill colonists, and a few became extremely rich. In the later years of the system, when the worst was over, convicts often looked upon exile as a kind of assisted emigration. Charles Darwin, in 1836, thought that transportation had succeeded "to a degree perhaps unparalleled in history" in converting useless vagabonds into active citizens, and by the time the system ended the sons and daughters of the transportees had indeed proved themselves remarkably law-abiding. A fine interesting race, the naval surgeon Peter Cunningham called them in his book *Two Years in New South Wales* (1828), intensely proud of their city, and only anxious to distance themselves from criminal association ("I should be afraid to go to England," one girl told him, "from the number of thieves there").

Nevertheless Sydney grew up, like a child in a bad home, inured to terrible facts, terrible sights. Penal Sydney was run in the first place by officers of a brutalized Royal Navy— offending marines were punished even more horribly than convicts—and cruelty was endemic. Prisoners were part of the street scene in the early years. They were clanking about in irons, breaking stones, building roads, digging sand, sometimes degradingly kitted out in frayed exotic uniforms taken from foreign prisoners of war, sometimes in a ragged mixture of prison dress and miscellaneous hand-me-downs. They were shackled like beasts to wagons. They were bonded as domestic servants or as laborers on private farms. Between 1788 and 1840 huge works of development and reclamation— the Argyle Cut through the Rocks, the Semi-Circular Quay, the road over the Blue Mountains—were accomplished by these slaves of the State, whipped mercilessly to their labors.

There was no closing one's eyes to the truth, in this little town. For the first decades of Sydney's history jails, barracks and labor yards were among its most prominent buildings— as one visitor remarked, all the best buildings "had something to do with convicts." St. Phillip's Church looked more like a prison than a house of God, and even Greenway's elegant St. James's had arrows stamped all over its steeple in case the copper sheathing was stolen. If you went to divine service you shared your devotions with sullen prisoners on compulsory church parade—"the most miserable beings in the shape of humanity," thought Captain Tench when he went to church one Sunday, "worn down with fatigue." As a matter of course artists included in their landscapes convicts laboring in chains, or pulling carts in which the muslin-dressed and sun-hatted womenfolk of officers reclined.

Sadism was institutionalized, and must have given the infant city a pervasive air of the macabre. The whistle of the scourge, the cries of flogged men, were familiar to everyone—you could be flogged just for the expression on your face, or for looking at a passing ship. The treadmill creaked and groaned the hours away. Women sat in the public stocks, or were ducked shaven-headed in ducking stools. The very first court that ever convened in Sydney, on February 11, 1788, sentenced its first prisoner to 150 lashes (he had abused his guards), and sent its second to spend a week alone on Pinchgut. Forty years later two delinquent soldiers were committed to jail with fifteen-pound fetters on their wrists and ankles, linked by chains to spiked iron collars riveted around their necks. On Goat Island, at the eastern end of the harbor, one is shown the rock to which a convict named Charles Anderson was sentenced to be chained for two years. An eighteen-year-old orphan, transported for smashing shop windows, during his time in Sydney he had already received 1,500 lashes for petty offenses; now he was forbidden any human contact, made to sleep at night in a crevice with a wooden lid locked over him, and fed like a mad creature with food on the end of a pole.[1]

Inevitably the administrators of the place, and the free set-

---

[1] Though the local folklore and guidebooks have him serving out this nightmare sentence, in fact the punishment went too far even for penal Sydney, and after some weeks Anderson was unchained from his rock; he was sent

tlers, were contaminated by all this. Gently nurtured families found themselves the slave drivers of felons. Priests who had given men the Holy Sacrament one day passed by them chained in road gangs the next. Children grew up with a contemptuous disdain for working people—for all working people in those early years were convicts—and sometimes horrifying vocabularies. Gentlemen got used to employing shackled prisoners around the estate, and the servant who brought your dinner, as Darwin observed with distaste, might well have been flogged the day before on the orders of your hospitable host; George Allen, the godly and teetotal owner of Toxteth Park, in the suburb of Glebe, thought little of ordering thirty-six lashes for a carpenter who took a day off, twenty-five lashes for a boy who drank.

People went out in their boatloads to stare at Anderson in his misery, and when a new jail was opened at Darlinghurst in 1841 crowds of citizens jeered and catcalled as the convicts were marched bedraggled through town to their new quarters. As late as 1846, according to David Mackenzie, a local clergyman, anyone standing at the door of the Sydney police office on a Sunday morning would hear a barbaric sentence pronounced from the magistrates' bench every two or three minutes—"Six hours to the stocks—twenty days to the treadmill—fifty lashes!" Another priest, J. C. Byrne, arriving in Sydney at about the same time, was shaken to hear that his assigned servant had received, at one time or another, an aggregate of 2,275 lashes.

For of course not everyone was desensitized. If children sometimes learned to despise their convict fellow beings, sometimes they learned to sympathize with them, and even to side with them against their parents. We read of Margaret

---

in the end to Norfolk Island, where he spent a few mercifully peaceful years as a cattle guard and signalman, before fading from his vale of tears.

Wightman, the Scottish wife of a farm superintendent, crying herself "almost into hysterics" because all night long she could hear the clank of chains as the convict laborers stirred in their sleep. And the writer Louis Becke, who lived as a child near the convict stockade on Cockatoo Island, at the mouth of the Parramatta River, remembered with compassion all his life the clanging of the bell on a foggy day that meant a convict had escaped, together with "the sound of someone panting hard in his swim for liberty."

Long after the ending of the penal system it remained a characteristic of Sydney that the genteel lived in intimate proximity with the disreputable. For years the Domain itself, whose centerpiece was Government House, was infested by ne'er-do-wells, and the gentry of Darling Point were neighbors to miscellaneous ruffians living among the reeds of Rushcutters' Bay. The prime example of such cheek-by-jowl propinquity was the Rocks. In the upper part of this small peninsula, by the middle of the nineteenth century, the Sydney bourgeoisie had built itself those agreeable terrace houses, that pretty village green, which tourists are still taken to see at Argyle Place. Just over the ridge, though, the rest of the Rocks fell away toward the harbor in almost indescribable squalor. At Argyle Place, any evening in the 1850s, the children said their prayers before bed, the ladies did their embroidery, the gentlemen came home from the office in their spanking carriages. A few hundred yards away the pubs and stews were warming up for business in a bedlam of drunkenness, foul talk and illicit transaction. Goats, whores and footpads indiscriminately wandered the back alleys of the Rocks, whale hunters and seal killers thronged the taverns, rats were fought, opium was smoked, violent gangs flourished, drunken seamen were kidnapped, there was a rip-roaring

Chinatown and a colony of destitute Maoris, and all down the steep lanes open sewers tumbled, "maintained in a constant state of moisture," as was graphically reported in 1858, "by new accretions of liquid filth."

With violent contrasts went violent shifts of fortune. Suddenness always seems to have been a Sydney characteristic, and sudden wealth especially. Almost from the beginning an explosive capitalism erupted here. Although the original settlement was ostensibly a bureaucracy of the most absolute kind, the officers of the New South Wales Corps very soon made themselves masters of its economy. They established corners in rum and many other commodities, and at least one opened a retail store—most of his customers were his own soldiers, and if they ventured to complain about his extortionate prices (he worked to a 100 percent profit) he merely threatened to have them flogged. In no time the cleverest of these moonlighters had been transformed from officers in perhaps the least fashionable regiment in the entire British Army to rich landed gentry: taken out to Sydney at government expense, paid government salaries, given land by government, assigned convict labor by government, they sold their produce to the government commissariat and became immediate aristocrats.

Speculators of other kinds made equally quick fortunes. Ships' captains, their holds crammed with goods from England, easily doubled their money on each voyage, and it is said that in the 1820s Sydney was a favorite and profitable outlet for stolen goods, smuggled from London for sale by George Street jewelers. Some of the emancipated convicts became very archetypes of *nouvelle richesse.* One year they were poor bondsmen, the next they were bosses of great concerns. We hear of one emancipist, in the 1850s, leaning stately on a gold-headed cane in a phaeton drawn by four ponies and driven by liveried postilions; of another, aged and illiterate, "dashing along in a perfectly appointed tandem, with a lovely girl beside him." Sometimes they threw vastly expensive parties: at a dinner given for the emancipated forger John Tawell, in 1831, one of the guests took a moment off to calculate that thirteen of his fellow diners possessed among them property worth £437,000—perhaps $A30m each by today's standards. The origins of great fortunes were well recognized. One mansion was frankly known as Frying-Pan Hall, because its owner had made his pile in ironmongery. Another was Juniper Hall, expressing its proprietor's indebtedness to gin. Sydney doubtless laid a collective finger along the side of its nose when J.G.N. Gibbes, collector of customs, found the wherewithal to build the splendid villa at Kirribilli that is now the Sydney residence of the governor-general of Australia, and it probably surprised nobody to hear that the well-educated and gifted Bradley of Bradley's Head, who had gone home to such a distinguished naval career, had been sentenced to death in London for his fraudulent practices, and very nearly shipped back to Sydney as a convict.[1]

From our distance of time it seems astonishing how quickly the struggling penal colony turned into a rich man's elysium. Everywhere comfortable houses sprouted—not vast English-style mansions, but agreeable neoclassical villas that fitted very well into the vaguely Mediterranean environment. All around the harbor they presently stood, and among the farmlands of the interior, with names like Curzon Hall or Tusculum, with terraced gardens and avenues of Norfolk pines, with elaborate outbuildings where the convicts toiled, with imported silver and furniture of polished cedarwood and even, whether by inheritance or imagination, family portraits. By the 1840s, when one sailed up the harbor, these pretty

---

[1] Instead, since he was by then an admiral, he was allowed to go and live in France, where he died in 1833.

buildings ornamented almost every bay and promontory of the southern shore. They looked urbane, but they all too often represented no more than crude opportunism. The early commerce of this city was elemental, and no-holds-barred. Its first industries were whaling and sealing. The booms that later enriched it were based upon wool and gold. These were abrupt, uncreative sources of wealth, and convinced Sydney people, perhaps, that they might thrive not by the old-fashioned means of making things, or even growing things, but by snaring, catching, grazing, swapping, digging things out of the earth or even, in later years, imagining things.

And how much of this old rawness, abruptness, bitterness of experience, keenness of opportunity, lack of scruple and abundance of gusto is really apparent in Sydney in the last decade of the twentieth century? One can only generalize, and I must start by saying that at its best the style of contemporary Sydney is delightful. Almost every foreigner thinks so (although almost every Sydney citizen is likely to say, as citizens say everywhere, that it's not like it was in the old days . . .). To my mind it still displays the "open sturdy manliness" that Alexander Harris, writing in the 1840s, thought characteristic of the plainer emancipists. Nine times out of ten the Sydney person in the street, in the shop, on the bus, will be friendly, polite and remarkably frank, and young people coming from Britain, in particular, immediately feel a sense of euphoric hope and liberty. The supranational, supraethnic fraternity of kind, educated, open-minded people, which exists like a freemasonry in every city of the world, is powerfully represented here, and a palpable sense of fellowship is apparent, too, in the camaraderie of pubs and clubs, and in a penchant for reunions. There was a reunion recently of mothers, babies and grandchildren at one of the city's maternity hospitals, and there are often gatherings of descendants of particular nine-teenth-century settlers, or immigrants from some Greek islet, or survivors of a destroyer crew from World War II: the re-union of the Anzac soldiers of 1914–18 is by tradition the one occasion of the year when the police turn a blind eye upon the old soldiers' gambling game of two-up, and the little band of veterans takes the chance, encouraged by all, to throw a bet or two in Hyde Park.

There is much goodness in Sydney. Every kind of charitable and altruistic organization flourishes here, bat defenders and seal supporters, environmental-protest movements and ab-original-protection leagues. Sydney people are hospitable to strangers rather in the way Americans used to be, before worldliness set in, and in most matters the city is outspoken and unshockable. I always admire the impeccably ladylike shoppers who buy their groceries so imperturbably among the porn shops, strip shows, and general scatologicals of Kings Cross. Startled though I was, I was impressed when, pausing in Martin Place to sympathize with a young woman who seemed to have difficulty in getting up from her bench, she thanked me courteously but added confidingly that "it was a good lay, anyway." I liked the sound of the man who wrote in a Letter to the Editor: "I always read Gittin's column, sometimes I wonder why I bother. I think February's effort was probably the biggest load of crap he's written so far."

"Melbourne people come as you are," said a Sydney card inviting people to a party in 1930s dress, and the joke exem-plified this city's cocky and lighthearted self-regard. Most Sydney people seem immensely proud of their city, im-mensely proud to be its citizens, and this happy confidence is contagious; it makes the outsider, too, feel proud to be there—when I look out from my balcony across the harbor I feel positively possessive, and nobody is more invariably moved than I am, I swear, by the two floodlit flags that fly so bravely in the evening above the Harbour Bridge.

At its worst, on the other hand, the Sydney style can be disconcertingly nasty. This city is still more hardened to the brutalities of life than most of its peers. Can one imagine people in Copenhagen or Vancouver looking up, as breakfasters at a Kings Cross café did one day in 1990, to see a man with a baseball bat clubbing a barking dog to death across a street? Would *Le Progrès* of Lyon include among a celebratory group of city worthies, as the *Sydney Morning Herald* recently did, a rugby player convicted of smuggling heroin from Thailand? Are there many opera houses, besides Sydney's, where a conductor in the pit has been seen pulling an imaginary lavatory chain when a soprano concludes an aria? On a single Sydney day the following local items found their way into my notebook:

- A television advertisement for a pickup truck shows two louts hitting each other with crowbars, butting each other's heads and kicking each other in the testicles, until one clinches the dispute by applying an electric sander to his opponent's face.
- A sixty-two-year-old woman is accused of murdering her husband, binding his corpse from head to foot and concealing it in a brick crypt below her rumpus room.
- A former premier of New South Wales having expostulated about the behavior of the clientele at his local pub, who go in for vomiting, urinating, copulating and self-injection in the streets around his house, a gentle acquaintance of mine wonders what he is making such a fuss about.
- The mother of a recently murdered homosexual millionaire throws herself under a train.

- Walking through the suburb of Newtown in the afternoon I hear a girl call to her lover on the other side of the street, as she might remind him not to forget the mayonnaise: "I work my fucking arse off for you, you don't even pay the fucking rent."
- A private detective complains to the press that policemen have been searching for a dead body under his tennis court. "It absolutely repulses me," he says, "that they would even suggest I have some poor soul buried in my backyard."

There can be poison to this crudity, too. The unfortunate Danish architect Jøern Utzon, returning home in despair after months of controversy concerning the building of his Opera House, thought the debacle as much malignant as incompetent, and called it Malice in Blunderland. He was by no means the only eminent alien to feel himself savaged by Sydney, and there are still suggestions that when in 1956 Eugene Goossens the conductor was caught at Sydney Airport with pornographic literature in his suitcase, he had been betrayed by ill-wishers. I was amused to watch the exchanges when one of the most celebrated of London newspaper harridans ran the gamut of the TV interviews in Sydney. Asked why she was so unpleasant about people in her column she replied, "I tell the truth, and that's why I'm famous, and not a little television reporter like you": but into the eye of that little television reporter there crept a gleam of loathing so pure, so well honed, so evident and so rooted in history that we all knew who won.

Sydney is notoriously racist. It was brought up to be so. Robert Hughes suggests, in *The Fatal Shore*, that the bigotry began with the convicts, despising the aboriginals "because they desperately needed to believe in a class inferior to themselves." In later years it was encouraged by membership of the British Empire, itself so racist and xenophobic that the official attitudes of this city were ingrained with fear of foreigners. Two world wars sustained the suspicions, and they were powerfully encouraged by the national policy of White Australia, rigidly pursued for several generations. The specter of the Yellow Peril was vivid here—"We don't want to fight," said a Sydney version of an old British *cri de coeur*, "but, by jingo if we must,/ We'll lick the yellow peril and leave it in the dust."

These emotions are far from dead, and appear to be self-generating: in the 1970s the children of Lebanese immigrants ("Lebs") found themselves horribly bullied at school, and even now women in Muslim dress are treated with open hostility and contempt. The immigrants of one generation project their own resentments on the immigrants of the next—sometimes of the one before, too. In 1989 there was a proposal for a new industrial satellite city which would greatly increase Sydney's industrial and technological power; support soon soured when it was realized that most of the money behind it would be Japanese, and that some 30,000 yellow men might be coming to work there. I am still taken aback by the attitudes of some otherwise cultivated Sydney gentry to the aborigines, whom they shamelessly call "abos"—like calling American blacks "niggers"—and whose very mention in a conversation can bring into the Sydney voice a disturbing steeliness, into the frank Sydney eye an involuntary glint of distaste.

So time and again one finds, exploring attitudes in present-day Sydney, that one is treading emotions of the past.

Land brought an early and lasting passion to the Sydney style. The aboriginals thought either that it was held in trust for everyone, or that it held everyone in trust. The whites thought it the one permanent and infallible source of personal wealth. The British authorities, disingenuously resolving that since the aborigines did not appear to do anything with it, they had no right to it, declared it all at the disposal of the Crown, and distributed wide tracts among worthy white recipients. Since the land was mostly thick bush, entirely unworked, it sometimes came in very large parcels. Emancipated convicts were allowed only a few acres, and the more humble kind of free settler could expect little more: migrants of means were soon playing about with thousands, amounting to gigantic if originally hypothetical estates.

I know a man in Sydney whose family owns one of the very same patches of land granted to it at the turn of the nineteenth century—then a small country property, now the site of a row of terrace houses. Many such Sydney clans established their well-being upon land given them by government (though not many still possess it), and the consciousness of land, its status as the ultimate form of wealth, runs deeply through the ethos of the city. The Lands Title Office swarms always with animated claimants and disputants, like a bank or passport office somewhere else. If there had ever been a Sydney constitution, an inalienable right to the pursuit of property might well have been written into it—also a right to the sale of property, for many of the original land grants were very soon split by their owners and sold off in lots.

The almost universal desire to own one's own house is part of this territorial instinct. So is the fascination, amounting almost to a public obsession, with house prices. Sometimes I think all Sydney life is governed by the price of property, so inescapable is the subject in conversation and the press, and so obtrusive the hyperbole of the estate agents: The Best Address on Earth, The Quintessential City Terrace, Possibly the Most Eloquently Contemporary Waterfront Residence in the World—Ever. Sydney realtese has a long and often irritating pedigree. When Vaucluse House went on the market in 1838 it was described as "a splendid and unequalled Marine Estate, commanding a perfect view of the head lands and sinuosities of the various Bays and inlets of the truly romantic Harbour in which it is situated." A century later D. H. Lawrence saw bungalows advertised as being 4 Sale or 2 Rent: nothing would induce him, he said through his surrogate character Richard Somers in *Kangaroo*, to live in a house thus advertised, especially when it was likely to have a name like Arcady or Racketty-Coo.[1]

Occasionally the fate of a house, its rising or falling value, its varying ownership and its future prospects become part of the general gossip. One such house was Swifts, a mansion on Darling Point said to be the most valuable house in the city. It was built for a nineteenth-century brewer in the Scottish baronial manner, was willed to the Roman Catholic Church as an archiepiscopal residence, and was bought in 1986 by a reclusive and enigmatic racehorse trainer. He paid $A9m for it and was soon refusing offers of $A38m, but got into the news when an eighty-four-year-old retired engineer threatened to foreclose on a large debt he said the man owed him. How the press loved it! A huge costly house with statues in the garden, a man of mystery connected with the Turf, an aged complainant ("ruining the last years of my life"), the Catholic Church, padlocked gates, enormous mortgages, vast potential profits —it was all Sydney wanted of a real estate affair.

Even more popular was the story of Paradis sur Mer, a lavish but unlovely mansion on Point Piper—Unparalleled Panoramic Harbour Views, Championship Tennis Court, Etc., Etc. This had become famous as the home of a particularly well publicized and amusing hostess, several times married and always to celebrities. It was bought for a fabulous price,

---

[1] Though Somers did eventually rent Torestin, and the house that Lawrence himself rented at Thirroul, some thirty miles south of Sydney, was called Wyewurk.

sold even more extravagantly, bought again by a speculator who lived in it for only three months, at an estimated cost of $A2000 a day, before selling it once more at a loss of $A3m. All Sydney waited to see what would happen next, but when on the following Sunday people picked up their newspapers, they found that Paradis sur Mer had been demolished overnight by its latest owner, who planned to build several more lucrative buildings on the site. Enthusiasts immediately flocked to Point Piper by boat, helicopter and jet ski, in the hope of picking up souvenirs among the ruins.

Whole neighborhoods in Sydney were destroyed in the 1930s, when the Harbour Bridge approach roads were built, and even now it is hard to keep up with the topography of the place, so drastically and frequently is it altered in the name of progress or profit. Sometimes buildings disappear almost overnight, sometimes they remain for decades in a limbo of uncertainty. In 1990 a new "heritage listing" plan proposed that more than a quarter of the downtown city should be declared protected property, not to be demolished: not a single city block would be without a protected building, which would probably make future commercial development more than ever subject to hook, crook and wheeler-dealing.

For if some people watch all these developments so passionately because they are concerned about the condition of their city, many others watch because there's big money in it. Sydney people do not seem to me terribly interested in small money, money as such. Easy come, easy go was noted as a Sydney financial maxim at least as early as the 1850s, and foreigners today often marvel at the insouciance of Sydney taxi drivers, who are not greatly concerned about tips, and indeed often reduce the fare to the nearest round figure. The political economist Andrew Wells recently suggested[1] that

---

[1] In *The Sydney-Melbourne Book*, edited by Jim Davidson, Sydney, 1986.

"the Sydney style has now elevated all forms of individual accumulation to an ethical imperative"; on the other hand it is said to be relatively easy to push one's way to the top of the plutocracy in Sydney, because so few people can be bothered. I get the impression that citizens are chiefly interested in other people's wealth—not so much in the power of it, either, or the morality, but simply in its ability to dazzle and entertain. The great tycoons of Sydney, however disrespectfully they are treated in the gossip columns, are civic stars really, and the melodramatic spectacles of high finance, the takeover bids, the bankruptcies, the venal internecine feuds, are watched with insatiable fascination.

To be extraordinarily rich is a properly native ambition. In many callings there comes a moment, if you want to be really in the big time, when you must abandon Sydney to practice in Europe or the United States. You can, however, become supremely rich without ever leaving home. Some of the older rich families have mellowed into a conviction of ample superiority, requiring no exhibitionism. Some have put their money out of sight, so to speak, into estates in California, country houses in Hampshire or Paris apartments. But there is something about the flash and easy conceit of Sydney that makes it the perfect setting for extravagance, and it is the lifestyle of the brasher wealthy that seems best suited to this city. Sudden wealth is the thing—not the long slog, but the bonanza. It was always so. The stupendously successful emancipist Solomon Wiseman was asked once if he did not regret his illiteracy. "What's the use of education," he retorted, "when the acquisition of wealth is the main lesson of life?" In 1850 the discovery of gold at Bathurst, beyond the Blue Mountains, galvanized the city: citizens from clergymen to laborers rushed off to the diggings, and countless firms found themselves without any employees at all. The last quarter of the twentieth century, with its emphasis on theoretical money, has suited Sydney admirably. Fortunes built on fantasy are very much its style, and in the 1970s and 1980s the whole paraphernalia of monetarism flourished mightily in this city. When the Yuppie first emerged in New York, he very soon found his clones in Sydney, and long after he fell out of mode elsewhere his local incarnation thrived. Nobody could be Yuppier than a Sydney Yuppie, nobody's B.M.W. was more carelessly parked beside the four-wheel-drive in the carport, nobody's trousers were more fashionably baggy, nobody flaunted his suspenders more dashingly, or spoke with such fluency about such multidigited sums over cellular telephones in public places.

There is a place called Hopwood's Terrace, at Blues Point on the north side of the harbor, where I used to love to watch the Yuppies perform. It is a modest row of buildings of the 1920s, with a quaintly ornamented roof line and shingled gables here and there, but it has been trendified. There is an Expo Oz Design House, a boutique, an advertising agency, Giuseppi's Italian Restaurant and something called the Image Bank. There is also a pleasant pavement café, and here the young executives, in the brave days of Yuppidom, loved to gather for Sunday-morning breakfast. One in particular always engaged my attention. He was an aging example, balding rather and a little too plump for the squash court, but he sported a proper Sunday-morning mode of T-shirt with whales on it, blue shorts and bare feet, while his companion had her blond hair in pigtails, and wore khaki slacks and sandals. Suavely he drank his cappuccino and ate his croissant. Knowingly but condescendingly he read out bits in the paper about people he knew. If his cellular phone rang he would saunter over to his Porsche talking loudly into his telephone as he went. How largely his laugh used to echo down Blues Point Road! How unsmilingly soignée his woman watched him as he returned, still talking and joking, across the road to the café, deftly flicking his diary pages as he came —successful, progressive, worldly, barefoot for all to see!

He was a gambler, I suppose, if only a gambler with other people's money, and Sydney has always liked a betting man. Sydney people will wager on almost anything, and as we have seen illegal off-course betting is a vice even among the sweetest of senior citizens; a popular two-up school, until it was flushed out by Authority, used to meet in a corner of Rookwood Cemetery. Alone among the big Australian cities, except only Canberra the federal capital, Sydney has no casino, but this is not surprising, because in New South Wales there are more poker machines per head (fruit machines, as they are called elsewhere) than anywhere else outside Nevada. In 1976 the money that passed through these devices, the vast majority of them in Sydney, amounted to one fifth of the entire disposable income of the State.

To gamblers as to all others, though, the tall-poppy syndrome applies. Many of the entrepreneurs who were Sydney heroes in the 1980s fell upon hard times at the end of the decade, and found themselves plagued by bankruptcies and criminal investigations. The press turned upon them then, and called them them collectively Greed Inc.

Sydney has traditionally prided itself upon being a classless society. There are no such obvious emblems of class distinction as there are in England, no such fearful contrasts between rich and poor as one sees in the United States. Slums are rare, the standard of living is high, and there are no more than a dozen families of any dynastic pretension. Houses generally pass from hand to quite unrelated hand. There is one called Mort's Cottage, in Double Bay, whose history has been metic-

ulously recorded by its present owner.[1] Its owners and oc-
cupiers have included a grocer, an umbrella and parasol
maker, a celebrated industrialist, a pioneering woman physician and John Tawell, the emancipated forger whose opulent
dinner party we glimpsed a few pages back. Egalitarianism
has always been a Sydney brag: it was said of the Anzac
soldiers in the First World War that they had never in their
lives known what it was to be given a direct order, "undis-
guised by a 'you might' or a 'would you mind'.[2]"

Nevertheless class always counted strongly in the style of
Sydney, as it did everywhere the British trod. Hardly had the
colony been founded than it evolved class distinctions of its
own. There were the administrators and military officers—the
official Establishment. There were the Sterlings or Exclusives,
the English-born free settlers—the colonial gentry. There were
the Pure Merinos, the sheep graziers who saw themselves
as the county folk of Sydney. There were the Currency Lads
and Lasses, white people born in Australia, whose nickname
implied a coinage good only in the colony. There were the
emancipists who were ex-convicts, and their subkind the
more modest Dungaree Settlers. There were the Ticket-of-
Leave men, who were more or less on parole. There were the
convicts, who included gentlemen felons called Specials, and
who preferred to be known as Exiles, Government men or
Empire builders. And there were the aborigines, grounding at
the very bottom in that lowest of the lowest of Sydney society,
the black woman. "Ladies, Gentlemen or Others" was the
formula used in the small advertisements of the day.

Much of all this was based upon English precedents, and
English social values were often anomalously applied—one
can imagine how bitter was the sense of caste among the 27

[1] In *Mort's Cottage*, by Jill Buckland, Sydney, 1988.

[2] By C.E.W. Bean, in the *Official History of Australia in the War of 1914–18.*

free women who arrived with the 775 felons of the First Fleet, and how reluctant they must have been to employ convict wet nurses. Those gentlemen convicts were put into a special camp, where unfrocked clergymen, cashiered officers, disgraced lawyers and exposed bankers got special treatment. One such was the naval officer John Knatchbull, member of an ancient Kent family.[1] Dismissed the service for behavior unbecoming to an officer, this patent psychopath was transported in 1825 for picking a pocket in London, but was not deterred. He beat a man to death on the voyage out. He tried to poison the entire crew of the ship taking him to Norfolk Island. He murdered a woman with a tomahawk. Yet he was given his own servant on the journey to Botany Bay (the man he beat to death) and to the very day of his eventual execution, by hanging in Sydney in 1844, he was surrounded by suggestions of aristocratic privilege. Lady Gipps, the governor's wife, was herself supposed to have agitated for his reprieval, and when he went to his death nevertheless he was wearing a handsome new suit allegedly supplied, for the sake of his class, by Her Excellency.

Then there was Sir Henry Browne Hayes, an Anglo-Irish squire transported for fourteen years in 1801 for having abducted an heiress. As one of life's irrepressible rebels Hayes did endure hardships during his sentence, spending some time in the penal coal mines at Newcastle, 100 miles up the coast from Sydney, and some on Norfolk Island; he once complained querulously that St. Patrick took no more notice of his prayers than if he were "some wretched thief in a road gang with manacles on my legs." For the most part, though, he was allowed to live as a gentleman should, attended by the valet he had brought with him from Ireland. He bought some land on the southern harbor shore, used the labor of fellow con-

---

[1] Into which Lord Mountbatten later married.

victs to build an agreeable stone house upon it, and filled a
ditch all around with 150 tons of specially imported Irish peat,
to keep the snakes out. Pardoned in 1812 by the intervention
of the Prince Regent, Hayes returned none the worse for his
experiences to live happily ever after at his delightful family
mansion in County Cork.

On the other side of the legal fence, but equally advantaged
by his rank, was Sir Frederick Pottinger, Baronet, a Pottinger
of the Berkshire Pottingers, whose father was the first governor of Hong Kong and whose cousin Eldred, "Pottinger of
Herat," was a celebrated hero of the Indian frontier wars. Sir
Frederick seems to have been a trueborn failure. He got into
money difficulties in his late twenties, and in 1860 he resigned
his commission in the Coldstream Guards and enlisted as a
trooper in the New South Wales Mounted Police, employed in
rounding up the outlaws known in Australia as bushrangers.
Although very soon promoted to subinspector when his bar-
onetcy was inadvertently discovered, he was famously inef-
fective in this role, his failure to catch one popular villain
being immortalized in a Sydney ballad:

> Sir Frederick Pott shut his eyes for the shoot
> And missed in the usual way.
> But the ranger proud, he laughed aloud,
> And bounding rode away!

But if Pottinger seldom succeeded in shooting a bushranger,
in the end this hapless toff succeeded in fatally shooting himself, accidentally with his own revolver while boarding a
coach. Through it all he remained the patrician anyway, and
his funeral was attended by the premier of New South Wales.

Some of the colonial gentry were bemused by English social
pretensions—in 1853 William Charles Wentworth, one of the
colony's most forceful politicians, actually proposed the estab-

lishment of a formal New South Wales aristocracy, with its own ranks of nobility ("Botany Bay Barons," his opponents mocked). Many shoots of snobbism took root, from a general toadying to visiting nobility to a preoccupation with suitable dress. The apparatus of visiting cards and proper introductions was rigorously upheld. The Bank of Australia (founded by graziers) was the bank for gentlemen, the Bank of New South Wales (tainted by convict association) the bank for the people. It was not the done thing to walk in the Domain on Sundays, because maidservants and their boyfriends went there. In 1838 a citizen was ejected from the Queen's Birthday Ball at Government House on the grounds that during his military service he had been only a sergeant-major: he argued in vain that he had married the daughter of a lieutenant. When in 1843 the first lord mayor of Sydney threw a popular fancy dress ball on behalf of his newly formed City Council, many of the city fashionables declined to come—they were, as a contemporary satirist wrote,

> *All pure merinos, trained to keep*
> *Their distance from your coarse-woolled sheep.*

There is plenty of snobbery still, too, whether it be expressed in footling dress codes at jumped-up pubs, or in the parade of bigwigs in medals, orders and tiaras that preens itself whenever royalty is around. It is not entirely a desire for an excellent education, we may be sure, which ensures that the great Sydney private schools have waiting lists of thousands, and anyone who thinks this is a city beyond convention should read the ten-page dress code issued to women lawyers in 1990 by one of its best-known law firms. Long-sleeved blouses, says this ineffable directive, "convey the most credible image," and with them suits must be worn, preferably navy blue, black, or charcoal gray (their jackets to be buttoned when standing, unbuttoned when sitting), together with antistatic slips five centimeters shorter than their skirts . . .

One of the sillier Sydney modes, copied like many another from Manhattan, divides restaurants into fashionable and unfashionable segments—some tables desirable and frequented by the famous, some (collectively nicknamed Siberia) absolutely unacceptable if you have any sense of status. On the face of it one table generally looks to the uninitiated very much like another, and it was fun when a mischievous journalist published table plans of the trendiest Sydney eating houses, clearly demarcating their Siberias, and puncturing not a few complacencies.

Where one lives is also more socially important in Sydney than in most cities of my acquaintance. It was a long time before an emancipated convict, however rich, was able to build himself a house on the harbor front, and those sprawling suburbs are largely identified by class.[1] I am told the districts used to be less homogenous, most communities including people of all ages and all kinds. Now sociologists say that to a degree unexampled elsewhere they specialize in old residents or young, rich or poor, immigrant or native-born. Social maps of the city, delineating its character by blodges of color, show heavy concentrations of blue (the rich color) in the northern and eastern suburbs, wide examples of red ("relatively poor" is as far as the sociologists will go) in the south and west. Even within the blue there are differentiations—the North-Shore suburbs are the place for high earning power, the eastern suburbs for great assets.

[1] Hence the old Sydney nicknames for first and tourist sections on aircraft—"Vaucluse" and "Woolloomooloo."

Some suburbs are of course still socially mixed: opposite an attractive row of small villas in Newtown I noticed one day a graffito saying GARBAGE-SUCKING SCUM LIVE HERE. Others are in a state of fierce social flux, as the energy of the market shifts their condition: the sociologist Peter Spearitt wrote in 1986 that "when Sydney gentrifiers invade a working-class Sydney suburb they know no mercy."[1] Others again maintain their social reputations more or less inviolate down the generations. La Perouse, down on Botany Bay, has never been able to escape its multiple social disadvantages (an aboriginal settlement, a prison, toxic inductions and an unlovely setting), while any Sydney citizen has a mental image of the kind of person you are likely to be if you say you live in Double Bay, St. Ives or Granville.[2] "This is not a baby area," an acquaintance of mine was told decisively by a shop assistant, when she asked for bottled baby food in North Sydney.

A charmer among these perennials is Hunters Hill, one of the most self-contained and gentlemanly of the suburbs. It is not on the flashier reaches of the harbor, but lies west of the bridge, where the Lane Cove River meets the Parramatta, and is compactly tucked away on a spit of land between the rivers. It is ranked only twenty-eighth in the suburban opulence roster, and is the smallest local government area in Sydney, but it is said that hardly anybody moves out of the place, so stable and villagelike is its character. It has a town hall, and a tea shop, and a post office with a postmaster in blue shorts and spectacles. It has lots of trees, verandas, cats, garden seats and narrow bosky lanes, together with a lawn-bowling club and, inevitably, CRUSH—Concerned Residents Under Siege in Hunt-

---

[1] In his contribution to Jim Davidson's *The Sydney-Melbourne Book*, Sydney, 1986.

[2] Double Bay very glitzy; St. Ives very conservative; Granville . . . well:
Q. What's there to do in Granville?
A. Go up to the Parramatta Road to watch the cars go by.

ers Hill. In Hunters Hill you see very old ladies being helped through garden gates by solicitous sons, and high-spirited children with trim satchels being met at school by personable young mothers in Volvos.

Nothing much changes in Hunters Hill. Everything has changed in Balmain, which occupies another peninsula not far away across the harbor. Balmain began life as the first commuter suburb, to be reached by boat from the city center, and in mid-Victorian times it was a favored residential area for the bourgeoisie. In the 1850s, however, a shipyard was opened there, with a dry dock and large repair yards, and Balmain was proletarianized. Hundreds of workers' cottages were built, dozens of pubs arose. By 1920 the Balmain Council was ambiguously declaring that Balmain's "industrial qualifications far surpass those of its residential claims"—which meant that it had become dirty, smoky, overcrowded and of low taxable value. By 1953 all the aldermen of the local council had been removed from office because of corruption, and a powerful criminal underworld had set up shop in the place.

Now the dry dock is only a memory, the Balmain Mafia is said to be dispersed, and the suburb has once again been transformed. It is still an untidy congeries of hilly streets, pub-speckled and poor in parts, but long ago the lift-off of gentrification occurred. Little workmen's cottages are pretty with trelliswork and bougainvillea. Pubs are popular with young accountants. Authors write novels, and at the bottom of steep lanes down to the water handsome launches stand on slipways. Chic invests the town center, where there are Japanese restaurants and real estate offices and gourmet shops and alternative medicine doctors' offices and a Float Tank Center. When I looked in one morning to catch an assault case in the magistrate's court, in this once-notorious hive of criminals, the victim failed to appear, the defendant could not be found, the police had no evidence to offer and I was the only spectator in court.

Chippendale, an enclave near the University of Sydney, is decidedly unclassifiable. It is a small oblong bounded by four noisy city streets, and though its own main street is called Myrtle Street, and is crossed by Rose Street, and bounded by Pine, it is uncompromisingly urban. Originally industrial, its architecture is unnoticeable, but its atmosphere is famously tolerant and eclectic. Chippendale is very tight-knit, very much its own place, colored on those maps a poorish red but in fact housing people of all kinds. I went to dinner there one evening at the house of one of Australia's most distinguished authors. My fellow guests, all near neighbors, included a politically active lawyer, another writer and two artists, and the food was brought in from the Lebanese take-out restaurant around the corner. After dinner my host took me a little way down the road to show me the site, perfectly located between a side alley and one of those busy boundary highways, of a well-publicized recent murder.

The name of Mount Druitt, in the west, has lately been adopted by the press as a synonym for working-class Sydney —distinctly red on the social map, where the poor bloody taxpayer lives, where the archetypal voter waits to be polled, where the cannon fodder would come from in a war. It is quite a pleasant place on the way to the Blue Mountains, but has an obscurely makeshift feeling to it—something messy, something temporary, with muddled shacks here and there, and more rubbish than is usual in this city. I take this to be because it is out here in the western suburbs that Sydney's newcomers generally settle, on their way they hope to bluer parts. Some such western suburbs have been utterly metamorphosed by the latest waves of Asian immigration. Cabramatta in particular seems for the moment at least to have been altogether detached from the rest of Sydney. Its center is an ordinary enough commercial fulcrum in a lightly modernist style, but walking through it is like walking through a provincial town in one of the more stable and prosperous countries of east Asia. Hardly a face, young or old, is not oriental. Whole classes of Vietnamese schoolchildren pass by. Vietnamese housewives emerge from every shop. There are smells of Asian cooking, sounds of Asian music. The population is very young, scrupulously clean, and impeccably tidy. Here and there one sees elderly white Australians bewilderedly wandering, as if in foreign territory.

Still, on the whole this is a naturally sociable and egalitarian city. Before very long those Cabramatta Asians will doubtless be talking Sydney English, and stylistically this famous dialect is the great binding force of the city. To foreign ears its sinewy sounds perfectly vocalize the place, and also seem more absolutely Australian than any others. The Australian vernacular was born here, after all, and it was Professor Afferbeck Lauder of Sinney University who first codified it.[1] Sydney English is strong, strident and lively—not as creative as the street talk of California or black America, but still always on the move.

It began with the cockney thieves' slang of the eighteenth century, the half-secret argot of the English underworld. This was brought out in many varieties and in full flow by the convicts of the First Fleet, and was doubtless crossed *en voyage* with elements of Anglo-Irish and English provincial dialects. Watkin Tench called it the "flash" or "kiddy" language. It was "infatuating cant," he thought, so obscure that it was some-

---

[1] In *Let Stalk Strine*, Sydney, 1965, a book described in its foreword as "above all, minatory and warmly human." The professor's alter ego is Alastair Morrison.

times necessary to have interpreters in courts, and its eradication among the convicts would "open the path to reformation." Not a hope! The language of their origin, craft and brotherhood was the one possession the convicts inviolably held, and they bequeathed its vigor and its potency to the free generations that succeeded them—perhaps its guild qualities too, for when in 1990 a crooked doctor and a bent solicitor were taped talking to each other about criminal ventures, they were found to converse in a semi-illiterate underworld jargon. In earlier years the Sydney dialect included cryptic elements of rhyme, like the East End slang of London: to go the barber was to go down to Sydney Harbour, Jimmy Grants were immigrants.

Sydney English has never lost its cockney twang, though its vowels have grown broader as the generations have passed, and its inflections have shifted.[1] The language is perhaps not so witty as Sydney citizens often suppose it to be. Much of it consists of an infantile preference for cozy abbreviation, so that a can of beer is a tinny, a bathing costume is a cozzy, a U-turn is a U-ie, sickies means sick leave, a pollie is a politician, a lippie is a lipstick, a westy is someone from the western suburbs, a greenie is somebody supportive of natural conservation, a ute (short for utility) is a pickup truck, Darlo is Darlinghurst, Paddo is Paddington, and brekkie, bikey and boaty are perhaps sufficiently puerile to be self-explanatory. Nor is the vocabulary of man-in-the-street discourse very striking, its chief characteristic being an ineradicable fondness for the endearment "mate." The humorist Nino Culotta (alias John O'Grady) published his book *They're a Weird Mob* in

[1] Semanticists believe it to have been influenced recently by the presence of so many New Zealanders in the city, so that Sydney people are more likely nowadays to drop their *l*s, saying "miuwk," for example, instead of "milk," and to flatten their vowels in some special way, so as to pronounce "six fat fish" as "sux fet fush." These are permutations too subtle for my ear.

1957, but his reported greeting between two workingmen still rings true today:

" 'Ow yer goin' mate orright?"

"Yeah mate. 'Ow yer goin' orright?"

"Orright mate."

Nicknames and idioms are far more interesting. Sydney has always loved them. Long ago immigrant girls used to be given the names of the ships they had arrived on, like Matilda Agamemnon, or Susan Red Rover, while for years Sydney policemen were nicknamed Israelites because most of them had sailed out from England on board the *Exodus*. Criminals, hermits and general originals have always been given colorful sobriquets, too, from old ones like Whaler Joe, Sudden Solomon, The Earl and Rock Lizard to Abo Henry or Disco George today. I like the words "bubbler" for a drinking fountain, "bludger" for lazy, "chook" for a chicken, "hoon" for a street hoodlum (formerly "larrikin"), "cockie" (short for cockatoo) for a small farmer. I am intrigued by the use of "identity" to mean "personality"—a TV identity, a Colorful Racing Identity. A "sly-grog shop" beautifully describes, it seems to me, premises illegally selling alcohol. Nine Nuns in a Rugby Scrum nicely sums up the Opera House, the Coat-Hanger is perfect for the Harbour Bridge, the Sydney Tower really does look just like a Plunger. "To perve" almost onomatopoeically expresses looking at someone libidinously. Silvertails is a good word for the well-heeled, rorting is horribly expressive of fixing the books, dobbing someone in is better than telling tales on them, Pom really does fit many kinds of Englishmen, Dinky-di encapsulates the purest kind of Australianness, and I know of no handier way of explaining your daughter's resident boyfriend than calling him her *de facto*—a euphemism which seems to have been in use since the first days of convict registration. "Take a squiz," says the shopgirl, inviting you to look around. "She's a rural," says a schoolgirl of a friend visiting from the countryside.

Built into this language is a caustic humor that is as old as the city. Sometimes it shows itself in pungent invective—a politician may be likened to a human suitcase, characterized as an archetypal son-in-law or be accused of having "all the menace of a tea urn." Sometimes it is just gently sardonic. When there was a search for an official tourist slogan for Sydney, someone suggested SYDNEY—SUN, SIN, AND SEWAGE; and the pupils of one of the Sydney schools have themselves translated their school motto, "I Hear, I See, I Learn," into the Latinism "Audio, Video, Disco."

Donald Horne the political scientist called Australia "The Lucky Country," and except during the city's cyclical periods of depression most Sydney people would probably accept the description. They are lucky and they know it, to live upon this generous and generally even-tempered shore. "No worries" is Sydney's habitual nonchalant assurance, "not a problem." Fortunately the consciousness of good fortune has not made the people smug, and even now they are innocently anxious to cast a happy impression, to show their city in the best light and prove it World Class.

The chief people-watching site in Sydney is unquestionably Circular Quay, which offers a kaleidoscopic view of the generic Sydney style, leavened by coveys of tourists, but representative of most kinds and classes. Here we may see the last of the Dinky-di Aussies, in their shorts and long socks, sometimes wearing bush hats and bearing themselves with a touch of bravado, like the kilted and sporranned Scotsmen who parade the streets of Edinburgh. Here we may see the Sydney office population en masse—on the whole a healthy, good-looking population, moving vigorously, laughing a lot. There are workmen with majestic beer bellies sitting on their haunches eating fruit, and ladies who are dressed as for royal garden parties, but are probably just going shopping. Groups of semipunks sometimes meander through, with yellow hair, silver-buttoned jackets and T-shirts incomprehensibly sloganed. A jogger pads by. A barefoot eccentric in a tam-o'-shanter disappears into the railway station. A postman lopes past in bush hat and shorts, with a rucksack of mail on his back. A man I knew thirty years ago as a lithe dark-haired young Italian looks back at me now over his café counter as a grizzled paunched Australian. Here and there along the quay solitary fishermen, in anoraks and baseball caps, bait their hooks with chunks of fish from plastic buckets. Around the corner at the oyster bar, businessmen are getting slowly and pleasurably sloshed on wine, beer, prawns and sunshine.

It is a great place for buskers. There is a Japanese playing "Danny Boy" on a kind of zither, and a very slow-motion go-go dancer in a yellow straw hat. A serious young woman plays Bach on her clarinet. A black comedian raises a burst of laughter along by Pier 4, and an evangelist maintains that One Cannot Live Without God ("quite untrue," loudly and briskly retorts a man in a dark suit as he hastens by without a pause). Somewhere somebody is winding up his bagpipes. Toward the Opera House we may see a dark-haired girl, ten or eleven years old perhaps, playing "Waltzing Matilda" earnestly on her violin; her even smaller brother waits to turn over the page of her music (bound, we may note, in the Australian flag) while looking up into her face in just the pose of a small Renaissance cherub in the foreground of a masterpiece.

All around us people are pottering about, or enjoying a late breakfast with the morning paper, or consulting their guidebook maps, or exchanging computer files over omelets and white wine, or strolling with beach gear and snorkels toward the Manly ferry. Except at rush hours, when waves of commuters come pouring through the ferry turnstiles, people are not half so agitated here as they are at most such city hubs. If they miss one boat they can always get the next. There is a train every few minutes. Another coffee? Why not, the office can wait. All through its history Sydney has been characterized as essentially easygoing, and easygoing it remains. It is a metropolis of the lucky country—lucky to get away with it.

PEOPLE

1 MAJORITIES

The people of Sydney are sometimes called Sydney-siders. Nobody is quite sure why. Some theorists believe it originally meant people living on the north or Sydney side of the Murray River, as against the south or Melbourne side, while others think it merely referred to transported convicts—they were sent to the Botany Bay side of the world, and later the Sydney side. Whatever its origins, it suits them. The word is sturdy, explicit and satisfied, and so on the whole are the people. Sydneysiders en masse are more easily recognizable, I think, than the inhabitants of most big cosmopolitan cities. Stylistically, historically and topographically theirs is a town of potent personality, and two centuries of settlement have created a citizenry to match.

Once almost entirely of stock from the British Isles, now embracing Greeks, Italians, Yugoslavs, Vietnamese, Maltese, Thais, Turks, Lebanese, Russians, Hungarians, Syrians and scions of almost every other race you care to mention, *homo Sydneyaticus*, whether male or female, has been molded gener-

ation by generation into a species of its own. Sometimes I
think it is the natural successor to the New Man travelers
thought they found in the North America of the nineteenth
century; perhaps it is even the celestial race that the poet Bernard O'Dowd hoped might evolve in Australia.[1] The climate
of this city, the food, the fresh air, the space and the general
ease of living soon mutate peoples of very disparate roots into
a recognizable kind—small island Greeks become husky,
women whose parents lived wan in Lancashire become marvelous golden girls, and it seems to take no time at all for a
slender Italian at a Circular Quay café to become a whole-hog
beer-swilling Aussie. If I spend too long in Sydney I sometimes develop recognizable Sydneyside symptoms myself.

By now this is a self-generating species. Immigrants still
come, but since 1981 more than half the people of Sydney
have been Australian-born to two Australian parents. Short of
some cataclysmic ethnic convulsion or climatic reverse, the
young native-born Sydneysider of today is likely to be, so to
speak, definitive. The mutation is, however, as much tempera-
mental as physical. It took guts to get to Sydney in the first
place, whether you came free or manacled in a convict ship. It
took patience or cunning to endure captivity, and spirit to
defy it. Force of character, if nothing better, was necessary to
administer the convict community, and a thick skin, if nothing worse, to act as its jailers. Complex feelings of rivalry,
scorn and rejection governed early relations with the
aboriginals. Only a keen eye for the main chance could exploit
Sydney's early disadvantages, and a fine discrimination between anarchy and discipline was necessary to evolve a free
society out of a prison. All these characteristics are still appar-

---

[1] *Last sea-thing dredged by sailor Time from Space,*
 Are you a drift Sargasso, where the West
 In halcyon calm rebuilds her fatal nest?
 Or Delos of a coming Sun-God's race?

ent among the mass of the Sydneysiders, passed down the generations through the collective unconscious.

D. H. Lawrence said that Sydney had no rulers. He meant that it had no hereditary elite, but of course it always had a governing stratum of rich and powerful people. In the very beginning they formed a military oligarchy—the first nine governors of New South Wales were all naval or military men —and later they evolved into a civil Establishment of officials and private citizens. They were the recognizable progenitors of contemporary Sydney's upper crust, and they are often honored in retrospect, at least by the more old-fashioned popular historians, with the sobriquet Father of This or That. Here are half a dozen examples:

- The unchallengeable Father of Sydney was Arthur Phillip, R.N. (1738–1814). His power over the original community was absolute, thousands of miles as he was from the nearest superior authority, and his commission was described at the time as "a more unlimited one than was ever before granted to any governor under the British Crown." He could be arbitrary when his temper was aroused: when one of his servants was murdered by aborigines he ordered a punitive expedition to behead ten natives in reprisal, bringing the heads back to him.[1] On the whole, though, he exerted his autocracy temperately. A small man, with a small, sensitive, melancholy face, childless from two marriages, he was the son of a German language teacher and his English wife, and during periods of half pay in his long naval career had twice been seconded to the Portuguese navy. This perhaps gave him a wider perspective than most of his contem-

---

[1] Later he relented, and said that two should be shot and four sent to Norfolk Island; but the only native the marines of the expedition could find was an old friend of theirs, so nobody was punished at all.

poraries (and experience as it happened of transporting convicts—to Brazil). From the start he saw Sydney as potentially "the most valuable acquisition Great Britain ever made," and sticking to this conviction against all odds, he went home to London sick and exhausted after four years on the job. When he died in Bath in 1814 Sydney was well on the way to a fine future, but he seems to have died a sad man anyway, by crashing his wheelchair through an upstairs window—perhaps on purpose. "A good man" is how Lord Nelson simply described the Father of Sydney, and 200 years later Sydney generally agrees.

• Lachlan Macquarie (1761–1824), the first soldier-governor, was a Hebridean with a sufficient conceit of himself: there are twenty-three streets named either Lachlan or Macquarie in Greater Sydney, together with nine roads, seven avenues, five places, two groves, a drive, a close, a terrace, a circuit, a university and a shopping center. He had served in the American War of Independence and for many years in India, and seems to have been a pompous but generally kindly man, of relatively liberal views, who believed that the future of the colony lay above all in the hands of the emancipated convicts. He invited ex-prisoners to functions at Government House, he patronized the forger-architect Francis Greenway, and a blackmailer-poet named Michael Massey Robinson became his unofficial poet laureate.[1] Macquarie was sporadically sympathetic to aboriginals and beautified the colony with his building program. Nevertheless he made many enemies—among the free settlers and the military officers, who thought him soft on criminals, sentimental about blacks and a threat to their own fortunes, and among his superiors in London, who thought him irre-

---

[1] And his eulogist—*His glowing Heart, at Mercy's Pleadings mov'd,/ Shares, as He yields the Boon to Worth approv'd:—/ Wipes the big Drop from Sorrow's glittering Eye,/ And opens the blest Path to Liberty . . .*

sponsible and extravagant. In the end he was accused by an imperial commissioner of unwarranted expenditures on public works, and went home bitter and disappointed, though fulsomely remembered in modern Sydney: he looks from his portrait a Scotsman through and through, and he lies on the Isle of Mull beneath the appositely presumptuous inscription FATHER OF AUSTRALIA.

• The first, most thrusting and most unappealing of the Sydney tycoons was John Macarthur (1766–1834), Father of the Australian Sheep Industry. Son of a Plymouth draper, he came to Sydney in 1790 as paymaster of the New South Wales Corps, and soon made himself a fortune on the side. He became a landowner, a hugely successful businessman and a pioneering sheep breeder. He founded one of the first Australian farms, Elizabeth Farm at Parramatta, naming it for his much more engaging wife, Elizabeth Veale, and he had visions of himself as a dynastic gentleman—the Macarthurs considered themselves descendants of King Arthur. He behaved all his life, though, like a vulgar parvenu. He quarreled constantly, fighting a duel with his own commanding officer, leading the rebellion against Bligh, plotting against Macquarie, and calling those he disliked Reptiles, Bloodsuckers or Cockatrices. He himself was nicknamed The Perturbator. Abnormally splenetic always, he went mad in the end, estranged from his unfortunate wife but able to fulfill his last ambition by supervising the building of the great mansion Camden Park, which he envisaged for his descendants—a properly Sydney denouement to an archetypically Sydney life.

• Benjamin Boyd (1800–1851), who might be called the Father of the Sydney Take Over, breezed into the city terrifically in 1842, sailing his magnificent armed yacht *Wanderer* through the Heads with an escort of four less glamorous vessels carrying his supplies and possessions. He had launched a bank in London to finance development in Australia, and he fell flamboyantly upon the New South Wales economy, acquiring thousands of acres of farmland, promoting whaling and export-import businesses and importing South Pacific islanders as indentured-labor. For a few years he was one of Sydney's heroes, like one of the fabulously successful corporate raiders of the 1980s, but before long his whole showy construction began to fall apart. Of course he turned out to have been cooking the books, his ventures were spectacularly in debt, his bank presently collapsed, his indentured-labor scheme was exposed as the next worst thing to slavery, and he sailed away again in the *Wanderer* for the California oil fields. Sydney never saw him again, for in pursuance of a later dream to establish a private kingdom among the Papuans he vanished without trace in the Solomon Islands, very likely eaten by cannibals.[1]

- Robert Campbell (1769–1846), very Scottish, very canny, very pugnacious, very efficient, was the Father of Australian Commerce. Campbell arrived in Sydney in 1798. He had family interests in Calcutta, and based his fortune upon the growing trade between Sydney and British India. His ships became familiar throughout the eastern seas, and his warehouses and fine house on the western arm of Sydney Cove were dominant buildings of early Sydney—Campbell's Cove it remains to this day. Campbell bred Arabian horses, imported Brahman cattle, kept peacocks, supported Bligh in his squabble with the officer corps and was in general an unimpeachably useful citizen, besides being enormously rich—the sort who gets honorary degrees nowadays from the University of New South Wales, and attends gala performances at the Opera House.

---

[1] The lovely *Wanderer* sailed on without him, to be wrecked off Port Macquarie, north of Sydney, and coveted by putative salvagers ever since.

• Thomas Mort (1816–78) celebrated his twenty-first birthday
on the ship coming out from England. "Of a truth," he
wrote then, "the sun had put on his most splendid and
magnificent attire to grace my manhood's dawn. I hoped it
was a bright omen of future Success." He gave it a capital *S*,
and it came true. Mort became the Father of the Australian
Meat Industry by introducing refrigerated ship services to
England, and he built the dry dock at Balmain, and founded
sundry marine repair companies and engineering works
and auction houses and real estate concerns, and built himself a mansion at Darling Point. He had advanced ideas for
the welfare of his workers, and was considered a model
Sydneysider—there is a grateful statue of him in downtown
Sydney still. For myself, all the same, I am rather haunted
by his report on a visit to the Destitute Children's Asylum
in the suburb of Randwich, which he contemplated as the
convenient nucleus of a silk industry. The asylum offered
three great advantages, he told his fellow promoters:
ground for the planting of mulberry trees, a big room for
the silkworms, and "the labour of the children free"—three
very important items, emphasized the philanthropist.

There are still no Sydney rulers in quite Lawrence's sense.
There are people with nonhereditary British titles, bestowed
upon them before New South Wales abandoned the imperial
honors system, and there are members of the Order of Australia, who put the letters A.C., A.O., or A.M. after their names.
But except among first-generation immigrants there are no
obvious distinctions of accent or physique; gone are the
stooped shoulders and rickety legs of the European poor, and
a patrician presence means nothing in a crowd of magnificently bronzed and muscular surfers. Physically at least this
really is a city of equals.

But here as everywhere there is an elite all the same, and I often see in it shadows of the early Sydney society. The first thing that strikes me is its proximity. It is not in the least remote. The political Establishment is as immediately to hand as it was in the days when the governors occupied their first little mansion above the Cove. Three quarters of the population of New South Wales lives in Sydney, its capital, and this makes the place much like a city-state, with its head of state always on view, if not actually next door. Everyone knows the premier, knows where he lives, knows his origins, knows a tale or two about his imprudences or his peccadilloes and seldom hesitates to tell them. Also there are generally a few ex-premiers around, making the presence of power more familiar still, and it is surprising how often women one meets turn out to have been, at one time or another, their wives.

The very rich, too, are as inescapable now as they were in the early days. People talk of them familiarly. They are not distant figures of legend, as they so often are in London or New York. They are like bank managers in some much more modest city, or perhaps squires in an English market town, so that the X family house is pointed out to visitors in passing, the Y family boat seems known to all, and the very day I lunched with one of Sydney's more influential editors he got a personal note from his proprietor, one of the richest men in Australia, giving him the immediate sack, effective that afternoon—what could be more proximate than that?

The moneyed and powerful of contemporary Sydney are often almost allegorically moneyed and powerful. When I first went to Sydney its rich women, in particular, had a famously scornful expression of face, noted by many observers: it was said of the novelist Patrick White's mother (née Withycombe and granddaughter of a Somerset innkeeper) that her mouth was "permanently set at twenty past seven."[1] Above the main door of the Customs House, on Circular Quay, the architect James Barnet put a bust of the young Queen Victoria which immortalizes that particular Sydney look. It is mercifully out of fashion now, but there is still no denying a predatory character to the Sydney elite. A hint of steel-within-the-velvet-glove characterizes its social style, and I would not care to make enemies among the Sydney jet set. I met a young man at a banquet once who was introduced to me as having just bought a television channel: "Two, actually," was all he said, without a smile. There is a dauntingly veneered and lacquered look to many of these people, who often seem rather too absolute to be true—too well coiffed, too expensively dressed at the wrong time of day, rather too glittery and enthusiastic. Gush is a well-known Sydney society failing, but so is the habit of interruption: among the upper crust here the art of conversation is mostly the art of competitive monologue, and I have seen souls from gentler milieus reduced to stunned withdrawal because they have never been allowed to conclude a sentence. Nor is delicacy a quality of the Sydney *hoi polloi* (as Sydney people, in a curious semantic inversion, call their society folk). I was proudly introduced one evening to a woman descended from one of the oldest and most eminent Sydney families, and never in my life have I encountered such an overbearing, loudmouthed, over-dressed, sozzled and insensitive old hag.

This raw but effective aristocracy is extremely well traveled, often owning properties abroad and sometimes sending its children to Europe or America for their education. There was a time when it was also passionately Anglophile and royalist, and one comes across survivals of the convention—any visiting peer is soon adopted by the partygoing classes. A Sydney

---

[1] From David Marr's biography *Patrick White*, London, 1991.

novelist once told me that a prime characteristic of Sydney-siders was their ability to tug a forelock and spit abuse at the same time, and the dichotomy is apparent even among the sophisticated, who are by no means unaware of their own elevation, but curiously susceptible to the altitude of outsiders.

With all this, there is something undeniably attractive about Sydney's higher society, in a cynical, glittery, hospitable way. It gives me the disarming impression that it enjoys life hugely, and if I tread warily in its generic presence, I tread with pleasure too. It is a small society. It meets frequently, knows itself intimately and is made homogenous by common success. At a single party in the city I met, one after the other, two premiers of New South Wales, two of Sydney's most notoriously expensive barristers, its most famous living architect, one of its most celebrated authors, the headmistress of its most fashionable girls' school, the director of its greatest library, the chairman of several of its most profitable companies and the man who had just bought the television channels. Almost all were equally charming to me, though some kept their eyes on the door behind my back, in case somebody more important walked in—Robert Campbell perhaps, or (far better at a party) Ben Boyd of the *Wanderer*.

If Sydney's original society was polarized between the jailers and the jailed, gradually there came into existence a powerful middle class of professional people, functionaries and politicians, and down the generations this was to produce some of the city's most memorable characters. Six of them, now:
• John Piper (c. 1773–1851) first arrived in Sydney in 1792 as a member of the New South Wales Corps, but so clearly realized the potential of the place that he returned in 1812 to take the job of Naval Officer—part harbormaster, but more

important part customs collector, which gave him 5 percent of all customs dues. He was an enthusiastic Scot, despite (or perhaps because of) German paternal origins. Handsome, dandyish and extravagant, he married a convict's daughter and lived headily, breeding and racing horses, throwing money around, while steadily making himself rich on the strength of his 5 percent. By the 1820s he had built himself so grand a mansion that he was known as the Prince of Australia; twin-domed and colonnaded, Henrietta Villa stood at the tip of one of the most delectable harbor promontories, and was the scene of glorious junketings. Piper had his own band, and his guests danced quadrilles beneath the verandas, being seen off in the morning with ceremonial salutes from miniature brass cannons on the lawn. Behind the house, as if in expiation, a huge Cross of St. Andrew was laid out in clipped hedges on the hillside. Alas, this endearing hedonist overreached himself. Obliged to resign his office because of inexact accountancy, burdened with frightful debts, one day he was rowed out into the harbor with his kilted piper, and jumped overboard to the playing of a lament. He was fished out anyway with a boat hook, but his glory days were over. Henrietta Villa was sold to pay off the debts, and Piper retreated from history to die in altogether more bathetic circumstances.[1] All that remains of him is the name of the promontory he made so fashionable—Point Piper, which at least is soigné still.

- Two violent clergymen bring zest to the old Sydney annals. The Reverend Samuel Marsden (1764–1838) was a gross eighteenth-century figure, a Fielding character. He was the son of a Yorkshire blacksmith, had a Cambridge degree, and

---

[1] At Bathurst, New South Wales, in 1851, supported by the charity of friends.

came to Sydney as assistant chaplain in 1794. He looks in his pictures a perfect horror—fat-faced, bull-necked, sour-mouthed—and he made himself a squarson of the old English school, at once landowner, magistrate and vicar of Parramatta. In 1807 he took to London the very first bale of Australian wool, and was presented to King George III wearing a suit woven from his own fleeces. He is remembered in Sydney, though, chiefly as an exponent of corporal and capital punishment—Flogging Sam. He ordered floggings at the drop of a hat, he fervently wielded a whip himself, and he ordered hangings without compunction. It is said he used to drive parishioners to church with a dog whip; he certainly sentenced one of his own servants to death for absconding, and then attended him on the scaffold. He was a famous proselytizer of the Maoris, but saw no salvation for the Sydney aborigines, declaring them to have "no Reflections, no attachments and no wants." Sam Marsden was a pillar of society, as a clergyman must be, a member of the Turnpike Trust, president of the Benevolent Society, committee member of the Bible Society, but even the generally temperate Macquarie was once goaded into calling him a Mendacious and Vindictive Cleric.

The other memorable man of God was the Presbyterian John Dunmore Lang (1799–1878), who was violent in a more forgivable kind. He was a flaming Scottish Calvinist who came to Sydney in 1823 especially to reform its morals. For nearly half a century he thundered and raged about them, attacking everybody from venal bankers to delinquent governors. He built his own Scots Kirk, he started two newspapers, he founded a college, he wrote innumerable pamphlets, he was a vociferous member of the Legislative Council. At his own expense he brought out about a hundred Scottish craftsmen and their families in order to elevate the quality of the Sydney proletariat.[1] He was a Napoleon of the manse! Nothing could restrain him in his headlong pursuit of the right. He infuriated officialdom by publishing a series of parodies supposed to be intercepted dispatches to London, and at the height of his fame spent four months in Parramatta Jail for libel. But he was undaunted, and carried on in just the same way, God's rabblerouser, until his death in 1878.

- William Charles Wentworth (1790–1872) was Sydney's prototypical politician. His mother was transported for theft. His father was a physician who had been charged with highway robbery in England, but had escaped punishment by volunteering as a surgeon for the colony, where he had greatly thrived and sired at least eight children by various women. W. C. Wentworth became famous in his early youth as one of the first three Europeans to cross the Blue Mountains, in 1813, and when he went up to Cambridge he became something of a poet: in 1823 he was runner-up for the chancellor's medal for his poem "Australasia," dedicated to Macquarie and full of apostrophe'd Sydney images (throng'd quay, lengthen'd street, column'd front, glitt'ring heaps and vent'rous tread). All his life, impelled perhaps by his slightly disreputable origins, he stood for the New Man, the self-reliant Australian-born. He called himself The First Australian, and started a newspaper called *The Australian,* which argued vehemently for self-rule in the colony, and was perpetually at odds with Government House. Wentworth had inherited a fortune from his father, and used it with brio, making his house Vaucluse the Henrietta Villa of his generation. It was there that the Constitution Bill was drafted, giving responsible government to the colony of

---

[1] True to form they built themselves a little Glasgow around Clyde Street, in the midst of the Irish Catholics of the Rocks, with McAusland's General Store on the corner.

New South Wales, and there that Wentworth cocked a famous snook at one of his chief opponents, the martinet governor, Ralph Darling: when Darling sailed for home in 1831
Wentworth invited 4,000 guests to a rollicking celebratory
party on his lawns, the climax of the evening being a fireworks display that spelled out the words DOWN WITH THE TY-
RANT triumphantly across the night sky. "Australia First"
was one of Wentworth's slogans, but it was not Australia to
the Last for him, because he went to England again in 1862
and died there ten years later.

• The two most celebrated Sydney politicians of later years
were Sir Henry Parkes (1815–96) and William Morris
Hughes (1862–1952). Both were born in Britain, the one of
English parents, the other of Welsh. Parkes was six times
premier of New South Wales and the dominant Australian
politician of his day. Hughes was prime minister of Australia during the First World War, the antipodean Lloyd
George. They were both unforgettable figures, and both began their careers humbly in Sydney—Parkes worked in an
ironmongery and kept a shop that sold ivory knickknacks,
Hughes mended umbrellas and ran a general store in
Balmain. The huge, richly bearded and lavishly whiskered
Parkes looks in pictures remarkably like an aborigine. The
small, jug-eared and gnomelike Hughes had long droopy
mustaches and melancholy eyes, and was known universally as Billy. Parkes's voice varied peculiarly from deep
bass to falsetto, and he bore himself like an actor-manager,
sometimes adopting a visionary expression of the eyes and
sometimes falling into what was once described as a "vast
and inexpressive weariness." Hughes became in his prime
an ardent British imperialist—"What fields are left for us to
conquer?" he demanded rhetorically of the king's subjects
after the victory of 1918. "We are like so many Alexanders."
Parkes, who was accused in 1885 of "an inane and tedious

vulgarity of rhetoric,'' was married three times, went in and out of bankruptcy and died very poor at the age of eighty-one. Hughes, who was a famously entertaining orator, sat in one assembly or another without a break for fifty-eight years, chose his first Sydney constituency because it was the only one within a penny tram fare of Parliament House, and was given a state funeral in Sydney, in 1952, which was attended by 100,000 people.

And here now on a North Shore pier stands a modern Sydney bourgeois, waiting for the ferry. Is he a Wentworth, one wonders, is he a Piper, is he at heart a Flogging Sam? He is in his early forties, perhaps, slim but florid. He wears an Italianate three-piece suit with double vents to the jacket and four buttons on each sleeve, together with a stiff white collar above a blue-striped shirt, and a tightly knotted tie of the old-school sort. His brown hat, tilted forward, has a wide and slightly curled brim. Under his arm he carries a not-too-bulging briefcase, and he walks up and down the pier, one hand in pocket, with a preoccupied air. Perhaps he is preparing a brief, or weighing a prognosis. But then we notice his shoes. They are expensive-looking, highly pol-ished shoes, but if we look closely at them, when his back is turned, we may see that they are pathetically down at heel. He is not what he seems—his clothes are a bluff, his brief-case probably contains nothing but the morning tabloid, and he hasn't the cash to get his shoes heeled. Let him be a lesson to us: the contemporary Sydney bourgeoisie, of which we thought him so substantial a member, is ex-tremely hard to pin down.

This is because it ranges, as it always has, from the crimi-nal to the genteel, freely mixing. We are quite likely to meet the man with the worn shoes at tonight's sixtieth birthday party for the professor, but equally we might run into him taking illegal bets on the 4:30 at Randwick. If fashionable Sydney is almost incestuously tight-knit, middle-class Sydney seems to me generously heterogenous, and is the least obviously Australian of the city's social layers. Let me take you to a dinner party among the better-off Sydney middle classes—a composite picture, so to speak, true in the detail but fudged in the whole. The style of the apartment is trendy—everything new, everything the newest in fact, pictures by the most admired Sydney figurist of the day, furniture in the latest Slav-Mexican mode, tulips in Chinese vases, fabrics in the muted cerise, streaked with green, which has recently been decreed by Australian *Vogue*. The food is excellent, the wine terrific. The conversation is partly about last night's *La Bohème*, and partly about real estate prices, and predominantly about other people, and is very catty.

One of the guests tells us without embarrassment that among her family connections are some of the best-known members of the Sydney criminal classes. Another recalls his happy time as a Rhodes scholar. A third explains the anticorrosion system which has made his family business so successful around the world. A fourth is that awful old harridan of eminent pedigree. Two more are, before the dessert is served, sitting on each other's laps in a corner of the room. A sixth is the man we saw at the ferry pier, who presently spills his glass of red wine over the brand-new and gleaming white carpet. They all laugh a lot, ignore those they choose to ignore, interrupt freely, eat wholeheartedly and repeatedly congratulate our host upon the rapidly rising value of his property. We enjoy it all tremendously. We are sitting among truly historical figures, clearly recognizable in the Sydney annals, and bringing to that well-appointed apartment of the North Shore resonant echoes of old habits and intentions.

It seems to me that the professional, artistic and business classes of Sydney have only recently found themselves. When I first encountered them, thirty years ago, they were still patently subject to what used to be called the Cultural Cringe—the general assumption that things foreign, and in particular things British, were necessarily superior. Today this old complex is mostly dissipated, and the middle classes are generally confident of their own merits—as well they might be, since they have produced in the last couple of decades an astonishing stream of distinguished representatives. They are proud and fond of their city, too: during Sydney's annual clean-up day in 1990 some 40,000 people, most of them undoubtedly from the bourgeoisie, volunteered to help.

If there is a generic failing to this class of Sydneysider, it is perhaps a tendency to the omniscient. *What* a lot they know, and how they talk about it! Do not even try to raise the subject of abstract expressionism—your host is certain to have just returned from the current de Kooning exhibition in Manhattan, and is very likely the author of a monograph on Jackson Pollock. You think you know Roussillon well? Not half as well as the woman at the cocktail party, who will very soon put you right about the origins of Catharism. Just back from Prague—great chum of Gore Vidal—living in Paris then—not as good as the Connaught—bumped into Tom Wolfe—surely it should be pronounced Portmyrion, should it not?—bottomless is the experience, liberal the advice, of the Sydney intelligentsia. I kept a note during one stay in the city, and found that in two months I had been helpfully instructed on the rules of cricket, how best to cook rice pudding, the Sykes-Picot Agreement, the architectural accomplishments of the Royal Navy, bats, postmodernism and the role of the Privy Council in the common law.

Of course there are some very conservative families in this varied milieu. The private schools of Sydney seem staunchly traditional still, and produce alumni of ordered and stoic mold. On a very hot day I once overtook a long line of girls from one such school laboring up the steep track to South Head, wearing thick school blazers over their cotton dresses: breathless but uncomplaining they climbed, too well disciplined to remove their jackets, until I heard a ladylike call come winging up the hill behind—*"You can take your blazers off—pass it on—You can take your blazers off—pass it on"*—up the line and past me, speeding on its way like a watchword, while one by one the girls peeled off their blazers dutifully in its wake.

There is also, though, a potent stratum of the unorthodox, if not the anarchic, among this bourgeoisie. A sizable proportion of it is homosexual, which gives it an agreeable element of the raffishly defiant, and there is much of the exhibitionism which has always been endemic to this city. One of the most extraordinary houses I know is an unassuming small villa in Neutral Bay whose flamboyantly individualist owner has turned it into a kind of grotto, its walls painted all over with trompe l'oeil and tomfoolery, where an apparently constant succession of casual, unannounced and sometimes it seems totally unknown guests drops in at random for drinks or meals, at all hours of the day, heartily welcomed by the owner, his dogs, and unidentified acolytes.

No need to find individual precedents for the Sydney proletariat. Its founding antecedents were a social condition and a historical phenomenon. Far more than the Establishment or the rentiers, it is still the blue-collar working people that set the tone of the city. Their bounding but indolent optimism strikes almost all visitors, and this is surely a legacy of old trials. To endure the road gangs without losing one's spirit, to emerge as so many convict families did into competence and respectability, to feel oneself the equal of one's former jailers, to have defied the law by surviving the worst it could do, to be able to sit back at last without being bullied or flogged—just to have achieved all this was surely to achieve a permanent spirit of euphoria. No other populace on earth has grown out of such handicaps, and survived them with such panache.

Often the convicts were heroically scornful of the authority that had them so terribly in its grasp. I am proud to say that the only Morris who arrived in Sydney with the First Fleet (seven years for stealing a pair of breeches and a waistcoat) absconded within five days and was never seen again, giving me the tantalizing fancy that somewhere among the aborigines there may be cousins of mine. Many others escaped, too—it was easy to abscond from this prison without walls. Some just wandered hopelessly about the bush for a few days, but a few got away in epic style. In 1808 a gang of convicts seized a trading brig that was lying in Sydney Cove itself, beside Campbell's Wharf and in full view of Government House; they got as far as the South China Sea before they were caught. More inspiringly still, one night in 1791 Mr. and Mrs. William Bryant, with their two small children and seven other convicts, stole the governor's own cutter and rowed it down the harbor past the sentries, through the Heads and out to the open sea. Mary Bryant, a sailor's daughter from Cornwall, was the captain of this desperate enterprise. It took them ten weeks to sail 3,000 miles in one of the great open-boat voyages of history

—repeatedly blown helplessly off course, once stranded on the Great Barrier Reef, once pursued by cannibals, only to be arrested in the end in Dutch Timor and shipped back to England. Mrs. Bryant lost her husband and both her children in the course of the adventure, but lived herself to be unconditionally pardoned, and became a nine days' wonder in Britain as "The Girl from Botany Bay."[1]   We read of marvelous courage in the suffering of punishments—men and boys who had been mere hooligans in Britain became stoic champions in Sydney, enduring year after year chainings, floggings and every kind of bullying. Their insolence could be indomitable. Maurice Fitzgerald, for instance, an Irishman sentenced to 300 lashes for his part in an insurrection in 1804, knocked both of his warders down the moment he was unstrapped from the triangle, inspiring his almost-namesake the poet Robert D. FitzGerald to write:

> *Could I announce*
> *That Maurice as my kin I say aloud*
> *I'd take his irons as my heraldry, and be proud.*

When in 1834 John Jenkins, an absconded convict, was found guilty of murder and asked if he had anything to say before the death sentence was pronounced, he told the judge that "he did not care a bugger for dying, or a damn for anyone in court, and that he would as soon shoot every bloody bugger in court."[2]   To be obedient or to be intractable were alternatives, to be fatalist was almost obligatory. You could keep your head down and count the years, you could spit at the

---

[1] A £10 annuity was settled upon her by a particularly enthusiastic fan, James Boswell. One of her comrades in the escape celebrated his survival and pardon by promptly volunteering for the New South Wales Corps and becoming a Sydney jailer.

[2] "The judge sat," reported *The Australian* convincingly, "in mute astonishment."

system and suffer the consequences. Either way, an acceptance of destiny must have been part of the communal ethos. The convict Matthew Eberingham, transported for the most forgivable of all crimes, obtaining books by false pretenses, died in 1817 after twenty-three years of exile, and expressed it on his Sydney tombstone:

> *Farewell vain world i have had enough of thee*
> *and am Carless what though canst say of me*
> *thy smiles i court not nor they frowns i fear*
> *beneath this turf my head Lies quiet hear.*

Doubtless all these miseries bred jealousy, treachery, and sycophancy, but they also bred in a few people an irresistible determination to win, however rotten the hands life had dealt them. A handful of convicts, almost the moment they had served their terms, launched themselves into careers of full-blooded capitalism and became extremely rich.

For example they called Sam Terry "the Botany Bay Rothschild," so wonderfully did he prosper after his time with the labor gangs (for theft, the records say, though his descendants preferred to think it "for political offences"). Emancipated in 1809, Terry began his free life as a publican, having married a usefully endowed wife. He went on by astute usury to be a landowner, with scattered properties all over Sydney and 19,000 acres in the country, worked for him by 100 assigned convicts. He was a rough crude man, only just literate, plain of appearance and miserly of instinct, but he built himself one of the largest houses in Sydney—it had stables, a coach house and a central courtyard, and somewhere within it, so legend said, Terry kept much of his vast fortune locked away in hard cash. Into it the Botany Bay Rothschild (by then himself proprietor of several convict transport ships) withdrew when he was paralyzed by a stroke in 1834; from then until his death he could move only with the help of two servants, making rare excursions, "pale and bloated," through the streets of the wondering town. Although his business methods were decidedly shady, if not actually criminal, Terry was buried with Masonic honors, and a regimental band played a funeral march for the old rascal.

His contemporary Simeon Lord was a more sophisticated entrepreneur, and looks back at us from his portrait with a disturbingly calculating gaze. Lord was transported for theft in 1791, aged twenty. At the end of his term he set up a retail business, dealing in everything from soap to sheepskins, and became one of Macquarie's token emancipists. He was appointed to the board of magistrates and shown off at Government House receptions. In time he came to have a hand in almost everything, every kind of business, every category of import, export, production or investment. He owned 18,000 acres of farmland and eighteen blocks of Sydney town. He had a mill at Botany Bay. He managed a fleet of whalers, sealers and transport ships. He manufactured beaver hats, he experimented in paper production, and he built himself a house which outdid even Sam Terry's—a three-story building, with verandas on two floors, which towered above everything else like a portent of things to come.

Most formidable of all, among these felon-plutocrats, was Mary Reibey. If it was hard for a male convict to become a millionaire in penal Sydney, it must have been almost inconceivably difficult for a female, yet Mary Reibey did it. When she was thirteen, in 1790, this Lancashire girl was sentenced to seven years' transportation for stealing a horse (or borrowing it without permission, as she preferred to say). When she was seventeen she married a free businessman, and opened her own retail store. When she was thirty-five she was a comfortably off widow with seven children and a thriving general business. When she was fifty she owned two ships, eight farms, many houses and a very large bank account indeed (the Bank of New South Wales was one of her tenants). When she was sixty she was one of the best-known people in Sydney, often to be seen driving stylishly around town in a carriage drawn by two white stallions. When she was seventy she had built herself a mansion and could be characterized by the Anglican bishop of Sydney as being "praiseworthy in the highest degree for her exertions in the cause of religion." When she was seventy-five she died, a round-faced, pink-cheeked, bonneted, bespectacled and beribboned old matriarch, leaving heaps of money and a grandson to become, in the fullness of time, premier of Tasmania.

Could such careers be paralleled anywhere else on earth— not just rags-to-riches, but actually manacles-to-millionaires?

More fundamentally, the penal experience gave rise to an egalitarian staunchness that has become traditional to the Sydney character. Volumes have been written about the Australian condition of "mateship," the male bond of working-class camaraderie which is thought to have been born in those penal days, and was certainly strengthened in war. To foreign sensibilities it always sounds a little sickly, but alongside it there did grow a philosophy of simple loyalty which was articulated by many a colonial poet and balladeer, most nobly for my tastes by Adam Lindsay Gordon:

> *This life is mostly froth and bubble,*
> *Two things stand like stone,*
> *Kindness in another's trouble,*
> *Courage in your own.*

The sentiments survive in Sydney still, if not always in comradeship, at least in communality. Trade union power is greatly diminished in Sydney nowadays, but fishermen, surfers, bowlers, policemen, criminals, yachtsmen, gamblers—all seem to work and play together with an uncommon intensity, as though they are kith and kin. The club spirit is strong, and so is the sense of brotherhood. BE READY, MATES, THAT'S ALL, says an epitaph I admire in Sydney's Rookwood Cemetery.

For modern mateship at its most vigorous one need only go to one of the innumerable working-class social clubs—Rugby League Clubs, Workmen's Clubs, or clubs of the Returned Services League. Originally, I imagine, these were much like British Legion clubs in Britain, or Veterans' Posts in the United States, but in 1956 the legalization of gambling machines in New South Wales fabulously transformed them. They became extremely rich, and around the batteries of poker machines that became their cores they built themselves lavish new premises, with excellent restaurants, glittering bars, dance floors with resident bands and every manifestation of popular hedonism. Some of them have splendid sports facilities too, and swimming pools. Hardly a rock star is too expensive to be beyond the fees of these clubs, and though they often stand in dingy streets in dingy suburbs, and sometimes look pretty dingy themselves from the outside, inside they greet you with a most hospitable verve. They are the Workers' Paradise sublimated, offering history a lesson in what communism might have achieved, if it had not been so priggish.

Not long ago the Sydney proletariat was altogether homogenous, being almost entirely of Anglo-Saxon or Celtic origin.[1] This was the citizenry that made the reputation of Sydney—to

[1] Even now it is claimed that every fourth Sydneysider has had a Scottish grandmother.

this day, when the world imagines this city, it imagines your cheerful, boozy, prejudiced, lazy, brave and disputatious Ocker[1] male (your Ocker female is somewhat mistier in the mind). He still exists. You see him a thousand times a day, in his stubby shorts and undershirt, heaving crates about, mending telephone wires, reading the tabloids at ten in the morning with his feet up in the cab of his delivery van, or squatting on his haunches with his mates outside pubs at dinnertime.[2] In him the Sydney male physique reaches its excelsis—no longer tall and stringy, but more solidly powerful—the thickset brawn of the surfer or the rugby player, the drinker's potbelly. His accent is rank and twisted. He can be horribly oafish and ill educated, especially when young, and is not always much fun on holiday in Bali, but in general his manners are blunt without being discourteous, and his humor is agreeably caustic. He seems, whatever his years, more or less ageless, and he possesses still a certain crude charisma that D. H. Lawrence attributed to another generation of Sydneysiders—"that air of owning the city that belongs to a good Australian." In many other great cities the populace has outlived its old stereotypes; the Sydney masses remain just as we expect them to be.

[1] Ocker: the archetypal uncultivated Australian workingman (*The Macquarie Encyclopedic Dictionary*, Sydney, 1990).

[2] As long ago as 1825 he was described as "making no efforts beyond what [is] necessary to supply [his] own animal needs." This is how Anon. put it, in a contribution to *A Book of Australia*, edited by T. Inglis Moore, London, 1961:

> *Me and my dog*
> *have tramped together*
> *in cold weather and hot.*
>
> *Me and my dog*
> *don't care whether*
> *we get any work*
> *or not.*

2 INDIGENES

Here since the beginning of Sydney, likely to be still hanging around if it ever comes to an end—here stand the indigenes. Today's Sydney aborigines are not people of the Iora tribe, which may well have been living here before there was a Sydney Harbour, but was extinct within half a century of the British arrival. They are migrants from other districts, drawn here like everyone else by the magnetism of the big city, and often by now with strong infusions of white blood. Australian aborigines they are, nevertheless, by conviction and by perception, and thus spiritual and historical descendants of the original inhabitants. They are at the heart of Sydney's meaning, they bring out the worst and the best in it, and they have a right to an allegorical position in this book—a central position, that is, in its central chapter.

I did not always think like this. I used to consider the aborigines a marginal people, empty, pathetic and almost irrelevant, and I remember two episodes in particular which seemed at the time to sustain this sad conviction. One occurred at La Perouse ("La Per" to the locals), the suburb on the north shore of Botany Bay that contains Sydney's oldest aboriginal settlement. I drove out there one morning just to look around the place, and finding myself in a decidedly unwelcoming cul-de-sac, where mangy dogs bit at my tires and groups of young blacks stared at me with a kind of listless suspicion—turning hastily around at the end of the street with a less-than-confident grinding of gears, I was just in time to see one aboriginal knock another out, there and then, with a massive punch to the jaw. The man went down like a log, the attention of the bystanders was momentarily but still apathetically diverted, and I got out of the place before anything worse happened.

The other occasion, years ago, was an aboriginal rally at

Alexandria Park in Redfern, where many black people live. This was to have been the conclusion of an Aboriginal Rights march through town, but it went sadly awry, and by the time I reached Alexandria Park seemed to have fizzled out altogether. All I found was a huddle of dark-skinned people around a bonfire, surrounded by rubbish on the edge of the park. They greeted me with concern, offering me beer out of an ice bucket, sidling around me and occasionally winking. A small thin boy with cotton wool stuffed in one ear wandered here and there with a black puppy on a string. Others kicked a football about in the gathering dusk, and around the fire a handful of old women looked sadly into the flames. A strong smell of alcohol hung over us, and the man with the bucket urged me repeatedly to have one for the road. Had the rally been a success, I asked? "Yeah," they said, and looked into the fire.

These dispiriting experiences, if they no longer illustrate my own feelings about the aboriginals, probably still confirm the views of most Sydneysiders—the indigenes are predictably reviled by the more racialist of the whites, and widely thought to be beyond redemption. But many citizens are sympathetic to their causes, and I imagine that few people nowadays would deny the unfairness of their destiny.

The first words the Europeans ever heard uttered by the Sydney aborigines were *"Warra! Warra!"* which meant "Go away!" Cook himself said that all the natives apparently wanted from his men was their immediate departure. They viewed the goings-on of the new arrivals first with fear (they thought they might be devils), then with superstition (they thought they might be the ghosts of their own ancestors), then with curiosity (seeing them swarm up the riggings of their ships, they thought they might be giant possums), then with apparent indifference (David Collins, of the First Fleet, says that during the first six weeks of the settlement only two aboriginals ever bothered to visit the camp), and finally with mingled responses of opportunism, disillusionment and hostility (Phillip himself was once speared by an aboriginal, and for years there was sporadic fighting in the countryside around). The Iora seemed to have behaved rather like cats, fading in and out of view, sometimes pretending not to notice events, sometimes ingratiatingly participating, sometimes scratching and spitting.

At first the British called them Indians, and thought them hardly more than animals. They seemed to have no abstract ideas. They apparently had no notion of property. They could not weave. They had never put a sail on a boat, let alone a wheel on a wagon. They had never built a hut. Their one attempt at agriculture was the cultivation of yams. They lived by hunting, by scraping shellfish off the rocks and by the most elementary methods of fishing. They went stark naked, and were smeared all over with rancid fish oil. "In no part of my voyages," wrote the botanist Joseph Cavanilles, who went to Sydney with a Spanish expedition in 1793, "have I seen our nature more degraded, or individuals more ugly or savage."

Could they possibly have souls? More improbable still, could they seriously be considered, now that the Union Jack flew above their hunting grounds and oyster beds, to be British subjects? The convicts by and large thought not, robbing and violating the Iora without much compunction. The more imaginative of the officers recognized human qualities in them, Spartan qualities in particular, and often befriended them. There was a time, according to Captain John Hunter of H.M.S. *Sirius*, when "every gentleman's house was now become a resting or sleeping place for some of them every night," and the commander of the 1793 Spanish expedition, Alessandro Malaspina, reported fastidiously that he and his officers had been guests at the same table with aboriginal men and women "entirely naked and disgustingly filthy." Watkin Tench recorded with admiration a moment when an aboriginal woman, attending the flogging of a convict who had robbed her, broke into tears at the sight of the terrible punishment, while another woman grabbed a stick to threaten the scourger. Richard Johnson the chaplain gave his daughter, born in Sydney in 1790, the aboriginal name of Milbah, and George Worgan, surgeon of the *Sirius*, summed up his own views on the natives thus: "active, volatile, unoffending, merry, funny, laughing, good-natured, nasty, dirty . . ."[1]

Governor Phillip's attitude to the aborigines was ambiguous. Though he responded bloodthirstily when they killed his servant, he forbade retaliation when he was speared himself, and gave Manly its name in tribute to what he called the aborigines' "confident and manly bearing." He had three tribal males kidnapped and brought to live at Government House, as he might have trapped a few kangaroos as pets. One died of smallpox, one escaped, but the third, Bennelong, became a popular member of the household and a favorite of the governor's, who built a hut for him on the point—Bennelong Point—where the Opera House now stands, and later took him on a protracted visit to England.

An unlimited supply of convict labor meant that the aboriginals were not needed as workers or servants, as indigenes generally were elsewhere in the British Empire. Nor did they pose much threat or competition to the infant colony. They could within reason be indulged. Macquarie settled sixteen families at South Head, vainly trying to make agriculturists of them, and he instituted an annual feast and corroboree at Parramatta. John Macarthur, perhaps imagining himself an-

---

[1] Worgan might well be honored as the Father of Australian Culture—he took a piano with him to Botany Bay.

other duke of Argyll, dressed some of them up in scarlet shirts, blue trousers and yellow neckcloths, and paraded them as a private bodyguard.

Whether out of naiveté or opportunism, some of the Iora played along with these attitudes, and became well-known characters of early Sydney. A few achieved a sort of official status, and wore crescent-shaped brass breastplates to show they were tribal representatives. The most assertive of them was Bungaree, nicknamed "the King of Sydney," who habitually met ships coming into harbor dressed in a cocked hat and an admiral's jacket, but shirtless and barefoot. Bungaree circumnavigated Australia as interpreter to the navigator Matthew Flinders in 1802, and was chosen by Macquarie to preside over the South Head farm village, together with his wives Boatman, Broomstick, Onion, Pincher and the paramount Queen Gooseberry. In his prime Bungaree was not only merry, but also dignified, and he was painted by many artists. Every governor knew and greeted him, and Admiral Sir James Brisbane, R.N., gave him that cocked hat and jacket. When he died, in 1832, his obituary occupied a full page in the *Gazette*.

But if he died a celebrity, he died ravaged and defeated—an alcoholic buffoon, slung around with trumpery emblems of mock authority, greeted by all those governors and admirals not with real respect, but with amused condescension. One of his later portraits shows him with a basket of beer bottles at his side; the last, by the Frenchman Charles Rodius, presents a face tragically sunken, degraded and reproachful, all its humor gone. In theory, in those early years, government policy aimed at noninterference in native affairs—royal instructions to governors said there must be "no unnecessary interruption in the exercise of their several occupations." In practice European civilization fatally interrupted all the occupations of the Iora. Its good aspects, hard enough to detect anyway in early

Sydney, had little effect upon them, while its evil cruelly rotted them. Even Phillip's friend Bennelong, having been lionized as a Noble Savage in England, returned to Sydney to die rum-soaked in 1813.

They had no chance—from the very first landing at Sydney Cove they were probably outnumbered by the newcomers, and they had no means of countering what Robert Hughes has called "the malignant gravitational field" of the penal colony. How could one reconcile the mores of a settlement largely of thieves with the customs of a people who left their canoes lying around for anyone to take? Early representations of the Iora, virile and interesting in the foregrounds of watercolors, presently gave way to more contemptuous images: of drunken men, bloated degraded women, potbellied children, brawling, swigging liquor at street corners and begging from passersby. Squabbles with the Europeans soon became more common, as the tribespeople came to seem less quaint and more irritating, and the Europeans turned out to be not ancestral spirits or possums, but bullying land-grabbers. Smallpox was endemic among the Iora, it seems, before the Europeans arrived; cholera, influenza and venereal diseases further decimated them. Their traditions were disregarded, their pride was destroyed, and the last successors of the Bennelongs and the Bungarees, dressed up still in the frayed remnants of their fineries, went ruined to their graves. Queen Gooseberry was last heard of begging opposite the Emu Inn in George Street, and by 1857 a man who habitually sat outside the house of the Speaker of the Legislative Assembly could be pointed out as the very last survivor of the Sydney tribes; people used to throw him coins as they passed by in their carriages.

"Well Mister," the last of the original Botany Bay aborigines told an official investigator, "all black-fella gone! All this my country! Pretty place, Botany! Little piccaninny, I run about here. Plenty black-fellow then; corroboree; great fight; all canoe about. Only me left now!"

Sydney has never been without its aborigines, because there has always been a steady coming and going of black people from elsewhere; but paradoxically they have become the one group of Sydneysiders who do not, like Lawrence's workmen, look around the city as though they own it. The city has generally considered them unimprovable nuisances—the inn sign of a pub called The Labour in Vain used to show a white man vainly scrubbing an aboriginal in a bucket of soap. In 1859 the writer F. Fowler described a group of them coming into town on the steamer from Newcastle, nearly all drunk, and tumbling about the boat "like so many hogs"; the women gave intoxicated boxing displays while the men went around begging for money. By the 1880s black families were directed into an official camp at Circular Quay, where they were given government rations to keep them off the streets; the compound became a spectacle of entertainment for the white people of Sydney, who went down there in their hundreds to gape at the prostitutes, the drunks and the brawlers. Then in 1895 an aboriginal reserve was set up on the seashore at La Perouse, far from the city center. Methodist missionaries worked hard to make Christians of its residents;[1] many of its young girls went away as indentured house servants under the auspices of the State Aboriginal Protection Board; but the aborigines did for a time reestablish an element of tribal tradition down there, living by fishing and by the desultory practice of crafts —as was reported in later years, a man might make one boomerang one day, three the next, two the day after, and then take the rest of the week off. La Perouse also became in

---

[1] Ambivalently defining the task, in their journal in 1901, as "the evangelization of the perishing people."

time a popular afternoon's outing for Sydney people. The aborigines sold them tea sets or slippers ornamented with shells, gave them boomerang displays and mystified them with their ability to identify incoming shoals of fish by species: "Mullet, bream, blackfish," spotters would sing out from the headland above, and sure enough, when the boats came back with their catch, mullet, bream or blackfish was what they had caught.

The official reserve came to an end in 1931, but the aborigines remained, living first in shacks on the beach, then in fibro houses built for them by the state, and many Sydney people of a certain age remember family housemaids from La Perouse. Today people still go out to "La Per" on a Saturday afternoon to buy wooden and shell trinkets, to watch the young men throw their boomerangs, and to see the Snake Man tip his assorted reptiles out of their sacks in the sunshine, as his father tipped them out before him. By now few of the residents are full-blooded aboriginals, and the streets in which they live, where I saw the man knocked out, have a Gypsylike air to them. Windows are often covered in blankets or rugs, scavenging dogs lope here and there, rubbish blows down the sidewalks. Nevertheless if there is a traditional center of native life in Sydney, a place where you may just imagine a link with the songlines and the rites of initiation, it is down there on the shores of Botany Bay, in the lee of the oil refineries, windy, sandy and raw.

Aboriginal consciousness of a more contemporary kind is concentrated in Redfern, whose name has become a metaphor for black activism in Sydney. Parts of this suburb are fast being gentrified, but the aborigines' patch of it looks like a disaster area—like a bomb site, or a no-go area of Northern Ireland. In a couple of dilapidated streets, the doors of their houses opening directly into rutted potholed roadways, a community that appears to be half-stoned, or half-drunk, stares blankly at the passerby. Some of the residents are more white than black, some more black than white, but most are classed as aborigines, and upon them is concentrated the distrust and dislike of Sydney's racist whites. A palpable sense of morose resentment hangs upon the air, heightened by the fact that every now and then the police raid the district in search of drugs, stolen property or wanted criminals.

For half a century this has been a haven for aboriginal drifters, but more recently it has also been the symbolic focus of a black revival movement. The world has come to recognize that there was always more to the Australian aboriginals than met the Western eye, and for myself I have come to think of them, as I have come to think of Sydney itself, in an entirely new way. A proper supplement to a visit to Redfern is a trip out to the West Head, not far from that shimmering marina at Akuna Bay, to see some aboriginal drawings on a rock there. Nobody knows for sure how old these are, but they seem to have sprung out of a society marvelously confident and exuberant. High above the sea, in a clearing in the bush, they are a vivacious gallery of portraits animal and human, not at all like the patternings and eerie X-ray pictures we have come to expect of aboriginal art. Wallabies bound, fishes squirm, birds flap, and a triumphant human figure in a tufted headdress holds a big fish in one hand, a boomerang in the other. Nothing could be further from the image of Bungaree with that wretched breastplate slung around his neck.

We realize now that, far from being the hapless incompetents the first settlers thought them, the Iora were perfectly adapted to their environment. They were superb hunters, and they had a masterly knowledge of herbal medicines and wild foods: scholars have listed eleven kinds of shellfish, thirty-two kinds of fish and seventy-four plants aboriginals ate in the

Sydney region then, not to mention crustaceans, reptiles, marsupials of many kinds, innumerable birds, platypuses, grubs
and bats.[1] Charles Darwin, meeting a party of tribespeople in
1836, thought they showed "wonderful sagacity" in the arts
of survival in the bush.[2] Their boats, dismissed by Lieutenant
Bradley, R.N., as by far the worst canoes he had ever seen or
heard of, could be made in a single day, and even the lieutenant had to admit they were wonderfully maneuverable. What
the settlers thought of as terrible wilderness was friendly and
familiar territory to the aborigines, and it was largely by using
old tribal tracks that the Europeans found their way out of the
Sydney beachhead into the Australian interior. Only now are
we beginning to appreciate the subtlety of the aborigines'
spiritual ideas, their conception of land as possessor rather
than possessed, their visionary grasp of the relationships between place, man and the rest of nature—the "incomprehensible ancient shine" that Lawrence detected in the aboriginal
eye.

The Sydney aborigines themselves, so bludgeoned by
destiny, seem gradually to have reawakened to a sense of
their own worth. In 1938 the La Perouse community held a
Day of Mourning to protest against 150 years of colonization.
In 1973, when the Opera House was ceremonially opened on
Bennelong Point, at the height of the festivities an aboriginal
actor appeared dramatically at the apex of the building to
represent the spirit of poor Bennelong himself. In 1988, when
Sydney celebrated its bicentenary, a popular graffito said INVA-
SION DAY, 1788, and a convoy of Freedom Buses brought pro-
testing aborigines into town. Today, as I have only belatedly
discovered, one can meet in Sydney some formidably articu-

---

[1] A menu presented in *A Difficult Infant*, edited by Graeme Aplin, Sydney,
1988.
[2] "Some few degrees higher in the scale of civilization than the Fuegians"
was his final evolutionary assessment.

late, talented and well-read blacks, confined to no ghetto, half-castes probably more often than not, but fiercely proud of their aboriginal origins and traditions.

The aborigines' one claim to respect used to be the all-too-often repeated reminder that they had lived in Australia for 40,000 years, but now they are liable to speak in very different tones. They speak of secret tribal initiations; they tell tales of long-forgotten battles against the British; legends of fearless guerrilla leaders feed the aboriginal confidence, and convince the activists that they are descended not from passive primitives, but from resistance heroes. The status of the Australian aboriginals is beyond the power of Sydney, and beyond the scope of a book about this city, but more and more I have come to feel that their presence here in some way *charges* the place; and finding myself greatly moved one evening during the performance of an aborigines' play, I recognized that in them above all was personified Sydney's nagging suggestion of transience or yearning—its one glimpse of epiphany.

Yet there are very few of them—perhaps 20,000 in all—and they do not often show. To the stranger their presence is mostly embodied in memory: in place-names like Allawah, Coogie, or Parramatta;[1] in rock carvings here and there around the harbor, often so worn by time as to be almost invisible except at sunrise or sunset; in the reputations of a few long-dead collaborators, Bennelong, Bungaree, or Jacky-Jacky, who is honored in an inscription in St. James's Church as having "tended his leader Edmund Besley Court Kennedy during his fight against aborigines in 1848"; in the reputations

---

[1] The first meaning "Stay Here," the second "Stinking Place," the third either "Head of River" or, preferably to my tastes, "Place Where Eels Lie Down."

of a boxer or two—there is actually a memorial to the most famous of them, Dave Sands, in the suburb of Glebe.

They seldom appear on the downtown streets. Rumor says that property developers are trying to force them even out of Redfern, and indeed their quarter there is so small, so ramshackle, so apparently irrelevant to the affairs of the city, that I would not be surprised, when I go there another time, to find it all vanished. Occasional drunks and layabouts haunt the city's more raffish quarters; around the harbor one sometimes sees the distant figures of black fishermen, scrambling over the rocks with strings of dangling bream, or poised statuesque at the water's edge. Some Sydney people would not mourn if even these fragile reminders were expunged. If the aboriginals are a blot on the conscience to many citizens of the city, to others they are just a pain in the neck. "The only aborigines I ever see are the ones who hang about Kings Cross," one gently brought-up Sydney lady told me, "and I hate them."

3 MINORITIES

Aboriginals apart, when you think of Sydneysiders you probably think first of white males—the image of this city is overwhelmingly masculine and European, and its attitudes are endemically mass attitudes. But of course it is never unanimous really, still less totally homogenized, and powerful social minorities stand beyond the civic stereotypes.

Demographically Sydney's women may not be a minority, but historically, here as everywhere, they have formed an underclass. International legend has it that Sydney women live in a permanently downtrodden state. Perhaps they did in the days when the mateship cult was at its apogee, between the world wars, and when a woman's wage was seldom more than half a man's. Tacitly or explicitly the Sydney of those days, Slessor's bunch-of-bananas, tram-ride Sydney, excluded women from most of its favorite public pursuits—drinking in pubs, watching cricket, playing rugby, reminiscing in servicemen's clubs, lifesaving on the beach—except in ancillary or decorative roles. Even when I first knew Sydney, the segregation of the sexes was very apparent, women still being confined to ladies' lounges in most pubs, and banished to the far end of the room at many social functions. A Sydney symptom that struck strangers then was the feminine habit of ending almost every phrase with a doubtful, interrogative inflection, as though anything a woman said was tentative, possibly foolish and vulnerable to mockery. Latin has an interrogative, *nonne*, which expects the answer *yes*: Sydney women's English most decidedly expected the answer *no*.

The earlier annals of this city, all the same, were full of boldly self-reliant women, ever since the days of Mary Reibey and the Girl from Botany Bay. Many of the earlier female convicts were desperate people. They were desperate in anger and sorrow, one imagines, when one remembers the scores of babies who died on the voyages out, but they were also desperate in defiance. The officers of the First Fleet seem to have agreed that the women convicts were more intractable, foulmouthed and lascivious than the men. A fifth of them were probably prostitutes, it has been academically estimated; in 1802 an Irish political prisoner writing home to his sister said: "In this country there is Eleven Hundred women I cannot count Twenty out of that number to be virtuous. The remained support themselves through the means of Ludeness." But at least one is left with an impression of spirited independence, and some of the early Sydney women transcended their vile circumstances to be remembered ever after.

Jolly Grace Lynch, for example, seems to have been the life

and soul of the Parramatta Female Factory, a combination workshop, lying-in hospital, old-age home, refuge, reform school and prison for the early women convicts. In this depressing place Ms. Lynch proved utterly irrepressible. We see her, coming across a chimney sweep in the factory kitchen, instantly throwing her arms around him and kissing him, covering herself with soot and sending the other inmates into screams of laughter. We hear her letting loose a flood of "dreadful Oaths" when her skimpy dinner is laid before her. Who she was, why she was there, where she came from, history does not tell us, but it recalls her with a smile.

Then there was Ann Smith, who arrived in Sydney with the First Fleet at the age of thirty (she had allegedly stolen a pewter pot). She was evidently an old lag, and she was certainly no wimp. On the voyage out she told everyone that as soon as she could she would abscond, and hardly had she landed than she did so. She was gone within a few days. She was never recaptured, but tantalizing clues about her fate have reached us. In 1790 a piece of linen found near Parramatta was supposed to be part of her petticoat. In 1798 fishermen sheltering in a cove at Port Stephens, about 100 miles north of Sydney, were told of a white woman living with aborigines. And in 1803, when a whaler was attacked by pirates somewhere off Alaska, among those killed was a woman said to be named Ann Smith, and to have come originally from Sydney.

A lurid figure was Angelica Hallett, who attached herself in the 1840s to the well-known local artist Samuel Elyard. Elyard was a chronic depressive, and he claimed that Angelica, having dismissed his doctors, brewed for him a medicine of her own that not only made him curiously befuddled and excited, but also persuaded him to marry her. She threatened that unless he signed over his property to her, she would have him committed to a lunatic asylum, and she eventually drove him into madness. Worse, however, was to come. Abandoning

Elyard, the appalling Angelica now stunned Sydney by revealing that she had all along been the mistress of the governor himself, Sir Charles Augustus FitzRoy, whose dear wife had lately been dashed to her death against that tree in Parramatta. Sensation! FitzRoy found himself pilloried as an immoral hypocrite, and for a decade and more the name of Angelica Hallett sent horrid frissons through respectable Sydney society.

Every Sydney decade has produced its memorable ladies. In the 1820s a resourceful Irishwoman known as "Pig Mary" lived by extracting lumps of offal from the swamp by the slaughterhouse at the head of Darling Harbour, and selling them from door to door. In the 1830s some of the old women of the Rocks were said to be so rum-soaked that when they lit their pipes blue flames flickered from their lips. In the 1850s, reported an English visitor, when young women of Sydney went walking "you hear the tinkle of their bunches of charms and nuggets, as if they carried bells on their fingers and rings on their toes." In the 1880s teams of women cricketers played in the Domain, wearing peaked caps and long striped skirts, and Grace Fairley Robinson, defying the opinion of the dean of the University Medical School that "she would be better employed if she got a nice frock and a nice man," graduated as a Bachelor of Medicine. In the 1890s Ms. Val van Tassell, "the only lady aeronaut in the Southern Hemisphere," having parachuted out of a balloon over Bondi beach, landed safely in the middle of a cricket match at Coogie. In the 1920s two women were among the most powerful bosses of Sydney's organized crime, rivals in the drug trade and in the management of prostitution in Darlinghurst:[1] if one can judge from the police photographs they were a tough pair indeed—Kath-

---

[1] Then the vice quarter of Sydney, and variously nicknamed Razorhurst, Gunhurst, Bottlehurst and Dopehurst.

leen Leigh from Ireland wears a fetching silk scarf and looks murderous, Latilda Devine from London wears a cloche hat and buckle shoes and looks speciously humble. In the 1930s six women pilots took their biplanes into the air to greet Amy Johnson at the end of a record-breaking flight from England. In the 1950s Mary Gilmore, poet, teacher, political activist, folklorist, feminist, Dame of the British Empire, reached the climax of her career as one of Sydney's most celebrated citizens, with streets, schools, scholarships and awards named for her, and a portrait in the State Art Gallery by William Dobell which, like Queen Victoria on the Customs House, memorably demonstrates the Sydney sneer (she was ninety-two when it was painted, and said it "captured something of her ancestry").

Sydney remains rich in women of forceful character. Today Sydney women seem as emancipated as women anywhere else in the Western world, and indeed the city has perhaps more than its fair quota of decisive if not pugnacious ladies, ladies of society, ladies of the TV screen, business executives and academics. They are often wonderfully adept at the monologic system of converse, and sometimes resort to a particularly penetrating timbre of voice, once daringly described by John Douglas Pringle as "a strident saw-like whine."[1] They can be very impressive, and they can be unfortunately lofty, like the wife of the politician who, looking around for a waiter after a gala performance at the Opera House, peremptorily handed her empty glass to the conductor.

I found myself recently at a school reunion at the former Fort School, above the Rocks, where a crowd of old girls were

---

[1] And instantly recognizable anywhere in the world. Thinking I caught a snatch of it recently above the polyglot hubbub of the Piazza San Marco in Venice, I sought it out through the crowds for curiosity's sake and found, sure enough, a woman in a T-shirt emblazoned SYDNEY YOU'RE BEAUTIFUL. Mr. Pringle was writing in his book *Australian Accent*, London, 1958.

greeting one another as old girls do. How admirable they were, I thought! How nice to each other, how kind to me, how full of smiles, how breezily beflowered of dress and carefully permed of hair, how jolly, how open and assured! They looked likely to live forever, so free of stress they seemed, and indeed one hears of some truly splendid veterans in Sydney— the seventy-nine-year-old ballet dancer, for example, who appears in the Australian Ballet's productions, and who made her debut in classical ballet when she was sixty-three, or the celebrated actress who, besides appearing regularly in stage plays, offers a popular cabaret act at the age of ninety-one.

But then many of the younger women are formidable too. No incorrigible transportee could thumb a nose at destiny more effectively than some of the strapping girls one sees, in stubby shorts and shirts, cleaning the streets of Sydney; and one of the most impressive people I know in this city is the woman pilot who flies, in tandem with her husband, the Aquatic Air seaplane services up the coast to Newcastle— immensely competent, dapper and good-looking, to be seen at the seaplane jetty between flights, her blond hair pinned up with a blue ribbon, simultaneously joking, drinking tea, checking the log and smoking a cigarette, like an image of Australian Womanhood in a propaganda poster.

Originals, male and female, have always been a well-recognized Sydney minority. The great mass of the Sydney population is probably as conformist as any other, but it likes to think of itself as a society of individualists, and has always cherished its exceptions. I suppose the convict system, which tried to reduce all its subjects to numbers, engendered a backlash that has never died.

Affectionate tribute is still paid, for instance, to William King, "The Flying Pieman," who came to Sydney as a free schoolmaster in 1829 but became a seller of hot pies and a virtuoso walker—he walked from Sydney to Parramatta and back twice a day for six consecutive days; he walked 1,634 miles in five weeks and four days; he pulled a woman in a gig for half a mile; he picked up 1,000 corncobs set a yard apart in less than an hour; and he performed various esoteric feats of pedestrianism while carrying goats, dogs, cats, rats and mice. William Bland, a convict surgeon who became the most fashionable physician in Sydney in the 1830s, and later a powerful advocate of colonial reform, is fondly remembered for his famous flying machine, a kind of airship called The Amotic Machine [*sic*]; it never actually flew, but was to be propelled originally by manpower, later by steam, and was supposed to be capable of carrying five tons of cargo from London to Australia in five days. In one of the official publications of the Royal Botanic Gardens a large photograph honors William James Chidley, one of the most peculiar of all the peculiar public speakers who have mounted their soapboxes in the Domain; for many years in the early part of this century he was always to be found there, dressed in a white Roman tunic, declaiming wild ideas on sex and healthy living, and periodically detained either on suspicion of lunacy or on charges of indecent language and offensive behavior.

Sanctioned by such illustrious examples, oddballs still seem to be generally tolerated in Sydney, and numerous eccentrics of one kind and another wander the Circular Quay, or sprawl magnanimously on the Hyde Park benches. Quirks and anomalies abound, and there is nothing wrong with showing off in this city. One often sees people in the street, old as well as young, rich and poor, blatantly soliciting the public amazement. When I first came to Sydney there was a local celebrity whose life and reputation gloriously exemplified these attitudes. In her time Bea Miles, who died in 1973, was certainly one of the city's favorite identities. She had been expensively educated (Abbotsleigh Church of England School for Girls), but had made herself into a walking emblem of bloody-mindedness in the heroic tradition of the early convicts. A burly woman of genial countenance, supported by private means, she stood for everything free, disrespectful and entertaining, and detested, as she said, all "priggery, caddery, snobbery and smuggery." Everyone knew her. She was usually dressed in an old cotton dress, a sun-visor and men's black shoes, carried a satchel containing books by fellow spirits like Swift and H. L. Mencken, and was often found declaiming Shakespeare by heart in the Domain. Sometimes she was seen diving into the ocean with a knife in her mouth, looking for sharks. For years this magnificent original maintained a personal feud against bus conductors (too officious) and cabdrivers (too arrogant): sometimes she spent all day riding provocatively around on buses, chivying bus conductors but greeting admirers everywhere, and once she hailed a taxi and told the driver to take her the 2,600-odd miles to Perth—which he did.

There is a café in the opulent suburb of Double Bay ("Double Pay" to the wags) which Sydneysiders from Central Europe frequent. I like to go there too, to observe in his fulfillment a minority figure who was not so long ago called The New Australian—the first-generation immigrant, that is, from a country other than Britain. On the terrace at the Cosmopolitan the New Australians are no longer new, and have clearly prospered since they first came to Sydney thirty or forty years ago. Their children are absolute Australians by now, but they themselves behave just as though they are in their distant capitals of long ago. Here four men with coats slung over their shoulders smoke small cigars and passionately argue about politics—generally in still heavily accented English, sometimes in Ruritanian. Here a couple of leathery ladies, furred and proudly diamonded, sit in lofty silence over aperitifs. There is a smell of coffee and Continental cigarettes. A few solitary men with signet rings read papers that ought to be called something like *Y Sblygod*, but are really *Sydney Morning Herald*s.

Yet there in the winter sunshine they look complacently at home, and they are indeed essential to the Sydney idiom. I engaged a couple of them in conversation once. They were Hungarians, who had come to Sydney half a lifetime before out of a shambled Europe, had astutely enriched themselves and lived happily ever after. When I remarked that they seemed very fortunate people, they heartily agreed: they were extremely fortunate, Sydney was incomparably beautiful, and Australia was without all question the Best Country in the World.[1]

Thirty years ago the New Australian was still an exotic and possibly a threat, even though in those days the immigrants all came from Europe. When the Sydney Municipal Board took to advertising itself in the various languages of its tax-paying citizenry—*MESTSKA RADA SYDNEY*, or *SYDNEY VAVOSI TANBACS*—old-school Sydneysiders thought the worst had happened. After all, I was told at the time, some of the immigrants had come from "the kind of country you take pills for." Yet in fact foreigners had always played important roles in the development of Sydney—beginning with the half-German Phillip himself. Phillip's surveyor general, Augustus Alt, was a native of the duchy of Hesse (and liked to call himself baron), and his superintendent of convicts was a Rhinelander named Phillip Schaffer, who went on to start a

---

[1] All the same I suspect some of them still pine for lost luck of a different kind. "How grand you all were," I said when another Hungarian told me why he had never learned to drive a car—in his youth they always had chauffeurs. "Yes," he simply replied.

thriving vineyard and was thus the Father of the Australian Wine Industry.

There were foreigners among the First Fleet convicts, too. Scooped out of the London underworld, their lives took a queer turn indeed when they found themselves shackled and confined on the other side of the world. There were two Swedes, two Frenchmen, a Norwegian, an Indian, a pair of unfortunates classified as "probably Scandinavian" and "probably Dutch," and at least twelve black men of various provenances. One of these, Black Caesar from Madagascar, was among those who never did knuckle under to authority. Transported for seven years for theft, he was twenty-three when he arrived in Australia, and he remained defiant until the day he died. He stole things, he ran away, he robbed aborigines and white settlers alike. Whether in chains or in solitary confinement, he never gave in. Nothing, he proudly declared, could "make him better." Finally he led a band of absconding toughs into the bush and became the first of Australia's bushrangers: and so, free to the end despite everything, contemptuous still of all officialdom, he was shot dead by another convict, in 1790, there being a reward on his head of five gallons of rum.

Another famous black man was Billy Blue, a favorite character of Macquarie's Sydney. He is variously said to have arrived in Sydney in 1810 on board an American ship, or to have been transported as a convict from England in 1796, but then much about him was equivocal, for he was an enthusiastic liar. Macquarie, who employed him as a boatman, or perhaps a water bailiff, or perhaps in the government stores, found him as entertaining as everybody else did, and gave him eighty acres of land on the North Shore, almost immediately opposite Sydney Cove. This made Blue's fortune. He started a ferry service across the harbor, and on the strength of it, like his exact contemporary the ferry captain Cornelius

Vanderbilt in New York, was known to everyone as The Commodore—later The Old Commodore. He was a great clown. Sometimes he made his passengers row the ferryboat themselves, just for fun, and even in his prosperity he was a shameless beggar—he habitually carried a sack over his shoulder to accommodate the takings. Nobody knew how old he was, but he himself claimed to be seventy when he married, and he was popularly thought to be a centenarian when he died. Blue's Point is named for him, and there is a pub up the road from his ferry station called The Old Commodore still.

Americans have frequented Sydney since the eighteenth century. They had just acquired a nationality of their own then, had seen their own penal colonies absorbed into the freest of Republics, and were perhaps given a certain *schadenfreude*, or alternatively a certain fellow feeling, by the spectacle of the transportees. They also very soon saw chances to be grasped. American trading ships were among the first to find their way to Sydney, and Americans were prominent in Sydney's early whaling and sealing industries—who but New Englanders would have called an inlet in Sydney Harbour Chowder Bay? They have made themselves at home in Sydney ever since, and the countless Americans living in the city now are almost undetectable. The author Paul Theroux once wrote that only in Australia—perhaps only in Sydney, I would guess—could Americans abroad convincingly submerge their nationality in another, and American women especially seem easily assimilated into the civic style, cheerfully putting on weight and developing opinions well beyond conventional perimeters.

As we shall later see, Frenchmen were the first foreign visitors ever to set foot in British Sydney, and they have often cropped up in the city's life. One of the ablest of the convict artists was the Frenchman Charles Rodius, who had been fool enough to get caught stealing a suitcase while on a visit to London in 1829; in Sydney he produced a series of lithographs of aboriginal notables—perceptive, compassionate and haunting, but actually intended for the information of phrenologists. Hunters Hill was founded by two French émigrés in the 1840s, as a speculative project, and was for years almost a French enclave—the French consul had a house there. It was a French valet who committed one of the most notable crimes of early Sydney. In 1845 Jean Videll, having quarreled with his employer Thomas Warne, bludgeoned him to death, dismembered him with an ax, stuffed him into a sea chest and tried to set the house on fire; failing in this intent, he enlisted the help of a couple of friends and took the chest down to the waterfront, where he hired a boatman to row them into the middle of the harbor. But Mr. Warne was smelling badly by then, his blood was oozing from the box, the boatman was disinclined to believe the French explanation that it contained bad pork, and Videll was hanged outside Darlinghurst Gaol, watched by a large and appreciative crowd.

Many Greeks and Maltese have been driven to Sydney by tough times at home, and of these the most historically interesting are the immigrants from the Greek islet of Kastellorizon, which lies a few miles off the southwest coast of Turkey. Kastellorizon's first contact with Australians occurred in 1915, when its entire fleet of caïques was sold to the British for the Dardanelles campaign, and helped to carry the Anzacs to their beachheads at Gallipoli. After that war the islanders so enthusiastically emigrated to New South Wales that there are more Kastellorizians in Sydney ("Kassies") than there are in Kastellorizon, and they have a famous club in the suburb of Kingsford. As for the island itself, most of its people are now Australian citizens returned home in their retirement, and its economy is largely sustained by contributions from down under.

Some foreign settlers have added exotica all their own to the Sydney scene. It was a West Indian Creole named George Howe—"Happy George"—who started the first Sydney newspaper in 1803, not only writing the whole of the often scurrilous *Sydney Gazette*, but editing it, setting it, printing it and personally selling it. Sydney's superintendent of police in the 1830s was the romantic and mysterious Captain Nicholas Rossi, an anti-Napoleonic Corsican who was popularly supposed to have got his job in return for some unexplained secret service to the British state—perhaps (and it sounds his style) in connection with George IV's divorce proceedings against Queen Caroline. Baron Carl von Beiren, a dubious nobleman variously described as Dutch, German and Dutch American, turned up in the 1890s and founded the Australian Gunpowder and Explosives Manufacturing Company—the suburb of Inglewood is named after his ever-hospitable house, Powder Works Road after his factory; but though the words ADVANCE AUSTRALIA were inscribed upon the gates of Inglewood, no munitions ever seem to have been produced. People came to suspect that the baron was a confidence trickster or even a German spy, and the last we hear of him he was in jail for embezzlement.

Then there were the Chinese who started a fish-salting works at Barrenjoey in the 1850s, and the seven Greek pirates of Hydra (captured by the Royal Navy off Libya in 1827) who worked in a vineyard at Parramatta. There was Mary Reibey's formidable female Fijian bodyguard Foo-Choo, and the magnificently named Russian Nicolai Nicolaevich de Miklouho-Macklay, who started a marine biology station at Watson's Bay in 1881. There were the brightly dressed Maoris and Portuguese who used to row the pilot boats, and there were any number of miscellaneous wanderers, dropouts, adventurers, deserters, mountebanks and beachcombers of every nationality under the sun, forever jumping ship, trawling Sydney for pickings, smuggling contraband or finding oblivion in the city's tolerant taverns.

Two minorities of un-British origin have played particularly fateful and permanent roles in the history of Sydney—the Irish and the Jews, both of whom have been represented here since the beginning.

There is a biographical dictionary of Australia's earliest Jews, and thumbing through its pages is a moving experience. Most of the first Jews were petty thieves from Fagin's world, the underworld of London.[1] They had usually been tried at the Old Bailey. Very few had been charged with anything violent, and most of them were from the poorest of the poor— peddlers, fruit sellers, old-clothes dealers, chimney sweeps, hawkers, errand boys, slop sellers, though we see an occasional silversmith and engraver, and at least one dentist. They were generally small dark people, and were likely to be well tattooed—Lewis Joseph, for instance, a molder and founder, transported for theft in 1829, sported the tattoos "Love," "Hope," "Love me little, love me long," an anchor, a sprig, a heart, and the initials EK and LJBK. Often they lived out their sentences in obscurity, eventually disappearing into the Sydney populace, but often enough they never submitted. Here is Samuel Lyons, a well known pickpocket transported in 1815, twice trying to escape and once trying to rob the government stores (200 lashes, four years in the Newcastle coal mines). Here is Lewis Lazarus, tailor, transported for theft in 1818, further convicted in Australia of robbery, absconding, assault, receiving stolen property, drunkenness, absconding again,

---

[1] But the man popularly supposed to have been Dickens's model for Fagin himself, Isaac (Ikey) Solomon, was transported not to Sydney but to Tasmania, where he was eventually freed and became in his old age relatively respectable.

theft again—136 lashes, six weeks on the treadmill, speared five times by aboriginals. Bernard Levy, transported for robbery with assault in 1813, was described as "the most notorious thief and pocket picker the colony has ever produced"— so beyond redemption that when he was pardoned at last in 1862 members of the Sydney synagogue suggested the congregation should raise the money to ship him back to England.

Turn a page or two of the biographical dictionary, though, and here we find James Simmons, convicted in 1813, aged seventeen, of having broken into the home of the Dowager Duchess of Devonshire, in very short order the owner of an inn and a store, a prosperous auctioneer, a charterer of ships and an alderman of the City of Sydney. Remember Sam Lyons, who tried to rob the government stores? Only twelve years later, home and free from the coal mines, here he is a spectacularly successful property developer, active in the synagogue, well known for good works, driving around Sydney behind a pair of his Arab thoroughbreds. And sometimes if the Sydney Jews failed in their lifetimes, their descendants made up for it: Michael Davies, for instance (false pretenses, 1839), came to nothing himself and saw one of his sons hanged as a bushranger, but his grandson became speaker of the Tasmanian House of Assembly, while Cashmore Israel (theft from his own family's house, 1817) was father to the auditor-general of the Commonwealth of Australia.

The convicts were soon followed by free Jewish settlers, and the very first male among these is perhaps the most celebrated. Barnett Levey came to Sydney in the wake of his immensely successful emancipist brother Solomon. He is remembered chiefly as the founder of Sydney's first theater, but he had many other interests too. He started a lending library. He issued bank notes backed not by gold or sterling, but by Indian rupees. He launched a housing project. He owned the Royal Hotel, a grandiose building, designed by Francis Greenway, which was in its day the tallest in Sydney —a "frightfully lofty temple" is how George Howe described it in the *Gazette*. Levey was frequently in trouble, legal or financial, but after endless altercations with officialdom, and repeated financial setbacks, in 1833 he achieved his chief ambition and opened the Theatre Royal; there he put on a racily eclectic repertoire of operas, operettas, classic plays, melodramas and sometimes bawdy farces. Alas, he squandered his profits away in drink and extravagance, and died poor but ever-mourned in 1837, aged thirty-nine—the Father of the Australian Theater.

Since those days Jews have become ubiquitous in the business, artistic and financial circles of the city, and in general they have thrived. There have been occasional spasms of anti-Semitism—in recent years particularly, the vandalizing of graves—but it has not been one of Sydney's habitual bigotries. Today the community is 60,000 strong, its rabbis are prominent civic figures, and it is worthily represented by the magnificent Great Synagogue in Elizabeth Street, consecrated in 1878. A grand structure in mingled Gothic and Byzantine manners, this has two towers, fine wrought-iron gates, and a big rose window overlooking Hyde Park. I went there for a guided tour once, and a most relaxed and entertaining member of the congregation led us into the fane, whistling as he went, while a video of the presiding rabbi, projected hugely on a screen above the pillars, told us all about it.

And what can I say of the Irish? They have been in Sydney since the beginning too, and they have remained as Irish here as they remain anywhere outside their own island—weakening in their style a little now, I think, as memories fade, religion falters and organized labor loses its predominance, but exceedingly Irish still. About a third of the convicts transported here were Irish, and they were often different in kind from the rest—older, more likely to be married, more rural, the women thought to be better behaved than the English, the men more often politically charged. Ireland was endemically in turmoil during the transportation era, and many a young Irish patriot found himself sent to the other side of the world for waving the green too exuberantly.

Some of the Irish convicts were extremely simple. They were leading progenitors of the theory that China lay just out of sight over the hills, and that a quick walk through the bush would get you there; the most ingenuous carried with them a homemade compass chart without a needle, believing that the compass points themselves would give them magic guidance. But there were some able and remarkable people too, especially among the political prisoners. The nearest Sydney can claim to a saint is William Davis, an Irish rebel transported in 1799, who for more than a year sheltered an illegally immigrated priest, Father Jeremiah O'Flynn; secret masses were held in his cottage on Church Hill, perilously close to the George Street guardhouse, until in 1818 O'Flynn was discovered and expelled. Irish ex-soldiers led the only concerted armed rising of convicts at the Sydney settlement, the so-called Battle of Vinegar Hill in 1804.[1] They were mostly men transported after the Irish rebellion of 1798, and put to work clearing forest and building roads north of Parramatta; they hoped to raise a general convict insurrection, but were deceived by a false flag of truce and put down with many casualties, floggings and hangings.

You can still be very Irish in Sydney, if you want to be. There are Irish pubs. There is Irish music. There is a Blarney Street on Killarney Heights, and though it is true that

---

[1] One of the two pitched battles between Europeans on Australian soil, the other being the affair of the Eureka Stockade in Victoria in 1854, which lasted only ten minutes.

Irishtown is no longer called Irishtown, it is still called Kellyville. The fifteen directors of the Australian Ireland Fund include two McGraths, two Burkes, two Cosgroves, two O'Reillys, one O'Neill and the Earl of Portarlington. I once went to a St. Patrick's Day breakfast, held in a big marquee outside a pub in the Rocks, and saw the Sydney Irish at their jolliest. Pipes played, flutes tootled, stout and Gaelic coffee flowed, all the best-known Irish citizens were caught by the TV cameras tucking into a hearty ham and eggs or dancing vigorous jigs. "Is there anyone here from Belfast, now?" rang the bandleader's inquiry fruitily across Sydney Cove, or "Here's a little song for all you good people from County Waterford." I had intended, since the breakfast cost fifty dollars a head, to watch these proceedings economically from the outside, peering through a flap in the tent, but a couple of cheerfully tipsy waiters soon pulled me inside and gave me a Guinness.

All these people are immigrants, every one, if only by descent—even the aboriginals have come from somewhere else. Thirty years ago it was easy enough to forget the fact, so settled and homogenous was Sydney's population. Now reminders are everywhere. Kilioni Uele, charged with the attempted murder of Haumomo Uepe of Homebush outside the Tonga Taboo nightclub, is arraigned before Mr. Alex Mijovich, Her Majesty's justice of the peace. Passionately defending the wearing of tartans on behalf of Comhairie Oighreachd Albannach (the Scottish Heritage Council) is Mr. R. Nicolson Samios. A black shoeshine boy struts around his stand in the Queen Victoria Building. Multiracial larrikins ride their bikes hilariously through the Botanic Gardens. Rahmat Ullah, seventeen, defects from the Bangladesh National Dancing Group and vanishes into Sydney, leaving a note for his producer: "Uncle, my luck in Bangladesh is very poor. So, I am out to search for my fortune."

I hope he has found it by now, and become a New Man like all the rest, or one of the Sun-God's race.

CONSOLATIONS

It is a nice paradox that Sydney, a city born in misery, should be blessed with a true gift for self-consolation. In 1850 Charles Dilke was already commenting upon its high capacity for personal pleasure, and it long ago developed a very different communal ethic from that of the more religion-bound and work-obsessed cities of North America. Nowadays the arrival of Friday arvo is a Sydney institution—the sanctioned moment when, at noon on the fifth day, much of the populace subsides into hedonism; but no matter what day of the week it is, or what time of day either, more than most cities Sydney seems to enjoy itself.

There were few Puritans, of course, on Australia's First Fleet, and a general lack of religious zealotry or remorse has undoubtedly helped to foster the Sydney euphoria. It could never be said that religion is the opiate of the Sydney masses —I know of no city where it seems less obtrusive. A century ago it was recorded that orthodox Christianity had little hold in the local mind, "neither belonging to the country nor yet adapted to its peculiar requirements": the 1986 census showed that apart from the faiths of immigrants, the fastest growing denomination was the one classified as No Religion. The Baha'i Temple stands proudly enough among the woodlands of the north, Greenway's St. James's Church is prominent, the Great Synagogue is resplendent, St. Mary's Cathedral is vast, but on the whole places of religion play an unusually minor part in the city's aesthetic ensemble.

For some years they played no part at all. An outdoor Anglican service was conducted on the first Sunday after the landing at Sydney Cove, the text of Chaplain Johnson's sermon being taken from Psalm 116—"What shall I render unto the Lord for all his benefits toward me?" No church went up, however, for another five years, until Johnson had one built at his own expense on a spot (in Johnson Place) now marked by a memorial. Its convict congregationalists were flogged if they failed to attend without good cause; wondering perhaps what they could best render unto the Lord for his mercies, they habitually spat, coughed and hiccupped throughout the services, and it was almost certainly some of them who burned the building down in 1798. A second church was soon built—the one that looked like a prison—but in 1826 Barron Field was still complaining that Sydney was "a spireless city, and profane." The first three Catholic priests, allowed into the colony at the start of the nineteenth century, were soon expelled on the grounds that they were inciting rebellion; the fourth arrived illicitly in 1817, began his underground pastorate under the protection of brave Mr. Davis, and was thrown out in 1818. It appears to have been only in the middle of the nineteenth century that religion assumed the social role it played in most English-speaking cities around the world, and even then it was largely an instrument of class—English Anglicans on one side, Irish Catholics on the other. Today it is administered by a Catholic cardinal, an Anglican archbishop, and countless ministers, rabbis and mullahs; yet it seems to me, as an agnostic outsider, relatively muted still.

Like any great English-speaking city Sydney has its quota of cults and enthusiasms, encouraged here perhaps by the quasi-Californian climate, but it has never been a great place for revival movements or sectarian bitterness. There was however one famous example of religious ecstasy in Sydney, and its improbable focus was the beach promenade in the suburb of Balmoral, on the Middle Harbour. This is now a very model of suburban contentment. It has a little white pavilion, a bathhouse and a rotunda for a band. An ornamental bridge leads to a public garden on a spit, and there a club of local friends meets every day of the year to have breakfast as the sun comes up. This modest esplanade was to acquire unexpected prominence when the mystical Theosophical Society declared it a site of profound sacred significance. The Theosophists were convinced that a World Teacher would soon be coming to rescue mankind from its ignorance, and some of their seers also believed in the existence of a lost continent, Lemuria, which lay beneath the Pacific and would eventually give up its ancient secrets for the salvation of mankind. After the First World War they determined that Sydney was central to these truths. It was, they said, "the occult centre of the Southern Hemisphere." They acquired a large many-gabled mansion at Mosman on the northern shore, and Theosophist pilgrims came there from all over the world—including the young Indian Jiddu Krishnamurti, whom some of them believed to be the World Teacher in gestation. They established a school and a radio station, 2GB.[1] They arranged vast amounts of publicity in the press. They attracted influential sympathizers, including Walter Burley Griffin up the road at Castlecrag.

---

[1] The GB standing for Giordano Bruno, the sixteenth-century philosopher who was claimed as one of Theosophy's progenitors.

By the 1920s their lodge in Sydney was said to be the largest in the world, and in 1924, on the unassuming beach at Balmoral, they built a great white holy amphitheater. It could hold 2,500 people in twenty-six tiers of seats, and it looked magnificently across the harbor, through the Heads and out to sea. Here was a place of Coming, it was said, where the World Teacher would reveal all when the time was ripe; and through those mighty bluffs would flow the knowledge of Lemuria.

The conviction faded when, in 1929, Krishnamurti publicly declared that he was not the promised Teacher, and in 1939 the site of the Coming was sold—an apartment block stands on the site now. Today it is hard to find signs of religious fervor in Sydney. I once saw a shirtless boy march into St. Andrew's Cathedral and fall in passionate prayer before the altar, but it seemed forlornly out of character. I went to the lying-in of a much-venerated Irish Catholic priest, expecting to find scenes of histrionic distress, but the mourners were restrained, tearless and altogether devoid of black veils. A group of charismatic Christians recently fed their conceptions of Jesus into the Sydney Police Crime Unit's Image Generator —their Identikit. He looked like a cross between a Bondi lifeguard and a small-time crook, with short hair back and sides.

Spiritually the most rewarding place in Sydney seems to me Rookwood Cemetery, which is one of the largest in the world, and includes graves of every denomination. It was founded in 1867, and by the end of the century was the very latest thing in cemeteries, eventually embracing 777 acres of land (well away from settled areas, we read, "so that adjoining land would not be devalued"). It had its own railway stations, and twice a day trains from Sydney stopped at stations en route to pick up "corpses, mourners or clergymen," the mourners and clergymen having to buy tickets but the corpses traveling free. It was splendidly landscaped, with gazebos and canals, and was famous for its flower beds—a green rose used habitually to blossom there. A park ranger lived in a lodge with a tower, wore a peaked cap with RANGER on it, and carried a revolver for the extermination of stray dogs and goats. People of all sorts were buried in this ideal necropolis. The very first was an eighteen-year-old Irish pauper, and among those who followed him were politicians, artists, bushrangers, entertainers and tycoons.[1]

The trains stopped in 1948. The showplaces fell into decay, and today Rookwood is a more realistic allegory of the natural condition. In its center it is still well kept, and the adherents of many creeds lie there in trim oblivion—disciples of Shintoism, or Assyrian Catholicism, or the Salvation Army, or Hinduism, or Judaism, or Islam—Greeks and Latvians and Hungarians and Assyrians and Italians—all in their own carefully demarcated and appropriately scripted plots. Joggers and cyclists pass among them, here and there people tidy up graves, or lay fresh flowers, but as you wander away from the heart of the place an organic decay sets in. Obelisks become more tottery, gravestones are cracked, iron balustrades stand bent and rusted, until finally the great place of death is regenerated at its edges into life. The remotest parts of Rookwood are pure bushland, and there snakes, frogs, tortoises, ginks and geckos flourish, hares and foxes hide, fig-birds and honey eaters flutter vivacious among the gums.[2]

---

[1] Not to mention, since this is a passage about religion, Jacob Pitman, died 1890. He was a religious pioneer whose brother was Sir Isaac Pitman, the spelling reformer, and his epitaph at Rookwood says he woz the ferst Minister in theez Koloniz ov the Doktrinz ov the Sekond or Niu Kristian Church.

[2] More than a million people are thought to be buried at Rookwood, and in 1981 the Society of Australian Genealogists transcribed all their surviving epitaphs onto microfilm. It took ninety people seven years to do the job, and their labor is recorded in a book, *The Sleeping City*, edited by David A. Weston, Sydney, 1989, to which I am much indebted.

Secular consolations have been more boisterously pursued. Sex in Sydney, for example, began with a bang on the night of February 6, 1788, when the female convicts were disembarked to join the males already ashore at Sydney Cove. No doubt in the fortnight since the raising of the flag the married officers and wives had comforted each other in their beds, and perhaps a few people of initiative, Peter Morris for example, had already found comfort among the aborigines. For the mass of the convict population, though, the barriers were lowered when the women at last came down the gangplanks onto Australian soil. It was a rough night. Violent winds and rains swept the settlement, lightning streaked across the harbor, but the moment the women stepped ashore the penal community threw itself into orgy. After eight months at sea, cooped up in sexual segregation and cruel confinement, both men and women were ready for it. The officials and marines were unable to control them—perhaps they did not even try—and the diarists seem to stand back aghast as they view the commotion beside the Tank Stream. Tench preferred not to mention it at all. Arthur Bowes Smith, surgeon on one of the transports, said it was beyond his abilities to give a just description of the scene. We can only imagine it, reading between the lines and remembering human nature: around the soggy tents and shacks of Sydney Cove that night, watched from a cautious distance by officialdom and the less impetuous of the felons, several hundred couples writhing and twisting in the mud, while oaths, drunken songs, laughs, groans and the clankings of irons compete with the thunder.

It is a scene not at all appropriate to Sydney. This is not a very orgiastic city. In modern times the relationship between men and women here has traditionally been self-conscious, while homosexuality, though prevalent among the convicts and common now has only recently become socially acceptable. It is true that the history books are full of licentious suggestion: "detestable vices" that could be satisfied in the Sydney of the 1790s, "scenes of immorality beyond description" in the Domain of the 1860s. However when in 1838 rumor said that Richard Davies was "doing something improper with a pig," his neighbor Mrs. Holland retorted indignantly that he was "not a man of that description," and most Sydney males today are not of that description either.[1]

Wowserism has never been as powerful here as in Melbourne—its name, indeed, was invented by a Sydney man of permissive instinct, John Norton the editor of *Truth*.[2] Still, the city has had its share of killjoys, and anyway the general delight in the sun, the sea and the sand has perhaps kept libidos in restraint. When the magazine *Tracks* asked its readers which was better, surfing or sex, 62 percent said surfing. To be sure 80 percent admitted they thought about sex when surfing, but then 51 percent said they thought about surfing during sex.

It says something about the survival of innocence in Sydney that its people are so touchingly proud of Kings Cross. Originally called Queen's Cross, in honor of Queen Victoria's Diamond Jubilee, the suburb was renamed when Edward VII came to the throne, and it used to be the center of Bohemia in Sydney, the one cosmopolitan part of town before the New Australians arrived. It was given a sleazy new reputation by the American servicemen who flocked there during the Second World War, and later during the Vietnam War, and at night nowadays suggests a red-light quarter in some kind of sociological exhibition, so compactly assembled are its strip shows, its pornographic bookstores and its upstairs massage

[1] Though Mrs. Holland was wrong, unfortunately: Davies was later caught in the act in his peach orchard, and sent away to life imprisonment on Norfolk Island.
[2] Supposedly, I learn from *The Macquarie Encyclopedic Dictionary*, Sydney, 1990, as an acronym for his ironic slogan "We Only Want Social Evils Remedied."

parlors. The necessary hard-looking unshaven men hang around the Alamein fountain, a whirling floodlit device like a dandelion head. The essential emaciated prostitutes parade the shadowy sidewalks of Victoria Street. There is the statutory scattering of drug addicts, transvestites, tourists, drunks, sailors and miscellaneous layabouts from around the world. You would have to be very unworldly to be surprised by the all-too-familiar sights of Kings Cross; yet Sydneysiders habitually recommend it to foreigners as a prime metropolitan spectacle, not on any account to be missed.

Anyway, if you go back to the Cross in the morning you will find it charmingly villagelike. The GIRLS! GIRLS! GIRLS! signs have been turned off, the adult movie houses are closed, those jowly men are still in bed, and now you find flower shops and grocery stalls, pleasant houses in back streets, one of the best bookshops in Sydney and some of the most agreeable coffee shops. Along Victoria Street, now revealed as a delightful leafy thoroughfare, dropouts and addicts of the night before sit demurely beside the blistered Volkswagen campers they are trying to sell, before going home to be certified public accountants.

Far more than sex, the delight and the despair of Sydney has been strong drink. Hardly a passage of this city's history is without a reference to it, from the very earliest days, when convicts always seemed to be able to get hold of it, to the fearful drunken-driving records of today. So far as I can discover the Australian aborigines, almost alone among the peoples of the earth, never learned to make fermented drinks—or perhaps never needed to, their elaborate otherworld of dreams, song and legend being quite intoxicating enough. Hardly had the British arrived, however, than alcohol became an essential adjunct to life, and rum, a generic name for hard spirits of all kinds, assumed the importance of money itself. Goods were bought in it. Laborers got their wages in it. Chaplain Johnson paid for his church in it. The rebellion against Bligh was named after it. The 44th Regiment mutinied for it. The New South Wales Corps, its officers having acquired their monopoly in it, became known as the Rum Corps, and for years the Sydney general hospital, which was largely financed by it, was called the Rum Hospital.

The original rum was all imported, from England or from India, but the settlers were soon making their own, together with wines, beers and more peculiar liquors. A spirit made of fermented sugar bags soaked in buckets of water proved popular among the aborigines. The leaves of the sticky hop-bush, chewed by the Iora as a cure for toothache, were adopted by the Europeans to flavor their ale. A beer sampled at the Parramatta Fair in 1824 was said to be so strong that "reason was de-throned and madness and folly reigned in its stead," while an early settler of the North Shore, experimenting with fermented peaches, reported that "one glas put parson in the whelebarrow."[1]

In the nineteenth century there was a proliferation of pubs (called hotels in the city to this day). They were socially important in the early years because so many men were without families or decent homes, and later they became nests of mateship, being generally out-of-bounds to respectable women. With their quaint inn signs and particular reputations, the taverns greatly enhanced Sydney's sense of picturesque antiquity, and they often had piquant names: The Help Me Through the World, The World Turned Upside Down, or The Keep Within the Compass (kept by a former policeman). Sometimes they had resident fiddlers, often they were fre-

---

[1] He is quoted by Ruth Park in *The Companion Guide to Sydney,* Sydney, 1973.

quented by gambling schools and haunted by whores. The massed taverns and sly-grog houses of the Rocks were so uproarious in their heyday that their cumulative noise could be heard miles out at sea. The bar rail of the Shakespeare Tavern, in the 1880s, had an electric wire running through it, enabling the puckish landlord to galvanize his customers. The Marble Bar at Adams's Hotel was a prodigy of colored marble from France, Italy and Belgium, supplemented by American walnut paneling, chandeliers, stained glass, and lubricious wall paintings.[1]

The pubs were open from six in the morning until eleven at night, and of course there were objectors to all this jollity. Temperance movements waxed and waned in Sydney—as early as 1837 the Quaker merchant John Tawell, whom we have met before, ostentatiously poured a large quantity of spirits into the harbor.[2] The real blow to the city's drinking habits, however, did not occur until 1916, when there was a mutiny among the troops at a training camp in the western suburb of Casula. Objecting to a new and demanding training program, several thousand soldiers raided the camp liquor stores, looted some pubs of their drink, and set off on a disheveled progress across the city, smashing windows, breaking up food stalls, seizing cars and wagons, attacking clubs and stores and terrifying civilians wherever they went. There was no denying that drink was the cause of this rampage, and so there came into force "the six o'clock swill." For nearly forty years every legal pub in the city shut its doors at six in the evening, leading not only to a plethora of speakeasies, but also to a headlong consumption of liquor in the last moments

---

[1] And still to be enjoyed in a new home at the Sydney Hilton Hotel: as a pamphleteer wrote in 1893, "the globe-trotter who visits the bar for his glass of whisky looks round him with astonishment."

[2] A watching seaman cried out, "That's real murder," and this was a curious form of prophecy, for when the pious Tawell went home to England in 1838 he poisoned his mistress, and was hanged for it.

before closing time, when people came out from work. The Sydney pubs acquired a new reputation for lavatorial crudity, and were mostly redecorated accordingly, with tiled walls for the easier cleansing of spilled beer and vomit. Everything most philistine, provincial and misogynist about Sydney was epitomized in the six o'clock swill: at the end of each working day (as citizens of vivid memory have described it for me) a tide of inebriated men came rolling out of their ghastly taverns, staggering into railway stations, barging on to buses or throwing up over ferry rails.

The rule was mercifully abandoned in 1955. Nowadays the pubs have mostly softened their ambiences, and welcome women with more or less good grace. Although beer and Sydney still go together in the world's mind, the per capita consumption of alcohol has lately declined, perhaps because of the new proportion of abstemious Italians, Greeks and Asians. Nevertheless Friday evening down at the Rocks, traditionally the quarter of chaos, can still be sufficiently rumbustious. Then the young people come into town from the outer suburbs, determined to live metropolitan life to the full, and the mounted police regularly move in to keep things in check. I was at a reception one evening at the Regent Hotel, the most luxurious in Sydney, which was a paragon of discreet conservative elegance. The older people were dressed expensively but not gaudily, the younger ones were in properly tempered derivations of street fashion. The music was provided, as is habitual at the Regent, by an elegant flute-and-piano duo. The refreshments were suave. Needing a breath of fresh air I took a couple of sandwiches and wandered through the foyer into the street outside; and there, not a hundred yards away, in the shadow of the expressway I found Saturnalia in full swing. A couple of dozen young people, reconditely dressed and impossibly drunk, were singing obscene songs in the half-light. There were beer cans in their hands, beer cans lined up for future consumption, empty beer cans rolling over the sidewalk. A youth in a wild and scraggly beard played the guitar. Three or four girls danced an abandoned go-go on a ledge. The men were husky and flushed, the women looked half-crazed, and they were all singing, shouting and waving their arms about like people in a dream.

I was rather sorry to leave this Boschlike gathering and return to the reception in the hotel, where a waitress instantly offered me a small shrimp canapé, and the flutist was into a Telemann sonata, I think.

Except for that brief grim period in the 1780s, almost nobody has gone hungry in Sydney. Perhaps it was this tradition of general plenty that made the city for so long indifferent to cuisine. Even twenty years ago the food, whether private or public, was a desperate approximation of English provincial cooking, its one famous dish being the Pie Floater—a meat pie floating in pea soup which has been sold since 1945 at the Woolloomooloo food stall called Harry's Café de Wheels. Fish generally turned out to be fish and chips in the old greasy style, few Sydneysiders were keen on oysters, and the cooking of kangaroos was illegal.

It is illegal still, innumerable patriots holding that to eat a national symbol would smack of treason, or perhaps sacrilege, but by now food has become almost a national symbol itself, and is certainly one of the prime Sydney consolations. The influx of foreign restaurateurs has changed everything—starting with the tea, now generally metamorphosed into espresso coffee. The restaurants have burgeoned café tables at last, besides climbing several hundred feet up the Sydney Tower and spreading themselves all around the harbor front. I can think of no national cuisine that is not represented somewhere in the city nowadays, and at private tables the food may be anything from roast beef to couscous. For a time *nouvelle cuisine* in its silliest forms seduced fashionable Sydney, and everything was stuffed with artichokes or grilled over herb-scented charcoal. Today the fad is over, and the best of the restaurants have come to realize that the true Sydney speciality should surely be fresh fish and shellfish, simply served. At Watson's Bay, on the harbor, the Doyle family restaurant has been preaching this gospel for several generations; now it has been joined by dozens of others, to be dropped in at while waiting for a ferry at Circular Quay, or flown to by seaplane on the Hawkesbury River, and serving Moreton Bay Bugs, Mud Crab Salad, Sydney Rock Oysters and all manner of fish washed down with good New South Wales wine beside lovely watery prospects.

It is sadly true, however, that to many foreign palates even the freshest and most straightforward Sydney food, even the juiciest Bug or most perfectly steamed Hawkesbury River Teraglin, seems disappointingly flavorless. It is glorious in the idea, enticing in the appearance, but tastes as though it has been cooked in unsalted water—or, in the case of the sea fish, caught in unsalted oceans. To my mind only the Sydney Rock Oyster, surely the best in the world, lives up to its promise.

"Seven Miles to Manly," it says above Pier 3 on Circular Quay, "A Thousand Miles from Care"—or as an earlier publicity tag put it, "Fourpence Spent on a Trip to Manly is Better than a Pound on Medicine." Essential to the full enjoyment of Sydney is a taste for the out-of-doors. The climate may not be as perfect as foreigners generally suppose it to be, but it is never really cold, and every year contains days of such unsurpassable beauty, such glory of freshness and stimulation, that they color all perceptions. For myself, though I have experienced this city in moods surly, dismal and almost alarming, when I think of a Sydney day I think immediately and deliciously of a rather northern kind of brilliance, as though the pale white clouds have drifted across the blue up there from Iceland or Helsinki.

And the setting is perfectly matched, providing the citizens of Sydney with unbeatable pleasure grounds. The harbor itself might almost have been designed for recreation, and there has probably been hardly a daylight moment, for 200 years, when there was not somebody fishing somewhere on its shores, sailing on its waters or having a picnic around its perimeter. The first registered owner of a Sydney pleasure boat was Robert Campbell the merchant, back in Macquarie's day, and in 1827 the Royal Navy officially sanctioned the delights of the harbor, as it were, by holding the city's first regatta: all the local worthies were among the guests, quadrilles were danced on board the warships in the harbor, and the Sydney professional watermen had their own race. By the mid-nineteenth century people of all ranks were out in boats, and swimming and rowing contests had become great Sydney spectator sports; 30,000 people went to the funeral of "Varney" Kieran, a champion fin-de-siècle swimmer, and an obelisk on a rock in the Parramatta River still honors Henry Searle, a star of late-Victorian sculling.

Fleets of excursion boats now indulged the Sydney penchant for a day out on the water. Even the ferry commuters often made a pleasure of necessity; for many years a society called the Hot Potato Club, formed by businessmen using the late-night ferry home to Mosman, kept a supply of pies and potatoes warm near the ships' engines, and washed them down each evening with a convivial drink. The Sunday harbor picnic became an institution, too—Kipling called this "a city of picnics." On especially picnickable days the path to Yurong Point, in the Domain, was lined with stalls selling boiling water for tea making, and there are innumerable pictures of the populace spreading its cloths on green swards, or hanging expectantly with wicker baskets over the rails of steamers. Picnic dances were popular too, and came to be known as Gypsy Teas; a favorite spot for them was Rodd Island, the exotic-looking islet we glimpsed from the planned suburb of Haberfield.

The harbor remains the greatest Sydney consolation. The weekend sight of it, with its thousands of yachts, is a very epitome of pleasure; the start of the Sydney-to-Hobart Race, and the spectacular passage of its yachts through the Heads, is one of the prime occasions of the Sydney year; the Australia Day ferryboat race must be one of the most entertaining of all sporting events—such a chuffing and foaming and lurching, as the tough little ships strain themselves along the brief course from Pinchgut to the Bridge![1] For many Sydney people a boat on the harbor is still the best of possessions, if only for lazing about on, drinking beer, in the shelter of some placid cove.[2] The harbor picnic may not be quite what it was, the Gypsy Teas are over, but Kipling would certainly recognize the spirit of a Sunday lunchtime at Watson's Bay—crowded white-clothed tables of restaurants, old ladies on benches eating seafood off plastic trays, families strolling beneath the palms of the little park, bright umbrellas everywhere, scavenging gulls, launches foaming in, yachts and tourist coaches, and away in the distance the flags on top of the Harbour Bridge just showing over Bradley's Head.

Excursion boat trips are still perhaps the most popular of all Sydney outings. Sometimes they can be rowdy disco charters —"hose-down trips," they are called, because the boats so

---

[1] And such embarrassment, too, when in 1984 the forty-eight-year-old ferryboat *Karrabee*, having done its best in the race, returned to its pier at Circular Quay and sank.

[2] "Wanted" (says a perhaps apocryphal small advertisement in a Sydney shop window), "woman to cook, clean fish, dig for worms and make love. Must own boat and outboard motor. Send photo of boat."

often need a good wash the morning after, and there were some disreputable cruises during the Vietnam War, when American servicemen interpreted Rest and Recreation as a synonym for sex afloat. Mostly, though, the excursion boats are as innocuous today as they were a hundred years ago, and one of my own sweetest memories of the harbor is of a wedding reception that came floating past my balcony one fine day in March. In the cabin of the boat I could just see the bride, a shimmer of satin happiness among a shirt-sleeved, summer-dressed crowd, and in the prow one of the bridesmaids stood alone and contemplative like a figurehead, her long pale dress fluttering, one hand holding the jack staff, the other a glass of champagne.

For years the harbor was enough. The ocean beaches came later. In 1857 Henry Gilbert Smith, a rich emigrant from Sussex, England, decided to turn the fishing hamlet of Manly, which straddled a spit between the harbor and the open sea, into an ocean resort for the city. Perhaps he was remembering Brighton, after which he originally intended to name it. Certainly he made of it an emblematic pleasure place, still a kind of blueprint of your ideal seaside town. From the ferry station on the harbor shore you walk down a wide pedestrian street, called romantically the Corso and lined with shops and souvenir stalls, until there opens out before you the wide surf-ranged crescent of the ocean beach, lined with now raggety Norfolk pines planted by Smith himself.

It was at Manly, in Edwardian times, that Sydney consummated its affair with the outdoors. Bathing had not always been a universal pastime here. In the earliest days genteel people thought it a practice only for convicts, who bathed to get clean, and in 1838 it was forbidden between six in the morning and eight in the evening "near or within view of any

public wharf, quay, bridge, street, road or other place of public resort." People swam in the early hours, or after dark, or
on secluded beaches, and there were inspectors to enforce the
law—at Manly a man with a big dinner-bell came around
each morning to signal the end of bathing time. On October 2,
1902, the proprietor and editor of the *Manly and North Sydney
News*, William Henry Gocher, put this preposterous law to the
test by openly, and with full publicity, donning his neck-to-
knee swimming costume and entering the Manly surf at midday.[1] The police declined to prosecute, the case aroused much
hilarity, and finally the law was ridiculed out of existence.
Sydney's obsession with sand, surf and sea, later to be dignified as the Beach Culture, began with Mr. Gocher's act of
defiance, and five years later he was presented with a gold
watch and a purse of fifty sovereigns as an expression of public gratitude.

The beach culture almost instantly exploded, in a splurge of
new tram and ferry services to take the populace to the sea
beaches, and Sydney appropriated it as peculiarly its own.
The sidestroke, hitherto used by all the fastest swimmers,
gave way to the Sydney speciality called the Australian crawl.
The great Duke Kahanamoku from Honolulu introduced the
city to the art of surfing. Lifesaving teams, stylizing their techniques into a strutting kind of pageantry, succeeded the old
Volunteer Fire Companies as expressions of local pride, and as
vehicles of working-class comradeship. The world came to
think of Sydney people as beach people, and they themselves
propagated the notion in posters, brochures, jokes and slang.
The name of Bondi in particular, the most popular of all the

---

[1] At least this is how Gocher himself remembered the occasion: according to
Alan Ross (*Australia '55*, London, 1955), a policeman on duty at the time
said the editor had gone into the water wearing a frock coat, striped trousers, and a bowler hat, with an umbrella under his left arm. "I can see it all
quite clearly," said the cop.

surfing beaches, went into the vernacular in many contexts. To go like a Bondi tram meant to go as fast as the trams which, urged on by enthusiastic customers, used to rocket across town to the Bondi beaches; and when in 1973 Ruth Park, writing *The Companion Guide to Sydney*, searched for an idiom to describe the fizzily eclectic architecture of Sydney Town Hall, she called it Bondi Renaissance.

The beach culture is often collated with philistinism, and of course it is true that there is nothing very cerebral to Sydney's weekend rush to the ocean. It is an instinctive escape to an environment where several Australian ideals can be fulfilled —perfect social equality, perfect freedom, perfect chances to display yourself, perfect idleness combined with strenuous physical exercise if you want it. They are wholesome ideals really. The declared ideals of the lifeguards are almost unctu-ously altruistic. The competitions of the Iron Men, stupen-dously demanding contests in swimming, running, rowing and jumping, are karatelike in their asceticism.[1]

The beach culture has weakened a little lately. The Bondi Lifesaving Club, where son traditionally followed father into the rituals, finds fewer competitive members these days. Fam-ily loyalties are weaker now, people have more and easier distractions, the object of young ambition is not so often to parade high-stepping along the sands holding a flag at a life-savers' carnival, or to be immortalized upon a clubhouse wall. Fears of skin cancer and pollution have reduced the magnetic pull of the beaches. Nevertheless on a fine weekend afternoon Sydney's ocean shore is still joyously crowded from the mouth of the Hawkesbury in the north to Botany Bay in the

---

[1] It was a 6'6" champion of Bondi, indeed, who was chosen to play the invincible extraterrestrial hero in the Japanese TV series *Ultra-Man*. The Iron Man cult began in California, but the first Sydney people to be called Iron Men were convicts who could withstand without a murmur the torture of the lash. In 1990 first place in the Narrabeen Iron Man Triathlon was won by the three pastrycooks of the Paris Cake Shop, Bondi.

south—one of the world's supreme hedonistic spectacles. I suppose there is no other great city with quite such a gift: the beaches of Los Angeles or Rio de Janeiro have none of the domestic appeal of these Sydney oceanfronts, which are like sand and surf extensions of the family suburbs behind them.

A passion for sport is part of Sydney's escapist talent—just look at the space devoted to it in the papers. They say the city has never been so sports-crazy as Melbourne, but Sydney-siders suggest this is because in Melbourne there is nothing else to do, and certainly by any other standards Sydney's devotion to racing, cricket, football and tennis would be hard to beat. It is a nonsectarian, extraclass devotion, shared by nearly everyone.

Cricket in particular has traditionally been fiercely played, rudely watched and spectacularly fulfilled, and the Sydney Cricket Ground is one of the historic sites of the game. It was here in 1929 that Don Bradman of New South Wales made 452 not out, the greatest score in first-class cricket, here in 1932 that England's body-line bowling tactics almost split the British Empire. The ground is also home to The Hill, the most famous barracking stand anywhere, whence an entire anthology of insults has at one time or another been shouted across the pitch, so I assumed that if I went to a match there at least I would not be bored.

Nor was I. I chose a match of floodlit cricket, Sydney's own particular contribution to the contemporary game, and it was terrific. It was the old charm of cricket with all the young thrill of football. Australia was playing New Zealand, and as evening fell upon Sydney feelings ran very high. The stadium glowed and throbbed in the dark. Bright beneath the floodlights the players themselves, colorfully dressed and using a white ball, were as much like performers on a stage as sportsmen on a pitch, and the mostly young audience behaved much as they would at a rock concert. Sometimes a vast tide of cheers, orchestrated by some invisible conductor, swept from one end of the stadium to the other, to break like a wave and return again as an ebb of boos. Sometimes, as a bowler began his run, he would be accompanied by a vast crescendo of banging feet. If a wicket fell, or a catch was missed, the crowd burst into instant and magnificent displays of emotion, throwing hats, paper cups and balloons into the air, banging the barricades, shouting, whistling, clapping, booing and cheering. Much beer and Coke was drunk, many chips were eaten, and as the match approached its last climax I felt a tremendous sense of restless and perhaps slightly menacing excitement—rather as one might feel it, I thought, in the hours before a revolution.

Nothing very terrible happened, of course (Australia won), but at one period of the evening I chanced to look over the balcony into an open space outside the stadium, and there I saw a succession of young men being hauled in handcuffed by plainclothes policemen—briskly questioned, photographed there and then with Polaroids, and shoved into a windowless van from whose interior emerged muffled thumps of protest. I don't know what they were to be charged with, but I did notice that a few yards away, within sight of the police but on the safe side of a high wire-mesh fence, three small boys were getting their own kicks by sniffing aerosol cans. . . .

But it would be wrong to end a chapter of consolations with scenes of squalor. Let me end instead with a Saturday afternoon I once enjoyed, doing nothing in particular, in the park at Parramatta, the wide expanse of rolling green, intersected by the river, that was originally the demesne of Government

House. A fair was happening just outside the park, so that everything was permeated by thumping music and the smell of hot dogs, and for the most part the goings-on were thoroughly traditional. There were people playing bowls, riding bikes, knocking golf balls about. There were the inevitable Sydney picnickers. There were jolly volunteers working on the Parramatta Steam Tram, an ancient prodigy which itself sometimes came snorting along its track beneath the trees. Small boys scrambled down the steep bank to the muddy Parramatta at the bottom. On one sward the Pike and Musket Society of New South Wales was practicing its tactics, marching and countermarching with gleaming breastplates, while in a glade nearby its ladies rehearsed a pavane dressed in becoming combinations of farthingales and cut-down jeans.

In a little gazebo, built in 1823 as a bathhouse for the governor and his guests, I came across another of those Sydney school reunions. Summer-frocked and gleamingly dentured, young Ockers and Sheilas of long ago sat in a circle inside the building, finishing off a buffet. They all seemed very fond of one another. "Didn't you have any enemies at school?" I asked one beaming lady, as she pressed me to a cup of tea. "How could anyone be an enemy to someone like *him*?" she replied—and she pointed to a benignly gap-toothed, red-faced old codger nearby, who sat on a chair with his knees apart and gave me a wink.

PURPOSES

1 FUNCTION

Sometimes, under the influence of drink or too many oysters, I feel a sense of amiable unreality in Sydney. It is
after all a most unlikely place. Born a concentration camp
thousands of miles from the next town, maturing so improba-
bly on the underside of the world, more than most cities it
seems artificial of purpose. It really need not exist at all. No
ancient crossroads or trading routes make sense of its location, it is not the center of anything, its indigenes did not
demand it and its annihilation tomorrow would not deprive
the world of anything essential to the well-being or the heritage of mankind. It is in short, say I to myself as I order
another half dozen, a self-indulgent place, created solely to be
itself. Sometimes I even find it possible to fancy that it has
never happened at all, and that I am resident in an agreeable
hallucination.

Two centuries ago this great city was nothing but an idea in
a few London heads—a wild intent to establish a settlement
upon an unsurveyed shore, visited only once by Europeans,

and that only for a stay of a few days. No reconnaissance party preceded the First Fleet. Sydney was an *ad hoc* kind of place from the beginning, and for me it retains a sense of permanent improvisation, making itself up as it goes along.

The city's first seal, struck in 1790, succinctly expressed its official purposes. It showed Industry sitting on a bale of goods receiving the convicts to their tasks, and is all too reminiscent of the slogan above the gates of Auschwitz—Work Shall Make You Free. Almost at the same time, however, Josiah Wedgwood of Derby, England, struck a commemorative medallion, modeled in Sydney clay sent to him by Governor Phillip. He based its design upon a poem by Erasmus Darwin—Charles Darwin's grandfather—called "The Voyage of *Hope* to Sydney Cove," which was itself prophetically inspired by the reports that came home from the penal colony:

> *There shall broad streets their stately malls extend,*
> *The circus widen, and the crescent bend;*
> *There, ray'd from cities o'er the cultured land,*
> *Shall bright canals, and solid roads expand.*
> *There the proud arch, colossus-like, bestride*
> *Yon glittering streams, and bound the chasing tide;*
> *Embellished villas crown the landscape-scene,*
> *Farms wave with gold, and orchards blush between.*
> *There shall tall spires, and dome-capped towers ascend,*
> *And piers and quays their massy structures blend;*
> *While with each breeze approaching vessels glide,*
> *And northern treasures dance on every tide!*

Fired by this prescient verse, Wedgwood produced a medal far more cheerful than the official seal. Hope presided over it, and bestowed her blessings upon Peace, Art and an unshackled Labor; and sure enough Sydney's original purpose was very soon overtaken by all the opportunities of a free society.

Just to be seen behind Hope's skirts, in the Wedgwood medallion, were the blades of an anchor, and very proper too, for Sydney's most obvious function is that of a seaport. At the very beginning, before the Blue Mountains were crossed by Europeans, the sea offered its settlers not only the one way into Sydney, but the one way out. Even when its hinterland was opened, the city remained primarily an outpost of a maritime Empire, looking to the ocean for its commerce and profits. Seals and whales, sandalwood and Tahitian pork—these were some of the first of the Sydney commodities, and for years this was one of the archetypal Conradian schooner ports of the South Pacific, where every captain came some time or other to sell his cargo, to look for charters, to repair or victual his ship, to replenish his crew.[1] In 1841 a newcomer counted 140 ships in the harbor—deep-sea sailing ships, coastal brigs and schooners, paddle steamers serving the Hunter River settlements, colliers from Newcastle, grain lighters down from the Hawkesbury River. It was to Sydney that the wool clippers came, in the epic days of sail. Sometimes eight or nine were in port at the same time, and for seven consecutive years in the 1880s and 1890s the most famous of them all, the *Cutty Sark* and the *Thermopylae,* sailed together through the Heads in a pageantry of canvas at the start of their long races home to Britain.

Even in the early twentieth century the maritime association was inescapable. A much larger proportion of the population then lived close to the harbor, and almost everything in Sydney proper still looked down to the ocean, the wharves, the Customs House and the warehouses. Whole families lived as seamen, dockers, ferrymen, fishermen or pilots. The

---

[1] Conrad himself came several times, though never as a captain.

wharfie, the Sydney docker, dominated labor affairs; suburbs like Balmain or Pyrmont depended upon the jobs of the quays and shipyards. The Peninsula & Oriental liner service from London was one of the municipal institutions, giving rise to a variety of local architecture called the P & O Style, and every old photograph shows the inner harbor gloriously crowded with riggings. Even when international air travel began, before the Second World War, it was to Sydney as a seaport that the first flights came; the flying boats of Qantas and Imperial Airways used a base at Rose Bay, on the south shore of the harbor.

The old sense of jostled maritime intensity is lost now. For one thing only a few cruise ships dock at Sydney Cove's Ocean Terminal, the rest of the quays being given over to ferry piers, while Darling Harbour is dedicated to tourism. Most of the big container ships dock at a terminal in Botany Bay. In Sydney as everywhere the picturesque old finger piers have mostly been demolished, or survive in rickety hazard, and the last of the regular P & O liners sailed for what was then still called Home in the 1970s.

Nevertheless this remains one of the best places to watch the ships go by, and when I walk out on my balcony at Mc-Mahon's Point there are almost sure to be vessels passing. Sometimes they are nosing upstream to the oil berths and coal docks still tucked away in unsuspected coves west of the bridge. Sometimes they are negotiating the bends into the Pyrmont wharves, where for the next couple of days I shall see their masts and upperworks protruding above the buildings. Often trim white Japanese fishery depot boats come by, and sometimes I am just in time to catch some gaudy cruise ship being nudged into the Ocean Terminal. A couple of tugs swing down the harbor to meet an incoming freighter. The pilot launch hurries toward Balmain to pick up a pilot for duty. Rusty Chinese container ships moor at Millers Point, opposite my window, gigantic vessels full of cars sometimes wake me with their sirens in the morning, and I was amused one day to observe that the crew of the Soviet freighter *Byelorussia* did not for a moment pause in their game of basketball as their ship steamed below the grand arch of the bridge, past the benedictory Opera House, past all the shine of Sydney to the sea.

El Dorado was ever the goal of Empire, and in Sydney from the start men dreamed of gold and other treasures of the earth. If the Blue Mountains beckoned some as a hint of liberty, they enticed many others as possible mining country. In the very first year of the settlement, in the very first of Sydney's celebrated frauds, a convict named James Daley (seven years for theft) momentarily galvanized everyone by producing a lump of gold he claimed to have dug up: he had made it by melting down a guinea and a brass buckle, and got 100 lashes for the deceit.[1] They really did find coal in Sydney, and it was briefly mined at Balmain, but in the end the city turned out to be El Dorado by proxy, as it were. For a time it was vastly enriched by the Bathurst goldfields, for which it provided not only so many of the speculators, but also the financial services, the supplies and the exchange. More permanently, it has prospered by the woolly gold of the sheep herds, grazing in their countless thousands beyond the hills. Sydney's first great magnates made their money in the sheep business, the huge wool warehouses of the nineteenth century were proclamations of the civic function, and to this day the bush (as Australians indiscriminately call both farm country

---

[1] Besides being ordered to wear a canvas smock with the letter R for *rogue* sewn on it.

and wilderness) plays its important part in the Sydney consciousness and economy.

By the nature of things Sydney, though a place chiefly of townsmen from the start, was born countrified. Cows, pigs, sheep, goats, horses and poultry were fellow migrants with the convicts, and Phillip, who had farmed himself during periods of half pay in England, did his best to make an agricultural go of things. His original government garden is preserved as a kind of shrine within the Botanic Gardens, planted with the same cabbages, carrots and beetroots: it was not much of a success in 1788, and the cabbages still look pretty moldy to me. Most of the original cattle soon ran away into the bush, but were discovered years later generated into flourishing wild herds. Lesser farm stock infested the streets of early Sydney; hens were all over the place, goats were a pest, pigs roamed the town as licensed scavengers. The surrounding countryside was a disappointment at first, and dreams faded of a plantation colony, reclining among palms and bananas in the West Indian kind. Soon enough, nevertheless, the first agriculturists were flourishing, some of them military men and officials farming on the side, some free settlers and ex-convicts.

The first of them all, and the first man to receive a land grant in the colony, was a convict from Cornwall named James Ruse (seven years for breaking and entering). He was one of the few farmers on the First Fleet, and Phillip gave him thirty acres at Parramatta. This was the beginning of Experiment Farm, whose house is now one of the two oldest houses in Australia, and whose acres are represented by an adjacent small and rubbish-strewn park. It was also the real beginning of Australian agriculture. Ruse failed in the end, and became someone else's farm overseer, but he was evidently conscious of his status as the Father of the Australian Farm, because he wrote for his epitaph, carved on his tombstone at Campbelltown:

> *My mother reread me tenderly*
> *With me she took much paines*
> *And when I arrived in this Coloney*
> *I sowd the forst Grain*
> *And Now With my Heavenly Father I hope*
> *For ever To Remain*

By the early 1800s farm settlements were spreading far into the bush. Although the free farmers and emancipees had convicts to work for them, still they were true pioneers, of the kind that were later to become emblematic of the imperial and American frontiers; the whole tradition of the Australian Outback, its squatters, its pastoralists, its homesteaders, its stockmen, its shepherds and its swagmen, was really born in Sydney town.

There were two kinds of agriculturists. The grazier, dealing chiefly in sheep, was the smart kind, the country gentleman, putatively evolving into the landed magnate. The cocky was the simpler sort, and was roughly subclassified as a cow cocky, a scrub cocky or a fruit cocky. The grazier's ambition was achieved when he found himself master of a couple of thousand square miles with a few hundred thousand merino sheep upon it. The fulfillment of the cocky's hopes was surely symbolized by the moment when, one day in the 1860s, Maria Ann Smith of Eastwood, near Parramatta, threw the remains of some Tasmanian apples out of her back door, and found them apotheosized into the Granny Smith. Both kinds of farmer looked to the city of Sydney for their markets and their urban needs. The driving of the herds into the Sydney slaughterhouses was part of Sydney life; many an inn along the Parramatta Road depended for its trade upon the cockies coming to market; shearers and farm laborers were familiars of the Rocks taverns; the more fashionable of the graziers would travel a couple of hundred miles rather than miss a Sydney ball.

The wealthy New South Wales grazier is still a potent figure of the Sydney social scene. He lives on his wide acres somewhere, in his ample station house, but he perhaps has an apartment in Sydney, he probably has a club there, he sends his children to Sydney boarding schools and he shows up aristocratically at grand functions now and then. Together with the cocky, he comes most visibly into his own on the occasion of the annual Sydney Royal Show, the Easter junketing of the Royal Agricultural Society that is one of the great events of the civic calendar. Then, for ten days, the country comes back to Sydney. The showground is part funfair, part exhibition, part show ring, part shopping mall, and to Go To The Show has been part of Sydney family tradition for a century. There are judgings of horses, sheep, cattle and farm produce. There are competitions of steer-riding, show-jumping, wood-chopping. There are displays of cats, needlework, jams and tractors. There are bands and roller coasters and Big Dippers. There is a monumental display of country produce, laid out in intricate patterns of apples, honey, oranges, pumpkins, corncobs, reaching from floor to ceiling in meticulous design. Everywhere are the farmers, unmistakable rurals, with rubicund bulldog faces, with sticks as often as not, preferably wearing moleskin trousers and a wide-brimmed kind of hat called an Akubra, and stumping around the place with an agricultural gait. They seem to me like people from an earlier Sydney, a Sydney without an Opera House or a single Vietnamese bistro, and indeed when I once told my acquaintances that I had been to the Show, some of them sneered a little, and said it was no longer relevant.

I would not have missed for anything, though, its greatest

spectacle, the Grand Parade of exhibitors around the big oval showground. This is likely to be attended by the governor of New South Wales, who arrives in a coach-and-four, and by nearly everyone who is anyone in the Sydney Establishment, but it is dominated by people from the bush. In the background the funfair proceeds, a Big Dipper rises and falls and an aerial cable car comes and goes. In the foreground the countryside presents itself in an astonishing crescendo of pageantry. The exhibitors parade in concentric circles. Dashing rodeo players on their ponies, tent peggers with lances, impeccable dressage competitors, lolloping cattle led by sturdy men in boots, immense shire horses, sheep trundled round on the backs of trucks—all revolve at a steady pace which, as the arena becomes increasingly crowded, and the circles tighten, and the excitement rises, and the dust billows, begins to look more and more like the movement of some beleaguered caravan—a huge ceaseless swirl of men, women and animals. On its perimeter, giving the scene a final thrilling touch of laager, scores of spanking pony traps whizz round and round, much faster than anything else, constantly outlapping the assorted livestock and driven by stern-faced, tight-lipped Australian gentlefolk, tweedy and bowler-hatted, who time and again race unsmiling past as though they are circling for the kill.

Heavy industry has never dominated Sydney, and is not much apparent in the central city now. A poet celebrating the International Exhibition of 1879 could suggest, as New South Wales's own contribution to the grand display of produce, only minerals, gold, wine, lusty herds and merry maidens, and it would be more or less true if Sydney were mounting an exhibition today. Cars were assembled here for a time, but the factories closed. Ships used to be built, but are not so often now. Reference books mention textiles, machines and transport equipment, but you would not know it. Although the statistics say that more than 300,000 Sydney citizens work in manufacturing industries, when I asked several informants what all these people made, nobody could suggest anything in particular.

The native Sydney industry is the industry of the entrepreneur, the middleman, and he came into his own with a vengeance during the boom years of the 1980s. All the service industries gave a new vigor to Sydney then, the dealers in futures and options, the real estate people of course, the publicity and marketing people, the computer kids, the brokers, the bankers, the art dealers, the lawyers, the auctioneers—and when boom turned to bust "new links were forged," as a Sotheby's spokesman smoothly put it, "between auction houses and the liquidation industry." Here as everywhere tourism, the ultimately unproductive industry, burgeoned, preened, and was given its own Sydney manner. More than in most cities, I think, in Sydney the state of the economy has a direct and immediate effect upon the citizenry. In good times almost everyone prospers, there and then; in bad times people go bankrupt all over the place, firms sack employees by the hundreds, TV stars find their salaries devastatingly cut and suddenly Sydney realizes that it, like any other city, has its fair share of the homeless, the unemployed and the unhappy. This is nothing new. Australia's economy depends to a dangerous degree upon world commodity prices, and throughout its history Sydney has been a place of capitalist ups and downs—in this respect if in no other, it has been said, the city was "born modern." Its blue-collar workers have to fight hard for security, its money-manipulating classes live on the edge of their nerves. GREED IS GOOD, said an advertisement I cut out from a paper one day, RESULTS ARE BETTER—not a very relaxing philosophy. At night in downtown skyscraper windows you may see the young merchant bankers at their work; it used to be only the flower-pinafored cleaners, scarves over their heads, now it is young men sprawling shirtsleeved in their revolving chairs, drinking out of plastic mugs and keeping an eye on the constant green flicker of the computer screens—when it is midnight in Sydney it is three in the afternoon in Frankfurt, and the markets are just opening in New York.

I imagine that, *mutatis mutandis,* similar young men have been similarly preoccupied in all Sydney's periods of economic thrust, only to slow down rather, or invite Sotheby's for a valuation, when recession sets in. Easy come, easy go. In Sydney "riches have wings," as a reporter for the *South Asian Register* reported in 1828, observing a former banker selling mutton pies in the street, and proper to the ambience, I think, is the text on the grave of Joseph Potts, infant son of an early bank manager of this city, who died in 1838 and is buried beside Botany Bay:

> *Let us not murmur at thy*
> *Dispensations*
> *Oh Heavenly Father. They were but*
> *Loans.*

It used to be thought that in functions of the mind Sydney was a backwater even by Australian standards. Melbourne was the place for culture and intellect. Sydney was all brassy show. Perhaps it was true. The possession of a piano may have given George Worgan a special status in the Sydney of the 1780s, but for 150 years or so Sydney society does seem to have been terribly philistine. Times changed very gradually, and at first according to strict English precedents. When Sydney University was founded in 1852 it was inevitably equipped with a medieval-style Oxbridge quadrangle, and at its inauguration one of the learned founders, Dr. John Woolley, prophesied that before long "the quiet bays of our beautiful harbour will mirror in their crystal depths many a reverend chapel and pictured hall and solemn cloister and pleasant garden like those which gem the margin of the Isis and the Cam." Fitfully, though, a more Australian intelligentsia came into being, the arts became more generally welcomed, until at last, with the opening of the Opera House, with the presentation of the Nobel Prize for Literature to the Sydney novelist Patrick White, with the intercontinental fame of the Sydney opera singer Joan Sutherland *(La Stupenda)*, with the distribution across the world of Sydney writers, filmmakers, painters and actors, in our own time culture became a civic function.

The press began the process. Some of the cleverest Sydney people had always been connected with newspapers, if only as mouthpieces for their own political ambitions, and had brought elements of public wit and debate to the mostly unlettered city. For the more educated young immigrant, journalism offered the nearest thing to an intellectual occupation, so that here as in New York the newspapers were nurseries of good writing and mental activism. The pyrotechnical young editor Edward Smith Hall, for example, who arrived in 1811, was a leader in the campaign for a democratic system in New South Wales, and maintained it with a torrent of editorials so fierce that he lived a life of lawsuits and imprisonments—he once characterized the governor of the day, Ralph Darling, as a tyrant outranked only by the Great Mogul, the czar and the emperor of China. The *Sydney Morning Herald,* founded in 1831, became one of the best-known papers in the British Empire. The weekly *Bulletin,* founded in 1880, developed into one of the most outrageously brilliant magazines in the English language: its declared aims included a republican form of government, the abolition of all private land ownership, a universal system of compulsory life insurance and an Austra-

lia entirely Australian—"the cheap Chinaman, the cheap Nig-
ger, and the cheap European pauper to be absolutely
excluded."

Then as now, it was a dangerous thing to cross the Sydney
press. The *Empire* said of a politician in 1853 that his oratory
was reminiscent of a dredger, "slowly and laboriously jerking
out deliberate buckets full of slush." The *Bulletin* called the
improvident Sir Henry Parkes, in 1887, "a cold-blooded, un-
grateful old vendor of mortgaged allotments." *Truth* said of
the generally idolized opera star Nellie Melba, in 1903: "Many
a stage star has shot an erratic course, but none has done it
with such vicious vulgarity, such bourgeois bumptiousness
and such indiscriminate cruelty." The art critic of the *Triad*,
reviewing two nudes painted by Tom Roberts in 1920, said of
them that "barring an occasional contour that would intrigue
a cheese merchant, they were hardly worth undressing." Patrick White was told in 1956 that he wrote "pretentious and
illiterate verbal sludge." Sidney Nolan's paintings were described in 1958 as possessing "a decadent, inbred, hill-billy
flavour of tenth-rate German expressionism." An American
film was described in the *Sydney Morning Herald* in 1990 as
"an egregious pile of mindlessly violent idiot fodder," and a
restaurant was said to offer "indifferent food, nonexistent atmosphere, appalling noise levels and Keystone Kop service."
Libel actions have naturally been incessant, and in recent
years even architectural and food critics have found themselves in court, having rashly maligned lobster salads or
mocked housing developments. Artists flourished in early
Sydney, when they were the indispensable memorialists of
history. Later they were treated with less respect, and Sydney
more acutely than most cities has suffered the usual phases of
artistic prejudice and reappraisal—now sneering at impres-
sionism, now deriding cubism, now laughing at abstracts and

finally realizing, late in the day but with a particular gusto, that there was money in them all. An indigenous Sydney school of painting did not really come about until 1886, when the Melbourne artist Julian Ashton came to the city and founded an art school. He was followed by many of the leading Australian painters of the day—Arthur Streeton, Tom Roberts, Norman Lindsay, Lloyd Rees—and for the first time Sydney and its harbor were interpreted not as reflections of European ideals, but as sources of beauty in their own right. It was the lure of the southern climate that attracted most of these artists, with its suggestions of mauve seductive twilights, Whistler-like nocturnes, languid dalliances in dappled gardens, Bohemian liberties and classical echoes: as the poet J.A.R. McKellar put it in a poem about a ferry trip through the harbor:

> *The lips of ocean murmur at delay,*
> *The lovely moon no longer will refuse,*
> *And from the arms of darkness slips away*
> *To tryst with young Ephesians on Vaucluse . . .*

It was also relatively easy for an artist to earn a living in Sydney. This might be an uncultured place still, but it always had its eye on the main chance, and an alliance between art and commerce was presently arranged. The carriage-trade Sydney department stores established art galleries of their own, and eventually Sydney became one of the most calculatingly art-minded of all cities. Nowadays the names of fashionable local artists are household words, and there is a lively subculture of art dealers, inhabiting parts of inner suburbia generically known as "the gallery belt." Some galleries flourish perfectly frankly as centers of investment rather than aesthetics, some are focal points of social networking, some make great fortunes for their owners—when the most prominent of contemporary dealers retired from the scene, he bought the billionairess Barbara Hutton's former house in the Casbah at Tangier. But there are highly civilized dealers too, and however mixed the motives, Sydney has become a city unusually concerned and familiar with art. Where else would one see advertised on the backs of taxis, as might be a rock concert or a revival meeting, a forthcoming competition for a portrait prize?

A civic interest in literature is less apparent. A handful of internationally celebrated authors are resident in Sydney, but the great city hardly seems to realize their presence; and anyway with one or two very visible exceptions they spend much of their time either abroad or plunged in hermitlike withdrawal, periodically emerging into the local limelight to be tall-poppied by reviewers or obituarists. There is no shortage of good bookshops, and an astonishing variety of literary prizes appears to be available, as one can see from the curricula vitae of Sydney authors, almost all of whom seem to have won one or another (not to mention the two authors, at least, who have won the Booker Prize in London). Literary people of the academic kind evidently fare well enough, if I am to judge by social encounters, and know all there is to know about structuralism, minimalism, contextualism, post-Marxist formalism or pluralistic imagery. Nevertheless this has often been stony ground for litterateurs. The balladeer Barcroft Boake, in 1892, hanged himself with his own stockwhip in the scrub at Cammeray, beside Middle Harbour. Henry Lawson, slowly staggering down the ladder of alcoholism, died in the suburb of Abbotsford sotted, impoverished and all alone in 1922, and wrote self-pityingly of himself:

> In the land where sport is sacred, where the labourer is a god,
> You must pander to the people, make a hero of a clod.

Many another Sydney writer, from his day to our own, has felt the need to run away abroad—it was the Sydney magazine *Truth*, after all, which observed in 1906 that if Australia had not been propitious to poets, it had to be remembered "what a drivelling, drunken lot most of them have been."

As to the theater in Sydney, it has been for the most part thoroughly populist. The very first play ever put on was Farquhar's *The Recruiting Officer*, presented by a cast of convicts before Governor Phillip in 1789. This seems to have been a great success: "I am not ashamed to confess," wrote Tench about it, "that the proper distribution of three or four yards of stained paper, and a dozen farthing candle-sticks stuck around the mud walls of a convict-hut, failed not to diffuse general complacency." Restoration comedy hardly proved the norm, though. The Sydney taste was more for melodrama, farce and burlesque. Barnett Levey gave the public just what it wanted, and the impresario who presently came to control most of the downtown theaters, the American J. C. Williamson, was above all a showman for the people—like the Harbour Bridge and the Manly ferry *South Steyne*, his firm proudly boasted itself The Biggest in the British Empire.

Sydney was a music-hall town, an extension of the British vaudeville circuit, and if ever a classical performer came, it had to be a star of stars whom everyone knew. Jenny Lind came, for instance. Lola Montez danced her celebrated Spider Dance, leaving behind her a reputation for heavy drinking and a cocktail called the Lola Montez—rum, ginger, lemon and hot water. Sarah Bernhardt came accompanied by two dogs, a bear, possums, parrots, a tortoise and 250 pairs of shoes.

There are three much-admired professional dramatic companies in Sydney, ranging in their work from the familiar classical to the incomprehensible avant-garde, but as a whole the theater is still dominated by big musicals from New York or London, and more serious plays are generally confined to fringe houses outside the downtown quarter. It is a theater, wrote the Melbourne playwright Jack Hibberd in 1986,[1] "obsessed with colour and movement, voluptuous effects, whimsy, corn, and sybaritic romps"—or as a critic more recently put it, "sweaty, sexy, fast and furious." Television entertainment too is mostly razzmatazz, or what the local industry calls "kid-led," but some distinguished films have been born here, enough of them to justify Sydneysiders talking about "our film culture," and there is ballet to see, and opera of course, and live rock music is everywhere, and it is a pleasure of the city that one often comes across theater people and theatrical events. In 1990 part of the Oscar ceremony was telecast direct to Hollywood from one of the restaurants of the Opera House in Sydney, and I went along to press my nose against the windows, joining a handful of fans or groupies there. Oh, the glamour of the show-biz scenes within! Through the windows on the other side of the restaurant I could see a fireboat spouting its hoses beneath the Harbour Bridge, and against this spectacular background the Sydney stardust glittered. Among the potted foliage were semifamiliar figures of TV or cinema, sweetly waving to friends at other tables, applauding lavishly when an Australian name cropped up in the ceremony, smiling all the more adorably, chatting all the more vivaciously, whenever a camera swiveled their way. There were hats, and many bracelets, and a pair of orchid earrings as big as soup plates. "Oh my God," cried one of the girls beside me, "isn't that Craig McLachlan?" "Oh my God," I echoed, *"could* it be?"

Better still, walking around the little park at Blues Point one day I came face to face with an actor pacing the path with a

---

[1] In his contribution to Jim Davidson's *The Sydney-Melbourne Book.*

script in his hands, silently rehearsing his lines—an extremely actorial actor, too, with presence and a flashing eye.

Visitors (and Sydney expatriates) still sometimes profess to find Sydney philistine, and it certainly has its yobbo elements, but for myself I am astonished by the energy of its cultural appetite. It is rather like Chicago half a century ago, brilliantly striving to catch up. The five Sydney universities burst with eminent scholars. The Sydney publishing industry is fertile. The Sydney Symphony Orchestra is very polished. The Sydney Dance Company is indefatigable. The State Art Gallery is crowded out every weekend. The State Library is superb. The Powerhouse Museum of Applied Science, occupying the former power station of the Sydney trams at Darling Harbour, is really a museum of nearly everything, and is generally agreed to be one of the best of its kind in the world.

We could do worse, in fact, than end our survey of Sydney functions with a remembrance of a Sydney intellectual: Lawrence Hargrave, who died in 1915 and was not only indisputably the Father of Australian Flight, but one of the world's great innovators of aviation. He was an inventor in the classic mold, a draftsman, an astronomer, an archaeologist and a bit of a crank. Sometimes to be seen walking on the water of Double Bay on inflatable shoes, he believed strongly that Spanish seamen had landed at Sydney long before the British, and claimed to have found rock inscriptions proving it. He was the inventor of the box kite, an immediate precursor of the airplane. In 1894 he was lifted sixteen feet off the ground by an assembly of four such kites, and this success seems to have had a seminal influence upon the Wright brothers when they came to make the first powered heavier-than-air flight nine years later.

Hargrave never patented anything, freely publicized his

ideas and shared his conceptions with anyone who asked. He sounds the perfect Sydney functionalist. He looks back at us now not only benignly eccentric in the city's memory, but with a visionary gleam from the back of the twenty-dollar bill.

2 SYSTEM

This immensely sprawled and complicated metropolis, held together physically by such elaborate means, must be the very devil to administer. It is hardly surprising that Sydney is heavy with bureaucracy. From the federal government at one end, by way of the state government, the city council, all the local administrations and multitudinous boards, trusts and commissions to the Hunters Hill municipal council at the other—from top to bottom the city festers with governmental and political activity. Perhaps this helps to foster Sydney's traditional contempt for the whole process. The general election of 1990 seemed to me to be followed in this city with the utmost cynicism; the graffito POLITITIONS ARE GANGSTERS appeared to express the public attitude very well.

The city's supreme political arena is the Parliament of the State of New South Wales, in its chambers on Macquarie Street, delightfully overlooking the Domain and lately fitted out with a roof garden and a swimming pool. Walking past Parliament House one carefree afternoon I decided on a whim to go inside and listen to the debate in the Legislative Assembly, the lower house. This was a shock to me. The chamber is small and intricate, and that afternoon it was jam-packed, both on the floor and in the galleries. Entering its confinement after the sunny liberty of Macquarie Street, I found that its sudden smallness, its artificial lighting and its feeling of intense privacy put me in mind of an eighteenth-century cockpit. There was a Rowlandson-like atmosphere in there. I forget the subject of debate, but it certainly raised grotesque passions. Sometimes even the gallery joined in, with shouts and sarcastic laughs, and down on the floor insults, vicious badinage, and reproach flew this way and that across the House—"mongrels," "long-haired gits," "deeply deranged." A government supporter angrily alleged that members of the opposition were passing bags of candy around. A minister, complaining that somebody had stolen his notes, was told to get stuffed. Disconcertingly prominent among the combatants was a man I happened to know, and thought of as a civilized and benevolent fellow. He was transformed. He strode around down there like a mad prosecutor, he called his opponents madmen, cheats, scoundrels, he waved his papers like spells or menaces. His face was distorted with malignancy. He was a man possessed.

But when I later commented to a colleague upon this alarming metamorphosis, "Oh" was the reply, "he didn't really mean it." Sydney politics is like that. So many interests are chafing against one another, such layers of authority are there to clash, that an archaic formalization of virulence seems more or less expected, as a kind of safety valve perhaps. In few other cities of the West would it be said, as it was said in Sydney in 1990, that voting for an opposing political party would be like a child knowingly accepting candies from a loony in a raincoat, or that an opposition candidate had as much charm as a used suppository. That debate in the Assembly was nothing special, and certainly nothing private. The chamber is open to everyone at all times, with a minimum of fuss, and it was really a family squabble, rather than a hole-and-corner sporting event, that I had wandered so innocently into.

The inflammatory urge in Sydney politics first arose, I suppose, when in 1808 the officers of the Rum Corps marched up to the Governor's House and arrested Bligh on the grounds of his authoritarian behavior.[1] It has never again erupted into rebellion, but it has never been exorcised either. It has been institutionalized instead. Groans, laughs, hisses, hoots, boos, cheers, cries of "Shame!" and sarcastic interventions have always punctuated reports of parliamentary debates—Henry Parkes, in 1880, said of his fellow parliamentarians that they beslimed the face of the earth with their unsightly and unclean carcasses. Visitors from Britain, inspecting the progress of this distant alter ego, were often quite taken aback. Not only were political proceedings in Sydney rowdy and unseemly, they also appeared to display an unstable tendency toward the radical and the democratic, not to mention the disloyal.[2]

In particular it was ironic to discover that in a colony founded upon such rigid principles of Authority, the voice of Labor was so disrespectful. Even in penal Sydney there was an element of labor power—convicts worked by task, rather than by time, and in their free hours they could sell their labor to anyone who would pay for it. The Masters and Servants Act of 1828 was severe indeed upon employees (up to six months' jail for negligence at work), but gave the employee rights of complaint too, and by the 1880s the formidable Mort, when he was building his dry dock, felt obliged to offer a freehold allotment to every laborer who completed his contract. In the 1930s the unions sometimes seemed all-powerful, and they still play a more subtly influential part in Sydney civic affairs than in most cities of the West: for example, mu-

---

[1] His daughter met them at the door with drawn parasol, but they found the governor under his bed, hiding state documents according to his own account, hiding himself according to the rebels.

[2] Even the socialist Beatrice Webb found the political scene distasteful; after meeting Sydney civic leaders in 1898 she reported that the lord mayor was illiterate in speech, awkward in manner, extraordinarily muddled and "heavily scented with whiskey."

nicipalities have lately been induced to pay their employees for sick leave they do not take, and the gravediggers' union has recently been campaigning for a monthly day off.

The powers of the lord mayor of Sydney, in theory the supreme civic official, have fluctuated down the years, because owing to incompetence or corruption his city council has repeatedly been superseded by commissions. In any case his writ has been circumscribed. He is lord mayor only of the downtown area, containing 2 percent of Sydney residents, which was constituted a city in 1841—and even within that the Commonwealth and state governments have enclaves under their own control. All around his fief other administrations hold sway in one degree or another, and attempts to create a Greater Sydney Council, on the old London pattern, have always failed. Greater Sydney makes up most of something called the County of Cumberland, but within it there are thirty-six municipalities and six shires, with territories ranging from just over a thousand square miles to less than three square miles.

The general assumption is that Sydney people are endemically anarchic. Nowadays it does not often seem so, and the city gives the impression of being fussily overgoverned. Generally speaking the Sydney suburbs run indistinguishably into one another. There often comes a moment, though, as one meanders through the unmemorable streets and innumerable traffic lights, when the place opens out a little, a few trees or municipal flower beds appear, and there stands the local town hall. It often has a tower; it sometimes has a courtroom attached; there may be a police station beside it, or a post office, a memorial of some kind, even a statue perhaps; it speaks of a long tradition of municipal dignity stretching back to the civic aspirations of Victorian Britain. Even in the most formless districts the civic buildings offer some probably specious promise of organization.

For despite this proliferation of mayors, aldermen and clerks across the vast metropolis, a strong sense of the slovenly pervades the Sydney system. "No worries"—"It'll do, mate"—these dear old Sydney mantras have all too often cast a spell upon the running of the place. Phillip's original Sydney was inevitably makeshift. Very few people in the First Fleet knew how to build a house or even plant a potato, and the most efficient officers of the Royal Navy were amateurs when it came to the business of organizing a colony. For the first thirty years there was no currency, and the economic system was based upon barter, debt, bills of exchange, military paymasters' notes, miscellaneous foreign coins and the Holey Dollar—a Spanish coin whose center was punched out, the ring having one value, the center another. Nearly everything had to be improvised, from the treatment for dysentery (using the leaves of the red gum tree) to the beer (brewed from the remains of the maize milled for the convicts' porridge, flavored with gooseberry stalks).

This slipshod survives. "Sorry, our computer's down" is one Sydney *cri de coeur*, and "Lift out of order" is another. When I went to board the McMahon's Point ferry once they had forgotten to bring the gangplank, so that elderly passengers had to be manhandled aboard, and one constantly hears of more extreme examples. A cat falls through the ceiling of an operating theater at the Prince Henry Hospital. A Vietnamese man rings the emergency number, 000, after four youths ransack his house and threaten his family with knives and a gun; he fails to make himself understood, so is told to fuck off. A lady, buying a bag of garden fertilizer, finds upon it a telephone number to call for advice about its use; she does so, and gets information about AIDS in the Macedonian language. When Sydney trains are running late, it is revealed, they are told just to ignore a scheduled stop or two, to make up time.

The most famous example of bumbling tergiversation was the building of the Opera House. No city ever undertook a task more daring or more admirable—to create as its architectural centerpiece an opera house and concert hall, designed by a foreigner in a style almost unexampled and with techniques altogether unproved, on the most prominent of all city sites. An international competition had found the architect and the design, much of the money was raised by lottery, but from first to last nothing went right in the construction of this lovely thing. It took five years to discover how to build the flying roofs. The cost rose from an estimated $A7m to a paid-out $A102m. The interior design was drastically altered. The schoolboy son of one of the lottery winners was kidnapped for ransom, and suffocated in the boot of the kidnappers' car. The opera stage proved so inadequate that performers have been complaining about it ever since. There was no provision for car parking. The original begetter of the idea, Sir Eugene Goossens, conductor of the Sydney Symphony Orchestra, was caught with his pornography and left Sydney in disgrace. The architect Jøern Utzon quarreled with everybody and left too.[1] State governments rose and fell around the issue of the Opera House, and when it was at last finished Utzon understandably refused to return for the opening, and has never been near Sydney since.

Few cities of the world have to depend upon such extended and multifarious lines of inner communication. These offer an impression of genial and fairly energetic chaos. Ferries were the original vehicle of public transport, and to the outsider they set the general tone of it still (though far more people

---

[1] BRING UTZON BACK, said a graffito of the time, but there was soon an addition to it: AND HANG HIM.

commute by bus or train—and even, it is claimed, by bicycle). Sydney's topography means that it is the second busiest ferry port in the world, outclassed only by Hong Kong, another metropolis divided by the waterway that is its raison d'être.

The very first Sydney ferry was a punt that took people extremely laboriously up the river to Parramatta, and it was followed by rowboat services across Darling Harbour to Balmain, and then by the Old Commodore's transharbor enterprise. The first Sydney-built boat was also used on the Parramatta run: she had oars and sails and was nicknamed *The Lump*, partly because that was what she looked like, and partly perhaps because she sometimes took a whole day to make the fifteen-mile journey. Sydney took a brave step toward mechanical water-transport with the Horse Boat *Experiment*, which was propelled by the energies of four horses and carried 100 passengers, but it was the arrival of steam that altered everything. Steam opened up hitherto inaccessible corners of the harbor, and allowed daily commuting from the more distant suburbs. Manly indeed was really the creation of the steam ferry: until the service opened in 1848 it could take days to get there from the city center, and only twelve lonely families had settled there—even as late as 1928, when the first road bridge was built across the Middle Harbour, Manly's freight went from Sydney by sea.

The ferries became essential to Sydney's functions. They have been blamed for delaying the coming of the railways, but for generations they offered the only sensible way of traveling around the harbor—even along its southern shore, which was corrugated by many creeks and inlets. Pictures of the 1920s show the Milson's Point ferry wharf, the busiest on the harbor's northern side, looking very like one of the Manhattan piers in the heyday of the Hudson River ferries: a cavernous shed with a clock tower, tall funnels belching smoke around it, hurrying crowds coming and going, and on the road behind a line of waiting trams. In the single year 1928 more than forty-six million passenger journeys were made on the ferries, and D. H. Lawrence wrote of Sydney people "slipping like fishes across the harbour," so accustomed were they to jumping on a ship somewhere. Most of the regular passengers were middle-class people, but there were busy workmen's services to and from Balmain, and there were always pleasure services too, so that the ferries were almost as busy on weekends as they were on working days.

Tales and images of the ferries went into the literature, the art and the folklore, and into the books and pamphlets of innumerable ferry buffs. Who had not heard of the bisection of the *Greycliffe* by the liner *Tahiti* in 1927, or the capsizing of the *Rodney* in 1938, or the time the *Baragoola* collided with the whale, or the farcical affair when the *Dee Why* went aground with 700 passengers on Christmas night, 1946? The tall-funneled steam ferries of the nineteenth century—the big double-ended craft between the world wars, which sometimes look to me like drawing-board mistakes—the rushing hydrofoils of today—all have become in their time municipal symbols, prominent in lithograph or color printing wherever Sydney has been publicized.

The boldest and biggest of them have always been the boats to Manly. This service demands of its vessels an average daily sailing of about 100 miles, and entails crossing the unprotected water just inside the Heads. It can be a rough ride— there are photographs of waves, sweeping in from the open sea, towering high above the ferry decks—and the ships have always been potentially oceangoing vessels, some of them sailing out to Australia under their own steam from shipyards in Britain. In former times they were often heavily overloaded, too, and sometimes wallowed precariously into their piers with passengers clinging like limpets all over them, gunwale to superstructure. The long line of these ferries, starting in 1848, stood high in Sydney affections, and even their names could stir the susceptible exile—*Bingarra, Kuringai, Burrabra* . . .

The ferries reached a majestic climax in the massive *South Steyne*, the last of the steam ferries and, as they said when she appeared in the harbor in 1938, The Biggest Ferry in the British Empire—seventeen knots, propellers fore and aft, 1,780 passengers, 1,200 tons (nearly twice the size of the *Cutty Sark*)! Very heavy looking, like a bulldog, or perhaps a London bus, with two squat bolt-upright funnels and bridge houses at each end, the *South Steyne* was a sight to see: she flew flags at prow and stern, and she stormed through the harbor for thirty-six years with a characteristic Sydney air of mingled toughness and festivity. When she left the scene in 1974, leaving only diesel-engined ships and hydrofoils, many were the lyrical words written about the lost smell of the grease and the steam, the pounding of the pistons, the warmth emerging from engine bays on winter evenings and the clang of engine-room telegraphs. It was sad to think of such grand old ships scuttled, as several of them were, in the deep water off the northern beaches.

Still, their successors are bright and bustling, and always exciting to watch (though earlier ones, built in Italy, ran at a deficit, frequently broke down, and were sometimes to be seen forlornly progressing to their yards high out of the water on lighters, propelled by tugs fore and aft). The hustle of the ferries is part of the fun of Sydney, and Circular Quay has always been a place of recreation as well as transport; for a time one of its piers was actually an amusement pier, and I can remember when deck musicians traveled back and forth on the Manly boats. The ferries are nearly all municipally owned now, but a private company runs a service between McMahon's Point and Circular Quay, including stops according to a complex timetable at two or three places along the way. This is usually maintained by a venerable launch, blistered of paint, creaky of woodwork and recognizably descended from the old riverboats, whose water-bug progress here and there, looking rather as though it has lost its way, gives the scene a piquant touch of frailty. Sometimes there hurtles across its prow a speedboat taxi, and I love to see the contrast: the ferry so quaint and elderly, the taxi like a crazy glass beetle scudding and bouncing over the water with an angry buzz of engines, driven most probably by a cheerful youth in an undershirt.

Besides, it is still the prerogative of your true Sydneysider unconcernedly to jump the gap between ship and shore just before the ferry docks.

In 1928 there were forty-six million ferry passengers; in 1933 there were twenty-three million. But the opening of the Harbour Bridge in 1932 not only shifted the pattern of function in Sydney, it changed the city's conception of itself—even its place in the world, for this was the largest of all arch bridges, and thus the first world-class artifact ever built in Sydney. The bridge was like an icon, an instantly recognizable symbol of Sydney-ness, satisfying civic visions and fulfilling one at least of Erasmus Darwin's prophecies. It was only proper that the poster announcing its opening should be dominated by a triumphant lifeguard, in those days the city's talismanic figure, supported by yachtsmen and sunbathers.

The harbor was so fundamental to the nature, the activity, and the reputation of Sydney that throwing an arch across it was like bursting through some great psychological barrier. They had been talking about it for 150 years, generally imagining a crossing at the site where the bridge was eventually built. Greenway was perhaps the first to propose a bridge, claiming that it would "bring magnificence, credit and glory to the colony." In 1840 there was a proposal for a floating bridge, forty-five feet wide, guided by fixed chains across the harbor and propelled by steam—"at incredible speed," claimed the proponent of the idea. Drawings survive of a scheme devised by an engineer, Peter Henderson, who had worked under the great bridge builders Robert Stephenson and Isambard Brunel in England. His spectacular construction would have been an unsupported flat span of cast iron, supported by towers at each end and lit by oil lamps all the way across. Then there were plans for a pontoon bridge, and a seven-span bridge, and there was even a suggestion that the harbor might be filled in between Milson's Point and Dawes Point. For years the matter of the bridge was a great public issue—"O, who will stand at my right hand" was an election cry in the 1880s of the old ham Henry Parkes, "and build the Bridge with me?" There were counterproposals for a tunnel, too, but finally in 1922 the Sydney Harbour Bridge Act authorized the building of a bridge. Its founding father was John Job Crew Bradfield, an implacable modernist who was the city's chief designing engineer, but Dorman Long of England won the tender for its construction, and the contract price was 4,217,721 pounds, eleven shillings and tenpence.

The bridge was built at the deepest point of the harbor; the height of its road above the water about equals the depth of water below. Many an old corner of the Rocks had to be demolished for its approach road, and many a humble terrace on the other shore. For seven years, as the great shape reached out across the harbor, Sydney waited with some skepticism for its completion—

> *Our 'arbour which art in Sydney,*
> *Good-o be thy name.*
> *Thy bridge be done,*
> *If not in '30, then in '31 . . .*

It was '32, in the event. The work was then declared complete, with its 1,650 foot span, its dual road, its four rail and tram tracks and its ornamental pylons in the Egyptian manner.[1] It was tested with a load of ninety-six steam locomotives and forty-eight coal tenders, buffer to buffer, and pronounced ready for its official opening.

This was to be the greatest public occasion ever known in Sydney. The city was fond of its bridge by then, if only because it had provided hundreds of jobs through the bleak Depression years. It was more than just a bridge, said the *Australian Worker*, but represented "oneness, unity, completion . . . symbolic of what shall yet become universal." The opening ceremony was broadcast live throughout Australia, and in Britain and the United States. The governor-general represented King George V. There were aerial displays by the Royal Australian Air Force, and a Venetian Carnival on the harbor. There were pageants, balls, a sailing regatta, a race meeting, a celebratory cricket match. There was a procession that included "lady life-savers," aborigines and surviving veterans of the Sudan War, 1885. For the first and last time the whole bridge was thrown open to pedestrians, to stroll over it as they would, and the first scheduled train crossed heavily crested and beflagged. A million people are said to have shared in the celebrations.

It was all very grand, all great fun in the Sydney tradition of festivity. But the touch that was to be remembered best of all, from a day of great memories, occurred at the exact moment of the bridge's formal opening. This was to be performed by the Labour premier of New South Wales, Jack Lang, "the Big Fellah," after the reading of a message from the king himself,

---

[1] Which are not actually connected to the bridge arch, though from a distance they look as though they are, and had no functional purpose until in 1990 the two northern towers were adapted as ventilators for the tunnel being built on the harbor bed below.

but the arrangement was not to everyone's taste. Lang was thought by many conservatives to be almost treasonably radical; the idea that he should perform the ceremony in conjunction, as it were, with His Imperial Majesty particularly stuck in the gullets of a right-wing paramilitary organization called the New Guard, who believed Lang and his government to be no more than a pack of Communist puppets—"We, a people of pure British stock, are under the domination of a band of imported agitators of low type . . ."

The moment came. The premier, the governor of New South Wales, the mayor of Sydney in his ermine, J.J.C. Bradfield, various senior officers with their swords and busbies, approached the ribbon that had been stretched across the southern entry to the bridge. The cameras were ready. The radio commentators in their booths busily set the scene. The governor-general's mounted bodyguard was drawn up behind. The crowd was hushed. And suddenly there erupted from behind the cavalry ranks a solitary wild horseman in Army uniform, brandishing a sword. Galloping up the roadway and through the astonished dignitaries, he slashed the ribbon with his sword and shouted that he had opened the bridge "in the name of the decent citizens of New South Wales."

He was pulled from his horse by the police, the ribbon was tied together again, and the ceremony proceeded.[1]

---

[1] The ebullient miscreant was an Irish member of the New Guard, Francis de Groot (1888–1969), the owner of a furniture factory who by this single act immortalized himself. He was taken to a psychiatric hospital but declared sane, and was later fined £5, with £4 costs, for offensive behavior in a public place. Charges of damaging a ribbon to the extent of £2 were dismissed. De Groot found many admirers—some say the governor-general's guard had lent him the horse—while within the year Jack Lang was dismissed from office by the governor of New South Wales, Sir Philip Woolcott Game, C.B., K.C.B., G.B.E., K.C.M.G., G.C.V.O., G.C.B., a future commissioner of the London Metropolitan Police.

The Harbour Bridge did for Sydney what the Brooklyn Bridge had done for New York half a century before—Bradfield declared in fact that the suburbs of the northern shore would be a Brooklyn to Sydney's Manhattan. He also foresaw that its existence would greatly intensify Sydney's centrifugal tendencies, encouraging people to live ever further from the city fulcrum. By now a vast web of roads has grown out of the original convict-hacked highway to Parramatta; parts of it have been given high-sounding names like the Great Western Highway or the Pacific Highway, which hold out some promise of clarity, but most of it remains a drab obfuscation. Suburban railways clatter in all directions, there are elaborately networked systems of buses and subways, hundreds of bridges cross creeks and inlets, there is a brief monorail track and there will soon be a harbor tunnel too, a few yards east of the great bridge, but built by Japanese.

A potent element in the Sydney system is corruption. It always has been. Mayhem was rampant in the penal days, and not only among convicts: the officers of the Rum Corps were crooked to the core, the doctors at the hospital sold its drugs at huge profits to their private patients, and I cannot help suspecting a whiff of nepotism in the result of the competition instituted by Governor Darling for a Government House design in 1827—it was won by his wife. In later years innumerable developments were accompanied by hints of jobbery: insider trading in land, for instance, where a railway was likely to be built, or untendered contracts for public works, or dubious complicity between architects and contractors. When the premier Sir Robert Askin died in 1981, it was alleged in obituary that illegal-casino owners had been paying him $A700,000 a year hush money.[1] More recently a famous scam surrounded the taking of driving tests, which were conducted by a system of organized bribery: seven faults was the official failure rate, but one woman, sufficient money having passed under the gearshift, was given her license after committing seventy-two. A private investigator, the Independent Commission Against Corruption was told in 1990, sent the following bill to an insurance company:

> To attend to your attorney's instruction to conduct certain inquiries in this matter, including the corruption of several members of the Police Force and obtaining printouts relating to the man's criminal form, then drinking with them for long periods, and reporting as attached: Hours, many, but say four at $A25 = $A100.

Most contemporary scandals have concerned the police. In Sydney they speak cynically of "the police culture," implying a general rottenness of morality. We are told standards have improved, but when an eminent villain was recently asked about the prevalence of organized crime in the city, he mentioned six conspiratorial groups—two Australian brotherhoods, one Lebanese, two Chinese triads and the New South Wales police. Certainly in the 1920s the police were blatantly in cahoots with the crime syndicates, and even in 1950, when the superintendent of the Metropolitan Police retired he was given a banquet by 300 underworld leaders, together with a generous check.

I have seldom been in this city when a Royal Commission

---

[1] Askin, a Grand Commander of the Order of St. Michael and St. George, was also well remembered for the order he gave his driver when, in 1966, hostile demonstrators threatened to block President Lyndon Johnson's motorcade through Sydney: "Run over the bastards."

of Inquiry has not been investigating some rort or other. The very first such inquisition was mounted by Commissioner John Bigge, who was sent out from England in 1819 to investigate the alleged extravagances of Governor Macquarie, and who by a combination of nitpicking and cheeseparing succeeded in squashing Macquarie's plans for the shape of Sydney. Since then Royal Commissions have inquired into every subspecies of public misdemeanor, and during my research for this book one was looking into the matter of Harry the Hat, a senior police officer accused by his own force, with maximum publicity, of having raped eight women over a twenty-five-year period of his career. The charges were later dropped, and the circumstances seemed to show lamentable degrees of misbehavior and worse within the police force. The inquiry into this odd affair was quite odd enough itself. Processions of poker-faced policemen appeared one after the other in the witness box, dressed for the occasion in high tight collars and business suits; the presiding judge looked remarkably skeptical throughout; a number of fearfully expensive barristers cross-examined; and in the front of the court, accompanied by his wife and sometimes putting his feet up for comfort on a chair in front of him, sat bespectacled and balding the man at the center of the case, so recently accused by his own colleagues of having been a sexual monster. He was exonerated absolutely, and his character was agreed to be so irreproachable that according to the Sydney wags it made Mother Teresa look like a sex maniac. On the other hand the police operation against him was characterized as incompetent, gross, slipshod and deceitful.

But then twenty years before, as a deputy police commissioner blandly deposed, looking on the bright side I suppose, Harry the Hat, secure within the closed ranks of the police culture, would not have been charged if he *had* been a rapist.

It is only to be expected that Sydney should be especially interested in matters of crime and punishment. They dominate whole pages of the newspapers, and they crop up frequently in conversation. For most of the original citizens, of course, crime was a natural way of life. The Newgate pickpockets of the 1780s did not lose their cunning when they came to Australia, but enthusiastically stole from their comrades, from their jailers and from the aborigines. Ralph Clark, having started a vegetable garden on his eponymous island in the harbor, found that no sooner did his vegetables start to grow than somebody stole them. Brick houses were conveniently easy to break and enter—householders of early Sydney often awoke to find a hole picked in the wall during the night—and when Governor Gipps moved into his new Government House in 1845 some of his silver was nicked on the way. Dead-end streets became so uncomfortably connected in the Sydney mind with thievery that well into the twentieth century town planners were reluctant to sanction them.

For years the city's natural instincts, like my own, were with the criminal rather than the jailer. Sydney's first public heroes were the bushrangers, convicts or adventurers gone feral and living by their wits as highwaymen. They had bold names—"Captain Thunderbolt," "Bold Jack," "Mad Dog Morgan"—and robbers and murderers though they were, and often anything but romantic, they were seen as popular champions of liberty, expressing in their lives many a pent-up grudge, and many a yearning for wider horizons. It would be hard for any poor convict of spirit, permanently ill-treated by destiny, to resist the appeal of the bushranger ballads:

Some dark night when everything is silent in the town,
I'll kill the tyrants one and all, and shoot the floggers down.
I'll give the Law a little shock; remember what I say—
They'll yet regret they sent Jim Jones in chains to Botany Bay.

or:

Come, all my hearties, we'll roam the mountains high,
Together we'll plunder, together we'll die.
We'll wander over valleys, and gallop over plains,
And we'll scorn to live in slavery, bound down with iron chains.

The most celebrated of all the bushrangers was the Irishman Jack Donaghoe, transported for life in 1825, who was sentenced to hang in Sydney for robbery but escaped between the courtroom and the condemned cell. For eighteen months he ranged the countryside west of the city, sometimes, so local legend said, appearing bold as brass in the city itself, suave in a blue coat and laced boots. Donaghoe appealed to many atavistic Sydney instincts, not just as a dashing defier of Authority, but as an Irishman cocking a snook at the English, and he was to live in the folklore long after he was caught and shot. He was the real hero of the ballad that has perhaps affected the Australian psyche more than any other:

He was scarcely sixteen years of age when he left his father's home,
And through Australia's sunny clime bushranging he did roam.
He robbed the wealthy squatters, their stock he did destroy,
A terror to Australia was the Wild Colonial Boy!

The Wild Colonial Boy—still perhaps, somewhere deep in the civic unconscious, a Sydney cynosure!

After the bushrangers came the Pushes, gangs of young hooligans, mostly based in the Rocks, who infested the whole downtown area and at once fascinated and appalled respectable citizens. Some of these were just groups of thugs, and their style was captured by a poem, attributed to Henry Lawson, in which one of their captains anathemizes an enemy:

May pangs of windy spasms throughout your bowels dart;
May you shit your fucking trousers every time you try to fart;
May itching piles torment you, and corns grow on your feet,
And crabs as big as spiders attack your balls a treat;
And when you're down and outed, a dismal bloody wreck,
May you slip back through your arsehole and break your fucking neck.

Other gangs aspired to dandyism. They wore pearl-button jackets and cocky narrow-brimmed hats, and their high-heeled boots were sometimes inlaid with mirrors, reflecting the finery above. Most Victorian memoirs have something about the goings-on of these tiresome but distinctive youths— knocking people's hats over their eyes outside the theater, indulging in noisy internecine fights, hitching rides on the backs of carriages or making curses of themselves at pleasure places of the harbor—*He put a rock in the heel of a sock/And went down the bay to Chowder.* In them the bushrangers' heritage was transmuted into the urban tradition of the larrikin, and if little else about them was very engaging, their disrespect for the established system perhaps still touched Sydney hearts. The word "Push," which the gangs invented for themselves, went into the language not entirely perjoratively: in later years various social cliques liked to call themselves Pushes, and when in the 1980s a group of historians published a journal concerning the origins of Australia, *Push from the Bush* is what they called it.

Later the swaggering kings of the syndicates were stars of a kind, and lived filmic lives. When the hoodlum Phil Jeffs died in 1945 the tabloid *Truth* began its obituary: "Phil the Jew,

Sydney racketeer, gangster, drug peddler, procurer, sly grog-ger, alleged phizz gig[1] for some detectives, gunman, wealthy friend of some politicians and many police, died on Tuesday." Richard Reilly, who was himself murdered by the syndicates, began his career as a dance-hall bouncer, became a wartime racketeer, ran a roadhouse called Oyster Lil's, drove a Maserati sports car, lived in a mansion and was known as the King of Baccarat. The gambler Chicka Barnes, murdered in 1957, was found to have four bullet scars in his abdomen, one finger shot from his left hand, two stab scars on his chest, a knife scar on his throat, bicycle-chain scars on forehead and shoulders, various scars on his chin and lips and the bullet hole in his back that killed him. When Colorful Racing Identity George Freeman died in 1990, the *Sydney Morning Herald* called him Big Crime's Artful Dodger. He was Mr. Big Enough for twenty-five years, the paper said, and it added that during all that time the best the police could manage against him was a couple of fines for illegal betting, though he certainly had contacts with the Chicago underworld and the Chinese triads, was generally assumed to fix horse races and run illegal casinos, was strongly suspected of heroin smuggling and had been refused entry to England as an undesirable. "His word was his bond," an old friend was quoted as saying, and many devoted Colorful Identities were photographed at his funeral.

I kept random notes of crime and misbehavior over a few months in Sydney, and the profusion was astonishing. Here for instance is a man on his seventy-ninth charge of having refused to pay restaurants for meals he has eaten: this time he

---

[1] A phizz gig was a police informer, a curious Sydney derivation from an old word which (so the Oxford Dictionary tells me) can also mean a frivolous woman, a kind of top, a harpoon or a silly notion.

has dined on soup, oysters, fillet steak, dessert, wine, cognac and Campari. Here another Racing Identity, convicted of stabbing a man to death in a street fracas, finds himself in the same jail as his twenty-one-year-old son, who has recently assaulted a Chinese cabdriver.[1] A gang of Fijians, Tahitians and Samoans clashes with a gang of bikies in the western suburbs. A senior railway official is accused of fiddling an expense account for an apple and a sandwich. The Maritime Services Board says that during the past eighteen months people with chain saws have stolen 200 solar-powered panels from navigation lights. Illegal hot-dog vendors, says a report, are battling with one another to preserve their territories.

What's this now? A visiting Commonwealth M.P. is bitten on the wrist by a female drug addict. Seven schoolboys, aged eleven to fifteen, are charged with breaking 300 train windows in two months. A surgeon is accused of deceiving patients: he pretends to operate on them for Ménière's disease, but a skull is presented as evidence to show that he never drills deep enough. A report says that the Philippines have become a second home for leaders of the Sydney underworld, who arrange many of their drug deals there, and control much of the prostitution. The Corrective Services Minister, sentenced to seven and a half years for taking bribes to arrange the early release of prisoners, appeals and has his sentence increased to ten years. Here is a complete newspaper story which was printed on 21 March 1990, but which had, I thought, something particularly timeless to it:

GIRL ROBBED

Four boys walked off laughing, after robbing
a 19-year-old girl of $150 outside Campbelltown

---

[1] The Racing Identity suffered from Parkinson's disease, and was described by a colleague as being as shaky as a dog shitting razor blades.

207

public library yesterday. One threw her empty
wallet back and shouted "You stupid bitch."

It sounds appalling. In fact I have never once felt frightened in Sydney. There are few places in this city where one cannot walk with safety, even after dark, and in recent years Sydney's murder rate has been considerably lower than London's, and something like one fifteenth of Los Angeles's. As to petty crime, it is probably no more common here than anywhere else, but I sometimes feel it is regarded differently—more as a folk custom perhaps. I remember well the goggle-eyed astonishment with which a young couple on holiday from Adelaide listened to a ferry deckhand, the very image of a Sydney larrikin or hoon, telling all and sundry how he habitually got home after night duty—he took a cab to a nearby address, asked it to wait for a moment and disappeared. And it was on a ferry too that a kindly woman warned me one day to be especially careful about pickpockets on public transport in Sydney. I thanked her for her advice, and when we parted she returned to me my wallet, which she had extracted from my handbag in the course of the conversation.

Sydney is born to show itself off. Like Venice, it is its own advertising slogan, forever blazoning its own merits. Elsewhere, as the poet Vincent Buckley once remarked, the play may be the thing: in Sydney it's the premiere. Perhaps it all began with the flash of criminals long ago. Certainly visitors to Sydney down the generations have commented on the swagger of things, the showy techniques of horse-tram drivers, the flaunting gear of larrikins, the confidence amounting almost to exhibitionism of workingmen. There is a street group called the Aussie Small Change Brass Band which might well represent the city at ceremonial functions, so alive is it with the authentic Sydney mixture of fun, fizz and chutzpah: its players are three very small boys in very large hats, with two trumpets, a tuba and extremely powerful amplifiers, and I can tell you they play "Puttin' on the Ritz" like nobody else. Virtuoso infant trumpeters—dress-up silks in the middle of the morning—scud of seaplanes off Rose Bay into the sun—chess players in Hyde Park concluding their game with majestic scowls, as though they have torn up a treaty—GORGE at the ice rink—Harry the Hat with his feet up before the Royal Commission—curly-wigged strutting barristers at the Supreme Court—bemedaled worthies at royal rituals, bowler-hatted trap drivers at the Easter Show—all these characters and glimpses, and thousands more, together with the Grand Guignol of awful memory, and the flourish of true achievement, add up to the histrionic purpose that is Sydney.

CONNECTIONS

Always, somewhere in Sydney's waters, gray warships can be seen: lying in dock, steaming out to sea, or standing morosely month after month in Atholl Bight, between Cremorne Point and Bradley's Head, waiting to be scrapped.[1] A pictorial album of Sydney is like a naval register, as the little *Sirius* of 1788 gives way to the bulky three-masters of the Victorian prime, to the prim-looking men-o'-war of the fin de siècle, to the rakish three-funneled County-class cruisers that gave a particular touch of elegance to the Sydney of the 1930s, to the bold carriers of World War II and the destroyers of today enmeshed in electronics. Sydney is the main base of the Royal Australian Navy, which hived off from its parent, the British Royal Navy, in 1911, but which still honors some of the old British traditions, and the naval presence is symbolic. The British Empire was a maritime dominion, built upon sea power, and of all the cities it nurtured from scratch around the world, Sydney is the most authentically imperial.

For the first decades of its existence it was entirely an Em-

---

[1] Old Sydney riddle: Why did Cremorne Point? Because it saw Atholl Bight off Bradley's Head.

pire town—a navy town, in fact, since its first governors were all naval men. Some scholars believe that its original purposes were more ambiguously imperial than London was ever to admit, and it was certainly not envisaged only as a penal colony. The first proponent of a settlement seems to have been the American-born James Matra, who had sailed to Australia as a midshipman with Cook, and who saw it, after the American Revolution, as a possible new home for dispossessed American loyalists. They should be accompanied, he suggested, by poor English emigrants, and supplemented by Chinese laborers, and in no time the new colony would be supplying timber and flax for the navy, produce of all sorts for the markets of the East.

One thesis argues that a fundamental object of the New South Wales enterprise was strategic. For myself I still have to consult the globe to grasp the historical significance of Sydney's geographical position—Mercator's projection grossly misrepresents it. The city lies about equidistant from South Africa, one of the key staging posts of the British imperial trade routes, India, the centerpiece of the whole imperial structure, and both the east and the west coasts of South America—Argentina going one way, Chile the other. One can see that it could indeed have been yet another stronghold to reinforce British control of the oceans. From Port Jackson, strategists argued at the time, Britain might conveniently threaten all the rival empires of the Pacific: the Spanish possessions of South America, the Dutch colonies in the East Indies, even Russian or American outposts on the coasts of North America. When Alessandro Malaspina brought his ships to Sydney in 1793, ostensibly on a voyage of scientific discovery, he was really spying for the Spanish government, and he went away convinced that perfidious Albion was establishing there a base for the extension of British power throughout the southern seas, from which armies of horrible

convicts would be conveyed by the Royal Navy to fall in loot-
ing and rapine upon the colonies of the Spanish Main.[1]

In hindsight he seems to have misread the signs of the settlement, just as one feels sure that his artist Juan Ravanet must
have been blinded by the sheer Britishness of the Sydney officials, who all look in his pictures supernaturally tall, slender
and gentlemanly. If a military role for Sydney was plotted
behind the scenes in London, it never came about, and no
armed expedition set sail from Sydney until the Sudan War of
1885. In fact Sydney never did fit easily into the pattern of
Victorian imperial expansion. It belonged really to an earlier
Empire. When Sydney was settled the American colonies had
only just been lost, while India, which was later to become
central to all imperial affairs, was still hardly more than a field
of adventure for private enterprise. Sydney was far from the
imperial trade routes, and in its early years offered little economic promise. It carried no evangelical banner, either: there
was no urge to raise the local aborigines to a higher state of
civilization, or to reconcile them to the Christian God—it was
many years before the missionaries advanced upon the indigenes, and by then all the Ioras of Sydney had gone.

Sydney certainly did not figure largely in the ambitions of
imperial administrators—*"My language fails!"* groaned Hilaire
Belloc's duke, finally abandoning all hope that his lachrymose
grandson Lord Lundy would ever make a success of life. *"Go
out and govern New South Wales!"*[2] For many years Sydney
remained synonymous in the British mind with Botany Bay.
Sidney Smith, "the wit of wits," refused to believe that a colony founded as "a sink of wickedness" could ever be im-

---

[1] Malaspina was treated with courtesy by the not terribly warlike British
officers, who were delighted to have visitors, and was obliged to admit in
one of his dispatches to Madrid that they had been very nice to him—"We
shall remain for the rest of our lives eternally grateful for the gracious
hospitality for which we have been obliged to the colony."
[2] *". . . and gracious! how Lord Lundy cried!"*

proved, and it was an English journalist, Henry Carter, who wrote the most famously contemptuous lines about the convict pioneers:

> *From distant climes o'er wide-spread seas we come,*
> *Though not with much eclat or beat of drum,*
> *True patriots all; for be it understood,*
> *We left our country for our country's good;*
> *No private views disgrac'd our generous zeal,*
> *What urg'd our travels was our country's weal,*
> *And none will doubt but that our emigration*
> *Has proved most useful to the British nation.*

But as the imperial pride swelled, the possession of Australia did become a rather hazy source of satisfaction to the British. To Dickens's Mr. Micawber it was a place not of exile but of possibility; and by the end of the century a representation of Captain Cook, implanting the flag for the very first time on the shores of New South Wales, was a favorite illustration in children's books about the glory of Empire. Kipling, in his "Song of the Cities," had Sydney singing about a birth stain "turned to good." "Farewell Australia," wrote Lawrence, remembering his departure from Sydney Harbour in 1922, "farewell Britain and the great Empire. Farewell! Farewell!"

In return many Sydney citizens cherished a revived pride in the Mother Country—not just a snobbish nostalgia, but a sense of comradeship in a great enterprise. The Imperial Factor, which had brought the city into being, powerfully affected its affairs for many generations, and is still apparent now.

The oldest surviving European graffiti in Sydney are on Garden Island the main naval headquarters—H.M.A.S. *Kuttabul* in service usage. This is not in fact an island any longer, but in 1788 it was still separated from the shore by a couple of hundred yards, and seemed a good place to establish a vegetable garden. Seamen were assigned to do the gardening, and it was presumably three of them who scratched their initials on a rock on the highest point of the islet, together with the date 1788—FM, IB and WB, now protected by glass pyramids like garden cloches. I was taken out to see them one morning by a retired civilian employee of the base, who had spent most of his working life there, who knew every inch of the place, and who had for years been puzzling out the identities of FM, IB and WB. I shall always remember this delightful man's comical consternation when I happened to see another set of initials—FP—on a nearby rock; through all those years of infatuated study, through hundreds of visits to the spot, he had never noticed them before!

Actually we came to the conclusion that they were a recent vandalistic addition (Sydney graffiti remain vandalism for a century or two, before they are protected with glass pyramids).[1] I think my companion's original dismay, though, concerned the defiance of tradition—that there should have been four pairs of initials, instead of the long-attested and Admiralty-approved three. Garden Island is soaked in the imperial tradition. For generations it was the Royal Navy's principal base in the South Pacific, and some of Sydney's most handsome buildings stand around the dockyard. Fine workmanlike structures in the Georgian tradition, they are the southernmost examples of the British dockyard architecture that dignified naval ports around the world—Simonstown and Bermuda, Bombay and Portsmouth itself. A succession of twelve British admirals presided over the fortunes of Garden

---

[1] Unless they are aboriginal, in which case they are never graffiti at all, but rock art.

Island from their enviable Admiralty House at Kirribilli across the water, and it was men of the Royal Marines who, in the 1880s, laid out its tennis courts above the sea.

Between the two world wars it was decided that the imperial navies must be provided with a dry dock for their largest warships at the southern end of the Pacific, supplementing the vast installations at Singapore in the north—a first confirmation, it might be said, of Malaspina's instincts. The Captain Cook Dock, which finally linked Garden Island with the mainland, was completed too late for the Second World War, but even so Sydney became one of the great naval ports of the conflict. Hundreds of Allied warships frequented it, hundreds of thousands of troops passed through it. Fabulous liners like the *Queen Mary*, the *Queen Elizabeth* and the *Aquitania* appeared as troopships camouflaged in its harbor.[1] For men all over the world Sydney was to provide a lasting memory of romance, gaiety, and hospitality—as Charles Causley remembered of his visit with the *Glory*:

> *O like maidens preparing for the court ball*
> *We pressed our number-one suits,*
> *Borrowing electric irons and starching prime white collars,*
> *And stepped forth into the golden light*
> *With Australian pound-notes in our pockets.*

Today much of the Australian fleet can be seen there at Garden Island any day—destroyers, frigates, repair ships, towered over by an immense cantilever crane which is one of Sydney's best-known shapes. The gray mass of it all, cluttered about with masts and superstructures beyond the Botanic Gardens, gives central Sydney a clout that I rather relish.

All around the harbor, too, the navy presence is familiar.

---

[1] The *Aquitania* had last been seen by many Sydneysiders standing offshore at Gallipoli a quarter of a century before.

There are repair yards at Cockatoo Island, and various depots and training places are dotted on headlands, and an enchanting little naval chapel, high above South Head, is one of the very first buildings to welcome vessels of the fleet back home. Minesweepers lie upstream, moored in a blaze of lights at Berry Island, and most compelling of all is the sight that awaits you at Neutral Bay, in one of the most thickly populated parts of the harbor's northern shore. A small park stands at the head of this cove, with shady trees and a cricket pitch. Pleasant houses stand around, and there is a yacht club. If you stroll down from the main road through the green you will probably find children playing, yachtsmen preparing to sail, pensioners eating sandwiches on benches, and even (I swear to you) an occasional lady in hat, coat and skirt practising her croquet shots. And down at the water's edge, there in the heart of the great amiable city, a pair of black submarines is almost certain to be lying alongside a pier at their flotilla headquarters—sinister predatory boats, but by now almost disregarded features of a saunter round the bay.

There are fortifications all over Sydney, but contrary to Malaspina's suspicions they have been motivated more by fear than by aggressive instinct. Until 1870 this was an imperial garrison town. The New South Wales Corps, mustered in 1790 and nicknamed the Botany Bay Rangers, was ignominiously abolished in 1810, to be replaced by a battalion of Highlanders. Thereafter battalions of fourteen British regiments came out in rotation to the Sydney station. Their main barracks were on George Street, and are said to have been the Empire's biggest. They were demolished in 1848, but two fine examples of Victorian military architecture survive: Victoria Barracks at Paddington, which looks like a toy fortress, and has sentries stumping up and down outside it, and the Lancers' Barracks at Parramatta, an elegant affair of sandstone and ironwork which has been in continuous use since 1820, and is thus the oldest military establishment in Australia. The Sydney garrison church was Holy Trinity Church, in Argyle Place, and this pleasant and beloved building is rich still in military mementos, flags, crests, pamphlets and miscellaneous ephemera that form, accumulated as they have been generation by generation, a kind of imperial palimpsest.

In the beginning the convicts were the enemy. Later defense works had the Empire's foreign enemies more in mind. It is said that Napoleon himself conceived the idea of seizing Sydney, and a French squadron that turned up in 1802 is thought to have been making a preliminary reconnaissance—certainly its cartographer mapped the settlement with exquisite care. Sydney's vulnerable isolation, however, does not seem to have worried the colonists much until one morning in 1830 the city woke up to the news that during the night four American frigates had sailed through the Heads, up the harbor and into Sydney Cove without anyone's noticing. "Had war existed," helpfully observed their commander, Captain Charles Wilkes, "we might, after firing the shipping, and reducing the greater part of the town to ashes, have effected a retreat before daylight in perfect safety." Later Governor Sir William Denison imagined such an event even more graphically—a few frigates might come in at night "and the first notice I should have of their arrival would be a 32-pound shot crashing through the walls of my house."

A fever of military activities ensued: Sydney was several thousand miles from the next British naval station, and in a world where almost every nation was a potential enemy of the British Empire, had nobody to save it but itself. The Americans were one possible threat, the Spaniards were another, the French a third, the Crimean War brought the Russian bogey even into these distant seas and in later years there was

always the Yellow Peril. There was a rumor once that ferocious Irish Fenians were on their way from California, and
during the American Civil War it was thought that Yankee
privateers, in what would surely have been one of the most
exciting of all skulduggeries, might raid the city for the gold
stored in its coffers. Successive administrations, backed by the
imperial authorities in London, accordingly turned Sydney
into a fortified base. "I had no idea," wrote Anthony Trollope
after viewing the works in 1871, "that the people of New
South Wales were either so suspicious of enemies, or so pugnacious in their nature": and to this day on almost every
headland or islet there are militant remains.

The center of the defense system was Pinchgut Island,
which we first saw as a wooded mount with a gallows on its
summit. This had been cut down to water level and converted
into a citadel. Renamed Fort Denison, after that apprehensive
governor, it was equipped with a Martello tower, one of the
last such fortifications to be built anywhere. For years the
island-fort was armed with muzzle-loaded eight-pounder
guns, during World War II it housed two antiaircraft guns,
and now it is one of the prime tourist sights of Sydney, looking very much like a surfaced submarine, or perhaps a moni-
tor of the American Civil War, a few hundred yards from the
Opera House. The daily one o'clock gun is fired from
Pinchgut, the tide records are kept there, and since it is occupied as I write by a caretaker with a large family, it is
equipped on its north side with a large rotary clothesline,
well-hung with the morning laundry.

Until World War II, when Australia took up arms against
Japan, nobody cared to test these works. By then the headland
batteries had been reinforced by a boom across the harbor
mouth, from Watson's Bay to the Sow and Pigs and across to

the northern shore. This had to be removed to allow the passage of any vessel, and a launch would hurry out to lift it whenever necessary—very frequently, during the daylight hours, if only for the Manly ferries.

In May 1942 an attack group of five large Japanese submarines arrived at a point some thirty-five miles out at sea, two of them equipped with aircraft, three with forty-six-ton midget submarines. On May 31 one of the aircraft was sent on a reconnaissance of the harbor, no doubt spotting the boom, and also noticing the presence of several warships, including the 9,000-ton American cruiser *Chicago*. That night the three midgets, each with a two-man crew, were launched from their mother ships and crept through the Heads into the harbor. One got tangled in the boom and blew itself up. One disappeared forever. The third, I-22, sailed past Bradley's Head into the inner harbor, and finding the *Chicago* in its sights, let loose two torpedoes, missing the cruiser but hitting the shore of Garden Island. One torpedo failed to explode, the other wrecked an old ferryboat, the *Kuttabul*, which was moored alongside a quay as a floating barracks; nineteen sailors were killed—the only people ever killed by enemy action in Sydney, unless you count those who died in skirmishes between whites and blacks in the early days of the settlement. Once Sydney realized what was happening, chaos erupted. Guns were fired all over the place, small craft buzzed around the harbor dropping depth charges, the night was alive with flashes and tracer bullets. The *Chicago*, firing one of its five-inch guns, chipped a small piece off the corner of the Pinchgut tower. Passengers on a ferryboat, reported the *Sydney Morning Herald* later, "had the thrilling experience of seeing large calibre guns blazing seemingly directly at them." The artist Donald Friend, watching the racket from his flat above Elizabeth Bay, decided there and then to spend all his money and enlist. I-22 lay low, but in the small hours was sighted by three patrol boats in Taylor's Bay, beside Bradley's Head, and sunk with depth charges.[1]

The Japanese claimed to have sunk two merchantmen and an American cruiser, but one takes it that the action was conceived chiefly as an attack upon morale, and six nights later another submarine, standing offshore in the darkness, lobbed ten shells out of the ocean toward Rose Bay, wounding two civilians. It seems to have worked. The morning after the submarine raid Kings Cross was full of removal wagons, taking nervous householders to suburbs further from the front line, and though most of these refugees soon returned the city seems to have remained jittery throughout the war. The firing of the midday gun was suspended, in case it alarmed the citizenry. Towers and belfries were removed from many buildings. Some (notably the Post Office tower) were taken down because it was thought they would act as markers for Japanese bomber pilots, presumably unable to recognize the Harbour Bridge, others (the dome of Balmain Town Hall, for instance) because it was feared that in an air raid they might fall off and hurt somebody. The worst never happened, though. There was never another naval attack on Sydney, and the nearest air raids were at Darwin, 1,500 miles away. One by one, when the war was over, most of the towers and spires went up again; for years the Post Office tower looked a slightly different color from the rest of the building, because they had taken the opportunity to clean it while it was down.

The wars of the British Empire, nevertheless, have left their

---

[1] The Japanese did destroy the *Chicago* in the end, off the Solomon Islands in 1943. In 1979 the officers of a later American cruiser of the same name presented a picture of their ship to be hung on Pinchgut Island, with the inscription: "The later missile cruiser U.S.S. *Chicago* made this presentation to atone for the bad gunnery of its predecessor."

sad mark upon this city. The first to involve Sydney soldiers was the Maori War of the 1860s, when several hundred Australian volunteers fought with the imperial armies, but the first proper Australian expeditionary force sailed away from Sydney in 1885, and is commemorated by a bronze plaque (paid for by a bequest from one of its soldiers) on the sandstone bluff behind the Opera House. The 750 men of the force, which was raised by the New South Wales government, had volunteered to fight in one of the most passionate of the imperial crusades, the campaign to reconquer the Sudan after the death of General Gordon at Khartoum. The expedition got off to an ignominious start, one of its troopships colliding with the cruiser *Nemesis* before it had even left the harbor, and its return was rather bathetic too, for it had reached Africa too late to see anything but a few skirmishes.[1] It had established a fateful precedent, though, and for the next century there was scarcely an imperial war in which men from Sydney did not fight and die.

This is a city of war memorials, so large a contribution have these conflicts made to the community's character and self-knowledge, and when I first came here the greatest of them all, the Anzac Memorial in Hyde Park, seemed to me central to Sydney's conceptions of pride, manhood and mateship. It was one of the keys, I thought then, to the Sydney character. It honored all the dead of World War I, but was associated in everyone's minds with the tragedy of Gallipoli, which had changed Australians' conception of their place among the nations. Never again would the leaders of the British Empire, far away in London, be regarded as infallible or omnipotent, and I interpreted the memorial as a permanent rekindling not

---

[1] The British had decided to withdraw from the Sudan after all, and it was another thirteen years before Lord Kitchener took the flag back to Khartoum without benefit of Aussies.

merely of sadness, pride and resolution, but of bitter disillusionment too.

I still consider it one of the most moving of all war memorials, but a Sydney generation has grown up now that hardly knows where Gallipoli is. Long ago I came to feel that the Anzac Memorial had lost its awful charge, and stood there in the park like a spent reactor. However sometime during any evening at a Returned Services Club a dimming of the lights is likely to interrupt the cheek-to-cheek dancing, the laughter at the bar, the slamming and tinkling of the poker machines. A hush falls upon the club, as the members one and all stand and turn in the same direction—toward Gallipoli? Toward Flanders? Toward the remote half-imaginary imperial country Sydney used to call Home? Many of them are Italians or Greeks nowadays, but they all stand silent as a sepulchral voice declaims over loudspeakers the great mourning dirge of Laurence Binyon—*"They shall not grow old, as we that are left grow old . . . /At the going down of the sun and in the morning/ We will remember them."* "We will remember them," mumble the revelers respectfully. Up go the lights, the band resumes the fox-trot, the poker machines crash back into action.

Imperialism often rode high in Sydney, in the heyday of the creed. Bishop Broughton said that while there was certainly "an eternal purpose" to the existence of the place, there was also a historical purpose: "the exaltation of the English nation, and its gradual extension of power to the limits of the habitable world." Charles Wentworth thought that one day Sydney might actually replace London as the center of British dominion. The memorials in St. James's Church would perfectly satisfy any vicar in Poona or Leatherhead, recording as they do so many officers, barristers, clergymen and other figures of the imperial Establishment, dying after esteemed careers in the public service, going down with their ships, killed fighting Germans, Turks, Blacks or "Natives in the valley of the Horokiwi." Loyalty to the Mother Country could sometimes be fulsome and sometimes ridiculous. One had to be fairly obsessed to name a slab of Sydney bush Chipping Norton, to build a Mortlake and a Putney on the banks of the Parramatta River, to cause the postmen in this brand-new country to be dressed up in the white pith helmets, scarlet jackets and striped trousers of British livery, or to equip St. Andrew's Cathedral with bits of stone not only from Westminster Abbey and St. Paul's Cathedral, but also from the Houses of Lords and Commons.[1]

An imperial occasion in Sydney could be imperial indeed. In 1868 the young duke of Edinburgh became the first royal personage ever to visit the city, and a Citizens' Ball was held in his honor. For this Sydney erected, in Hyde Park, one of the largest wooden structures in the world. It had a ballroom 250 feet long, a supper room almost as big, and its fountains spouted varying colonial perfumes, courtesy of E. H. O'Neill's, Druggists, King Street.[2]

But then the city had grown rich by virtue of the imperial connection. Once the East India Company had relinquished its monopoly of British trade with the East, Sydney soon became a lively participant in the Empire's oriental trades; and

[1] Though when, in 1863, Sydneysiders wished to honor the future King Edward VII's new wife by naming a suburb for her, they spelt it wrong, and it has been Alexandria ever since.

[2] The duke was followed to Sydney by a well-known prostitute he had got to know in Melbourne, but not invited to the ball was the family of William Augustus Miles, a former Sydney chief of police, who was an illegitimate son of William IV. Miles is buried in Camperdown Cemetery, and his epitaph there says pointedly that though his beating heart sank into death unmourned, it *might* have been Blessed by Thousands—he might, in short, have been William V.

when the imperial economic system reached its Victorian climax, and for a time the British Empire seemed likely to become a permanently self-supporting unity, the one part of it providing raw materials, the other manufactured products—then for a few brief decades Sydney appeared to have a secure and rational function, part of a system, part of a generative process.

Out through the port went the wools and the gold, in came the machinery, the clothes, the books and the spectacle cases. Sydney's currency was the pound sterling; its ultimate exchange was the City of London; its carrier was the British merchant fleet; its ultimate legal sanctions came from the English courts. Its economic partners were London and all the dependent cities of the Empire, with whom it was linked first in the fraternity of Free Trade, later in the device of Imperial Preference—the emblematic devices on the Customs House represented the West Indies, South Africa, Canada, Calcutta, Singapore, Cape Town, Quebec, Hong Kong, Durban, Rangoon and Vancouver, as if nowhere outside the Empire really mattered. British money sustained the growth of Sydney, and more often than not British settlers wishing to move to Sydney, as part of the natural imperial process, could often rely upon a government subsidy to help them—it was well after the Second World War that the last of the £10 immigrants filed dubiously down the gangplank (for by then the whingeing Pom was in full flower) to the transit camps of this city.[1]

All this meant that for generations the imperial factor was inescapable in Sydney. Other Australians often thought the city excessively loyal, and the writer Francis Adams, looking at it in 1886, could only marvel at "the appalling strength of the British civilization," so powerful were the influences of

---

[1] How well I remember their pale images, still dressed as I recall them in suits, cardigans and trilby hats, lining the rails of their ships, and sometimes patriotically waving, as they passed through the British-held Suez Canal!

Empire. The rich shamelessly aped the British, in the noonday of British prestige, and if they could not actually send their children to England to be educated, saw to it that their schools in Sydney were impeccably British in style. Most of the ships that lay at the Sydney wharves flew the Red Ensign; when the flying boats came to land in Rose Bay they were, if not those of Queensland and Northern Territory Aerial Service (QANTAS for short), those of Imperial Airways. What a thrill when, in 1930, telephonic voice contact was first made with London, the Mother City! How moving to hear, every Christmas courtesy of the British Broadcasting Company's Empire Service, the crackling voice of the monarch himself, sending his message of paternal goodwill to his subjects wherever the flag flew! As late as the 1950s the directors of the *Sydney Morning Herald* were claiming their newspaper to have "the largest circulation in the colonial empire," and in 1958 Frank Hurley's book *Sydney* still felt itself to be describing the Empire's "second white city."

Even now imperial vestiges survive. The governor of New South Wales, up there in his castellated mansion above Sydney Cove, still wears on ceremonial occasions the plumed hat and striped trousers of the British colonial administrator, and strives through presentation and garden party to cherish the imperial strain of gracious ceremonial. It is true that his powers are limited to "assenting in the Queen's name to bills passed by the Parliament of the State," and that all too often the Court Circular in the morning paper records only his opening of a new primary school, or his reception of a delegation from the New South Wales Cheese-Making Society. Nevertheless it seemed very proper when one recent incumbent was Sir Arthur Roden Cutler, V.C., who had only one leg and looked indeed like a hero of the frontiers. The governor's superior, the governor-general of Australia, also lives in sovereign spaciousness, when he comes to Sydney. His official house at Kirribilli is full of fine portraits, ancient silver and mementos, and when His Excellency arrives there from Canberra, to look out over the harbor from the spacious bedroom of the Admirals, he must feel that he is indeed surrogate to the queen of Australia herself.[1] Titles, though abandoned in New South Wales now, are still much in use here—in 1990 there was a knighted minister of the United Church in Sydney, and a knighted cardinal too—and there are plenty of people in this city to whom the imperial conventions are important. When British royal persons come here, as they are rather fond of doing,[2] part of the populace greets them with indifference or derision, but another part reverently puts on its tailcoats and flowered hats, prepares its curtsies and perhaps reminds itself of its own family links with the English nobility—enough to send a shudder down a Welsh republican spine.

In some ways Sydney is still much like a British city. Most of its people are of British stock—in 1986, 220,000 of them had actually been born in Britain—so that even now I often find it difficult to determine whether a stranger is an indigene or a Pom. The line between the two is hazed, too, by practice and relationship: thousands of Sydneysiders spend parts of their lives in Britain, thousands of Britons are always at large in Sydney. Sydney motorists still drive on the left, Sydney lawyers still wear wigs, Sydney schoolchildren are still dressed in flannel shorts and blazers, Sydney letters sometimes get posted in a mailbox with a crown on it. Television here is still partly British-inspired—they even call the A.B.C. "Aunty,"

---

[1] The prime minister of Australia has an almost equally enviable official house, just around the corner, but of course he is just a Polititian.
[2] Though Elizabeth II is the only reigning monarch to have set foot in the city.

which is what the British call the B.B.C.—and the *Daily Express* in London actually publishes a special Sydney edition for suitable expatriates living here. British investment is still enormous. Sydney rabbis go to London for their training. Everything most horribly English is stoked by the young women who come here from London to work as personal assistants to friends of Daddy's, or public relations persons in Sydney branch offices, and whose supercilious manners and nasal distortions of the English language they themselves seem to suppose evidence of superiority.

But sometimes I am touched by reminders of the imperial past. The Strand Arcade, an antipodean version of London's Burlington Arcade, can give me a momentary frisson of homesickness, with its faintly Dickensian suggestion of bright lights shining comfortably on damp winter evenings, and its stately uniformed beadle perfectly equipped to say "Morning, m'lord" to familiars walking through to Albany.[1] Some of the more venerable apartment houses of the Older Money suburbs can be evocative too: dark wood, polished brass, ornate and sluggish Edwardian elevators, nameplates by the door announcing the residence of Professor This, His Honour Judge That or Sir Manly Parramatta, Q.C. What could be more essentially British than the Frank Cash Memorial Prize, awarded annually at Shore School to a boy who (1) is a regular chapel attendant, (2) achieves steady progress in schoolwork throughout the year, though *not* achieving a top mark, (3) is neat and tidy in the care of his clothes, (4) is a willing hand at chores and (5) is "a likeable fellow with his mates, respectful and thoughtful to others"?

I poked my nose one morning through the doors of the fire station at the downtown corner of Castlereagh and Bathurst

---

[1] Though once when I inquired after him I was told I would probably find him taking refreshment at Mrs. Sippy's Coffee House.

streets, designed by James Barnet in 1887. The inevitable icon of Queen Victoria guarded the establishment, flanked by sculpted fire helmets and axes, and attended rather inappropriately, I thought, by a flaming torch. Inside there was no sign of life, but impeccably hung upon a line of hooks were the firemen's uniforms, their helmets shining, the brass buttons on their heavy serge jackets superbly polished and aligned. How tellingly they spoke of a grand old heritage—the pride, the diligence, the comradeship, the dutifulness which, together with many less commendable abstractions, Queen Victoria's Empire distributed around the world![1]

KEEP AUSTRALIA BEAUTIFUL: SHOOT A POM. By the historical nature of things, not everyone in Sydney regards the British connection with affection, or is sentimentally stirred by brass-buttonry. The penal origins of the city, the prevalence of Irishmen, the growth of republican sentiment, the unfortunate habits of visiting English people have all helped to make Sydney's Anglophilia less than unanimous. "The Old Dart," an ancient Sydney pejorative for England, implies scheming and hypocrisy; many Sydneysiders thought it proper that when in the bicentennial year a memorial was erected at Circular Quay to commemorate the imperial connection, it should contain parts of a gigantic sculpted chain—bonds of friendship in one interpretation, links of a shackle in another.

I suppose the first Bloody Pom was Governor Bligh, who so antagonized the local Establishment with his stiff-necked English regard for the proprieties, but republicanism certainly existed in Sydney from the beginning, when many of the convicts must have pined for the new liberties of the United

[1] The qualities survive, I am sure, among the men of the Castlereagh and Bathurst fire station, but shortly after I paid my visit the fire service decided to give up brass buttons.

States, and countless Irishmen detested the very notion of the Crown. That ardent Presbyterian Dr. John Dunmore Lang argued fervently for an Australian Republic, and hardly had the young duke of Edinburgh been feted at the Citizens' Ball than an Irishman tried to kill him at a picnic.[1] By the end of the nineteenth century, in the scurrilous heyday of Sydney political journalism, there was probably nowhere in the British world where Monarchy was more enthusiastically reviled. The *Bulletin* did not hesitate to call Edward VII "a little fat dismal person with pig-eyes," while *Truth* thought him a turf-swindling, cardsharping, wife-debauching boozer. Even Queen Victoria herself, the ultimate Briton, was far from sacrosanct. In the celebratory year of her Golden Jubilee, observed with sickly sycophancy almost everywhere else in the Empire, a public meeting at Sydney Town Hall turned down a proposal for a Sunday school fete on the grounds that "to impress upon the children of the colony the value of the Jubilee years of a Sovereign is unwise and calculated to injure the democratic spirit of this colony." Sydney cartoonists delighted in lampooning the Queen-Empress's dumpy figure and jowled features, and the *Bulletin* once definitively dismissed her as a fat old hunk of sauerkraut.

The antipathy has faded. The colonial chip on the shoulder is almost gone, and I get the impression that in general Sydney's attitudes toward its progenitors have matured into indifference. English people may still find themselves teased and patronized, but they are unlikely to be abused simply for being English. The imperial factor is an irrelevance now, and most people do not appear to care much whether Australia is monarchist or republican. The old trust in British power, at once debilitating and inspiring, was terribly weakened by the catastrophe of Singapore in 1941, and was symbolically dis-

---

[1] The Irishman it was that died—on the gallows.

missed in 1951 when the Anzus Defence Treaty was signed, linking Australia not with Great Britain, as in effect the protecting power, but with the United States. Since then American warships have been more familiar visitors to the harbor than the ships of the Royal Navy, and when the Royal Australian Navy celebrated its seventy-fifth anniversary the Americans marked the occasion by sending the immense battleship *Missouri*, more powerful than any warship the British ever built, to tie up at Garden Island opposite Admiralty House.

The constitutional connection with Britain is now remote indeed, having been weakened in stages down the decades. Once governed directly from London, Sydney became first the capital of a self-governing colony, then the capital of a state within an independent Australian federation, so that there are now no direct administrative links between this city and the old imperial center. An agent-general of New South Wales is stationed in London, but is hardly more than a trade representative; the British maintain a consulate-general in an office block overlooking Sydney Cove, like any other foreign power. Britons need visas to come to Sydney now. "My first feeling," wrote Charles Darwin of his introduction to Sydney, as so many British travelers wrote then about so many imperial stations, "was to congratulate myself that I was born an Englishman." Now not one visitor in ten thousand, I would hazard a guess, thinks of this city as British at all.

It was inevitable. Sydney was always on the far perimeter of the British Empire, and was bound to break away in the end. Founded in English contempt, and inhabited by people often genetically Anglophobe, it was remarkable that the place remained so British so long.

The first foreign intervention in the affairs of this city occurred before the city even existed. Six days after the First

Fleet arrived in Botany Bay, the day before the move through the Heads, Phillip's men were astonished to see the masts and upperworks of two strange ships approaching from the sea. "At first I only laughed," Tench recorded, so improbable was the event. They turned out to be the French frigates *La Bous-sole* and *L'Astrolabe,* commanded by Jean-François de La Pérouse, on a voyage of discovery through the Southern Hemisphere. Taken aback by their arrival, the British embar-rassingly managed to collide four of their own vessels as they beat their way out of Botany Bay, but put a brave face on the presence of their old enemy as they set about establishing the settlement at Sydney Cove. "All Europeans are countrymen so far from home," La Pérouse declared, and he and Phillip became quite friendly. Some of the convicts, having been dis-embarked at Sydney Cove, very soon found their way over-land back to Botany Bay, hoping for asylum with the French (or at least sympathy from La Pérouse's lieutenant on *La Bous-sole,* who was Irish) but they were all rejected, it seems, and perhaps they were lucky, for when La Pérouse sailed away six weeks later he, his ships, and all his men vanished into the Pacific forever—wrecked, it was discovered long afterward, in the New Hebrides.[1]

It was manifest then that Sydney could never be insulated against the world and its effects, and the bizarre arrival of La Pérouse in the first week of Sydney's history has never been forgotten. The suburb that is named for him, with its aborigi-nal settlement, stands at the place on Botany Bay where his ships anchored, and a little enclave down there commemo-rates his stay. There is a memorial obelisk, a museum tells the

---

[1] La Pérouse was well known to the Empire. He had spent two years as a prisoner of the British after the battle of Quiberon Bay in 1759, and during the American wars he had destroyed two British forts on Hudson Bay in Canada, courteously leaving some supplies behind for the use of their scat-tered garrisons.

sad tale of the expedition, and a French chaplain who died while they were in the bay lies in his tomb nearby—just down the road from the Snake Man. The crews of many French warships have paid their respects at this melancholy spot. It is not true, as legend suggests, that it is actually French soil; but until 1983, when French nuclear tests in the Pacific soured relations with Australia, it was customary for the La Perouse aborigines to celebrate Bastille Day, and the children would scramble for sweets showered among them by the French consul-general.

Very soon Dutch, Spanish, Danish and American ships were coming to Sydney, and as the nineteenth century progressed foreign vessels of every nationality took to using Sydney as a port of call or repair. It may not have seemed so at the time, but it was really a prophetic moment when, in 1908, Theodore Roosevelt's Great White Fleet arrived in the harbor. This spectacular squadron, of sixteen battleships and four auxiliaries, was circumnavigating the world allegedly in the cause of peace, really in pursuit of American prestige, and it was by far the largest foreign force ever to be seen at Sydney, easily outdazzling the elderly British cruisers which then represented the South Pacific squadron. Sydney adored the Great White Fleet, its spanking (if varyingly effective) warships, its good-natured matelots. It was true that after a reception for civic leaders on the battleship *Connecticut* some of the silver was found to be missing, but in general the Americans were given an extremely warm welcome. The city was plastered with American flags, eagles and portraits of George Washington; innumerable speeches of cousinly goodwill were exchanged; a five-story model of the Statue of Liberty was erected; the American admiral got hundreds of fan letters. During the week's visit a million passengers were taken by the Sydney Ferry Company to view the fleet, and thirty American sailors jumped ship for good. It was, though, more than a mere social triumph. America was displaying itself as a common enemy of the Yellow Peril, by then seen as the main threat to Australian well-being. As the correspondent of the New York *Sun* reported, in their effusive welcome to the fleet the Sydneysiders were "telling something extremely important to Great Britain"; and perhaps the Great White Fleet did impress upon the civic mind the realization that there were other powers but Great Britain in the world, and other ideals but Empire.

Nowadays I am constantly struck by Sydney's breadth of foreign interests and connections. Ships from unknown ports frequent the harbor, the *Sydney Morning Herald* regularly carries weather forecasts from the South Pole, and while I was working on this book there arrived at Sydney Airport the world's largest freighter aircraft, loaded with a cargo of 1.6 million diapers from Kiev. Tourists from everywhere come to this city nowadays: a young man I once saw clumping up the steps of the Opera House in roller skates turned out to be a Frenchman who had skated across half the world to this, the object of his pilgrimage. Some people claim to find Sydney Americanized, and call it a little Manhattan. I feel no sense of cultural annexation, though. The city feels to me no more Americanized that it did when I first knew it—no more Americanized than London.[1] It is not the impact of America that impresses me, every time I return to Sydney, but the ever-growing impact of Asia.

Nobody talks of the Yellow Peril now, and every year Sydney is more enmeshed with Asia. Sydney soldiers have fought in two post-imperial conflicts independently of the British, and they were both in Asia—in Korea and in Vietnam, in each case a war to prevent hostile Asians extending their power

---

[1] But then I am of the opinion that most "Americanization" is simply modernization, and that the Big Mac springs directly from the human heart.

further to the south. Asian power gets closer anyway. Japan has long replaced Britain as the main customer for the commodities that pass through Sydney's port, and here, as everywhere in the Pacific world, is now a mighty investor too. Asians from Vietnam and Hong Kong have flooded into Sydney, and a Chinese community that used to be thought of as a coterie of unhygienic restaurateurs, gamblers and opium smokers is fast becoming a formidable economic force. Every time I go to Sydney, Asian faces are more common in the streets, the papers carry more references to Asian affairs, and the ships that sail beneath the Harbour Bridge are more likely to be flying Asian flags. When I was there recently one of them flew not the innocuous moon ensign of the Japanese merchant fleet, but the blood-red rising sun of the Japanese Defense Force, successor to the Imperial Japanese Navy. I thought this reminder of old enmities might arouse disagreeable emotions in Sydney, since it was probably the first time the flag had flown anywhere near the place since the submarine attacks in 1942. In fact nobody took the slightest notice.[1]

Perhaps the truth is that this city has accepted its geographical destiny. The British Empire is dead and gone, the very concept of Australia is tenuous, and the world is really divided into three or four enormous geopolitical units. Seen in these terms, Australia is the southernmost island of the Indonesian archipelago, reaching down from south Asia, China and Japan, and Sydney is no more than a regional port of the Pacific—its peers, partners and rivals now are not Liverpool, Bombay or Baltimore, but Singapore, Osaka, Hong Kong. Sydneysiders are perfectly conscious of these inexorable developments. Sometimes they respond with racist expostulation, sometimes they seem unnerved by the cleverness and

---

[1] And when the ship sailed out again beneath the bridge I saw four of its officers on the helicopter deck pursuing an amiable ritual of contemporary Japan: taking each other's photographs.

diligence of their new Asian fellow citizens, but generally they appear to look forward fatalistically into a world very different from the comforting constructions of the lost Empire. Easy come, easy go! One evening I sat in a café at Kings Cross, its television flickering all-but-disregarded above the counter, contemplating the cheerful scene around me. The noise level was high, the customers were young and fun. Thinking how prosperous the place seemed, how sure of itself, and how high-spirited, I caught out of the corner of my eye a very different scene on the television screen. It showed a boatload of refugees from Cambodia arriving half-starved, destitute and wide-eyed somewhere on the Australian coast, I missed where. They were clinging all over their rickety vessel, hanging over the gunwales, draped over the wheelhouse.

It reminded me of old pictures of those overloaded Manly ferries, and just for a moment I thought it really might be one of the Sydney ferryboats that the refugees had commandeered. The Australians on the screen stood aghast to see them come, and remonstrated for a while, but in the end they had to let them land—as it were on Sydney Cove just down the road, or at Balmoral beside the bandstand. What else could they do?

RETROSPECT

W hat a fine and interesting city, all in all! What an attractive people! Yet I find I cannot end this book about Sydney without that streak of wistfulness returning. I used to think it was because beyond the Blue Mountains, just out of sight from Circular Quay, there extended an empty wilderness inhabited only by inexplicable primitives. I used to quote the poet A. D. Hope's indictment of Australia:

> *The river of her immense stupidity*
> *Floods her monotonous tribes from Cairns to Perth.*

Now the Australian Outback feels empty no longer, we think of the land itself in a more comradely way, and we understand a little better the arcane ideas of the aboriginals, but still Sydney feels on the edge of some more metaphysical blank. Most of the world's great cities have something inevitable about them, as though God decreed them come what may. In Sydney, even now, I catch myself feeling sometimes that the place need never have come into being in the first place.

It ought to be a simple city to write about. Started from scratch in modern times, developed according to elemental economic principles, well-documented throughout its history and almost untouched by war, Sydney should offer its chroniclers a straightforward task. It does not seem an introspective place. It is frank about most matters. Its icons are there for all to see, and it has never been overburdened with spirituality. Sydney, one might suppose, is Sydney is Sydney.

Yet the effect of this city upon its visitors is far from simple, and strangely fluctuates. Sydney is about the same age and size as San Francisco, yet it inspires a far wider range of reactions. Hardly anybody hates San Francisco, but plenty of people hate Sydney. Once you have evolved a view on San Francisco you are likely to stick with it, but in my own experience one's responses to Sydney shift from decade to decade, day to day, even moment to moment. The citizens of Sydney are themselves ambivalent about it, and combine pride with doubt, assertion with apology. The only constant of all Sydney opinion, the one leitmotiv of writing about this city since the very beginning of its history, is the beauty of the harbor. It is as though Sydneysiders feel the harbor to be their one unassailable satisfaction. Every single Sydney man and every single Sydney woman, Trollope reported in 1873, asked him if he did not find the harbor "rather pretty," and in a cartoon of half a century later Sydney is stuck all over with posters screaming "You Should See Our Harbour," "Have You Seen Our Harbour?," "How Do You Like Our Harbour?," "What Do You Think Of Our Harbour?," "Have You Ever Seen Anything Finer Than Our Harbour?" It is extraordinary still how often Sydney people comment upon their harbor's beauty; and perhaps by now it is a matter of self-protective convention, like the British conversational obsession with the weather.

For I daresay a latent uncertainty gives this often boisterous city its oddly dappled character. The civic motto is a gnomic one—"I Take but I Surrender"—and the destiny of the city is equally unclear. Dazzling though Sydney can be, it has always stood on the fringes of history—repeatedly spurned by history, I sometimes think. There was a time when it possessed real power, at least in theory. Its early governors were granted, by their royal commissions, hypothetical authority over more than half of what is now Australia, and "all the Isles adjacent."[1] It was from Sydney that Norfolk Island and Tasmania were originally governed, that the first European expansionists burst into the Australian interior, that Matthew Flinders sailed to circumnavigate the continent, that the colony of Port Essington was established on the Cobourg Peninsula at the other end of Australia.[2] Then for years Sydney was the capital of an imperial province, subject only to London; New South Wales was virtually a nation, with its own armed forces, fiscal policies, postage stamps and currency. Even Melbourne was subject to Sydney until 1851, and when the Commonwealth of Australia was brought into being in 1901, it was in Sydney that the delegates from the six colonies sealed the

---

[1] Australia was never annexed as an imperial entity, but when in 1840 a French official asked the colonial secretary, Lord John Russell, how much of it was British, "I answered him 'the whole,' and with that answer he went away."

[2] An unsuccessful settlement whose forlorn ruins poignantly suggest to me how Sydney might look if Phillip had not seen it through its first cruel years: the little Government House stands deserted on its eminence above the sea, the quay below is crumbled, tangled foliage covers brick works, sawmills, sergeants' mess and all, and one of the tombstones in the cemetery says simply: SACREAD TO THE MEMOERY OF THE DR OF THE SETTLEMENT.

agreement—a memorial in Centennial Park remembers the event.

Little by little this consequence was reduced, and the vast authority of the early governors shriveled. Tasmania and Norfolk Island went first. Port Essington was transferred to the new colony of South Australia. Melbourne was lost when Victoria was separated from New South Wales. It was Melbourne, not Sydney, that became the first capital of the Australian Commonwealth, and Canberra that was eventually chosen to be its permanent seat of government. Sydney has been left feeling rather high and dry, like a metropolis of its own disbanded Empire.

Indeed it stands to its remaining dependency, the State of New South Wales, much as Vienna stands to Austria. It is too big for itself. It frequently lives beyond its means, and especially in the flashier things of life, aspires beyond its station. It is neither one thing nor the other. On the one hand when most people think of Australia, they think first of Sydney and its images, and many of Australia's national institutions are based here, from the Arts Council to the secret service. On the other hand Sydney is really nothing but a provincial capital, the equal of Perth, Adelaide, Hobart or Brisbane. The city looks out tentatively to the world at large, as though it is not sure of its status. Where does it stand in the order of things? Is it *really* world-class? Better perhaps to content itself with easier comparisons—livelier than Melbourne, brighter than Adelaide, the richest in the Southern Hemisphere, or even, as statistics sometimes solemnly suggest, the biggest in New South Wales. Better still to content itself with itself. There is remarkably little news about the rest of Australia in Sydney's newspapers, and even the old competition with Melbourne, which used to be real and vicious, seems to have subsided now into a kind of half-humorous convention, like the rivalry between Harvard and Yale, or calling the House of Lords "the other place."

But what mere provincial capital ever aroused such passions and speculations? The vast momentum of the world proceeds far away from Sydney. Ideologies triumph or are discredited. The balance of the continents shifts. Yet it is still possible to wonder if it is here that a New Man may emerge. The peculiarity of the place, its originality of style and history, the fact that the new moon lies the wrong way round in the old moon's arms, as it rises pale over Barrenjoey—all these help to place Sydney beyond the usual category of cities. Its glittery image, propagated so jubilantly, does not do justice to the place. It is an image far too explicit. Tower Bridge may emblemize London, the Eiffel Tower says the right things about Paris, but the Opera House and the Harbour Bridge do not begin to epitomize the true sensations of Sydney, which seem to me tantalizingly ambivalent.

We think of it as a young city, but it is not so young really. Many a great city is younger—Toronto, Chicago, Hong Kong, Singapore, Washington, Johannesburg. Sydney, though, *feels* young: if not young physically, young in an abstract way, as though the generations succeed each other extra quickly here. There is something fugitive to the fascination of the place. Charles Causley, who responded with such affection to the natural generosity of Sydney, felt this elusive quality too, beginning and ending his poem, not so many years after his visit with H.M.S. *Glory*, with a gentle hint of it:

> *Now it seems an old forgotten fable:*
> *The snow-goose descending on the still lagoon,*
> *The trees of summer flowering ice and fire*
> *And the sun coming up on the Blue Mountains.*

An old forgotten fable—not the metaphor one expects of so splendid and apparently confident a city. "Sydney," I wrote myself when I was young, "is not one of your absolute cities." I was looking perhaps for the black-and-white, sharp-edged resolution that usually characterizes showy young towns of ambition, and all I found instead, I thought, was aloofness and introspection.

Sydney is still not your absolute city, but what seemed to me so long ago an affront to my sensibilities now seems a seduction—a kind of divine opacity, making me feel that perhaps the city was God-given after all.

I began this book with a harbor prospect on a sunny Sunday afternoon. Let me end with an evening stroll after the opera. Violetta, being a particularly robust specimen of local talent, has not unexpectedly recovered from her decline in time to take several rousing curtain calls. The lady in the next seat has remarked to nobody in particular well, thank goodness it could never happen in this day and age. We leave the great building euphorically, entranced into the Sydney evening.

There is something phosphorescent about Sydney Opera House. It glows almost merrily in the daytime, with the sun on its flying wings, and it glows refulgently at night. Walking now out of its foyer onto the wide terrace is like emerging into a holograph, so that we feel we are being absorbed into light itself. Beyond this luster there is a panoply of lesser lights—moving lights of ships, towering lights of waterfront skyscrapers, beacon lights, lights of oyster bars, coffee shops, restaurants, fairy lights glittering all over a tree at the foot of the Domain. High above is the hump of the Coat-Hanger, with its stream of cars hurrying over it, and on the highest point of its arch the two jaunty flags are floodlit in the breeze —surely the proudest flags in the world.

But we will find ourselves some secluded harbor spot, above a little-used pier perhaps, where all those bright lights are far away, the rumble of the traffic is almost silent, the great city around us seems astonishingly remote, and a more ambiguous magic settles on the scene. The evening is warm, with a scent of night flowers somewhere. Very likely there is a flash of torchlight from the jetty. A couple of men are fishing with lines down there, and we hear snatches of an unidentifiable language—Indonesian, perhaps, or Thai. When the torch goes out only the ember of a cigarette remains, looking rather like a wavering firefly, and in the voluptuousness of the moment we may be surprised to find ourselves feeling a little sad. Why, I wonder? The harbor is all at peace, the city is one of the world's happiest, those fishermen are delighted to be there, the recession is officially said to be past its worst, the bridge is strong, the Opera House is lovely, the flags are fine, Violetta is even now enjoying a hearty turf-'n'-surf with Alfredo. Yet at such moments as this, in the velvet sensual darkness on the harbor shore in Sydney, I sometimes feel myself haunted by a sense of loss, as though time is passing too fast, and frail black people are watching me out of the night somewhere, leaning on their spears.

THANKS

Countless kind Sydney people helped me to write this book about their city, and I thank them one and all. I am particularly grateful to a number of friends and colleagues who honored me by reading the book in typescript, in part or even most generously in whole, saving me from many errors and offering me many new perspectives: they include Rowena Danzinger, James Hall, Ian Hicks and Anthony McGrath, and I hope they will not think this final version has let them down.

I have acknowledged in my footnotes the books I am chiefly indebted to, but I must mention here two general essays about Sydney that I especially admire: the final chapter of J. D. Pringle's *Australian Accent*, London, 1958, and Gavin Souter's *Sydney Observed*, Sydney, 1968—both illustrated, as it happens, by my oldest friend and benefactor in the city, George Molnar.

Finally, my warm thanks to Charles Causley, whose poem *H.M.S. Glory at Sydney* has provided a melodic line for my book.

Trefan Morys, 1991

INDEX

Index

ABOUT THE
AUTHOR

JAN MORRIS is the author of over twenty books, including *The Pax Britannica* trilogy, *The World of Venice, Oxford, Spain, The Matter of Wales, Journeys, Destinations, Manhattan '45, Hong Kong, Conundrum, Pleasures of a Tangled Life,* and the fictional *Last Letters from Hav.* When not traveling, she lives in Wales.

ABOUT THE TYPE

The text of this book was set in Palatino, designed by the German typographer Hermann Zapf. It was named after the Renaissance calligrapher Giovanbattista Palatino. Zapf designed it between 1948–1952, and it was his first typeface to be introduced in America. It is a face of unusual elegance.

994.41
MOR

11/92

Sydney and environs

——— Main Highways ·—·—· Railways

0 — 5 — 10 — 15 km
0 — 5 — 10 miles

N

RICHMOND WINDSOR

Hawkesbury River

PENRITH MT DRUITT PARRAMAT

CABRAMATTA

LIVERPOOL

George River

Darwin

NORTHERN
TERRITORY

QUEENSLAND

WESTERN
AUSTRALIA

SOUTH
AUSTRALIA

Brisbane

NEW SOUTH
WALES

Perth

CANBERRA Sydney

Adelaide

VICTORIA

Melbourne

TASMANIA

Hobart

0 — 1000 km
0 — 500 miles